To my brother, Matt
Thanks for all your help. Much appreciated

CONTENTS

INTRODUCTION

FEW PLAYERS HAVE embarked on the type of football journey that Cristiano Ronaldo has taken in his short career. Even fewer could have imagined his transformation from villain to hero in the wake of the 2006 World Cup. At the age of just 23, he stands at the summit of the English game and is regarded by many as the best footballer on the planet. In his five years at Manchester United he has already completed his set of domestic medals – an achievement that took even the great Ryan Giggs more than a decade to accomplish. He was the inspiration for United's dramatic double success this season, scoring more than 40 goals. His performances during the 2006/07 season were nothing short of magical as he, more than anyone, led United to their first title in four years. In addition, Ronaldo has transferred his increasingly impressive club form onto the international stage, starring in Euro 2004 and taking an even more central role in Portugal's run to the World Cup 2006 semi-finals. He represents the future, not just for Manchester United but for Portugal too.

For some this would be a burden too big to bear, but Cristiano is made of sterner stuff.

He has worked incredibly hard to reach the top level in Europe. He has played in three very different cities, with two different languages and two different styles of play. He has not lived at home in Madeira since the age of 12 and has thrown everything into his football education, taking on all challenges alone. The experience during his time at Sporting Lisbon developed Cristiano's character and prepared him to tackle any obstacle in his life. The main asset that Ronaldo had in his favour was that he was born with the ability to play football. Some players go through their academy days and apprenticeships having to give every ounce of sweat just to keep up with the other players but Ronaldo was special. He worked hard, of course, but the dribbling, ball skills and fancy footwork came naturally to him. Technically, he had a God-given talent and the quality to entertain crowds.

While he did not sample the kind of youth team experience that the likes of David Beckham, Gary Neville and Paul Scholes enjoyed, he quietly got on with his job in difficult circumstances and his progress was exceptional. Family problems troubled him and made it hard to settle in Lisbon, but his inner drive carried Ronaldo into the Sporting first team, where he caught the eye of scouts in the space of just one season. He was clearly destined to play at the highest level.

His move to Manchester United was the making of Cristiano. Sir Alex Ferguson's watchful eye and knowledge of dealing with young footballers enabled Ronaldo to blossom into the attacking threat that so many had predicted he would become. It was a gradual process. Every season at

Old Trafford, Ronaldo would show indications of improvement and a greater understanding of his team-mates' styles of play. He was as happy as anyone when United won two trophies in his first three seasons, but he had set his sights on the top prizes that had thus far evaded him.

He liked to keep a low profile away from the football pitch and Ferguson rarely had to worry about his young star's behaviour. But the 2006 World Cup shattered any hopes Cristiano had of remaining out of the headlines. Despite a brilliant tournament, his role in Wayne Rooney's red card in the Portugal–England quarter-final made him public enemy number one. It was the make-or-break moment of Ronaldo's short career. He could either wilt under the spotlight or use it to fuel his determination for success.

Luckily for United, he chose the latter option after persuasion from Sir Alex, who had travelled to Madeira to discuss his future. From being one of a galaxy of stars, the departures of Roy Keane and Ruud van Nistelrooy pushed Ronaldo to the forefront. He was now the man to whom United turned for inspiration in times of crisis and he rarely let his team-mates down. Ferguson had called for more goals from his winger and Ronaldo responded by hammering in an amazing 23 during a remarkable season that put him amongst the best in Europe.

His effort levels and creative flair have made him a crowd favourite at Old Trafford and he has truly continued the wonderful tradition of the United number 7 shirt. Against the odds, he turned the feeling of a nation from loathing to admiration in the space of 12 months. The same man who was vilified after the World Cup was even being tipped by neutrals as their player of the year. His fellow professionals agreed as he scooped the PFA Player of the Year and Young Player of the Year double to cap an incredible campaign.

Incredibly, he even eclipsed those efforts by helping United land a Premiership and Champions League double in 2007/08. Again, he dominated the end of season awards, and deservedly so.

Love him, hate him, respect him or distrust him, Cristiano Ronaldo is a player who always provokes a reaction.

CHILDHOOD

CRISTIANO RONALDO DOS Santos Aveiro was born on 5 February 1985 to parents Maria Dolores and Jose Dinis. He is the youngest of four children, joining sisters Cátia and Elma and brother Hugo; this family unit offered Cristiano stability throughout his youth.

He grew up in the town of Santo Antonio in Funchal, the capital of Portuguese island Madeira. Funchal has a population of approximately 104,000 and is named after its mass production of fennel ('funcho' in Portuguese). His upbringing could not be described as privileged, despite his proximity to some of Funchal's more prosperous areas, including the lavish hotels on the seafront. The family bungalow was rather small, making conditions cramped at home – in fact the house was so crowded that the washing machine was kept on the roof. Ronaldo spent plenty of time with his siblings, who remember a very happy childhood with him. Cristiano always had a smile on his face.

His mother, Dolores, worked as a cleaner while Dinis, his

father, was a council gardener. It was a humble beginning for Ronaldo but it taught him the value of family and the importance of hard work. He developed a strong bond with his parents – he quotes his mother as his greatest support and inspiration – and both encouraged him to become involved in football and to make the most of his considerable talents. His parents had marked him out for stardom. The 'Ronaldo' part of his name is taken from the US President Ronald Reagan – not through his parents' love of politics but because Cristiano's father admired Reagan's acting ability. Perhaps he was destined to find fame. Also, it just so happened that a young Brazilian would later burst onto the world stage and make the name Ronaldo famous.

However, despite his tightly knit family, growing up was not easy for Cristiano. His father suffered with a drinking problem that put a strain on daily life and caused a lot of pain for those close to him. As Dolores told the *Daily Mirror*, 'Time and time again Cristiano offered to pay to get him treatment but Dinis kept on drinking.' Dinis's dependence on alcohol was a worrying situation that stayed with Ronaldo throughout his childhood.

The problem would eventually escalate to the point where Dolores felt that Dinis could not be helped and so the pair decided to separate. Although the split was amicable and both continued to live in Funchal, the difficulties in his parents' marriage deeply affected Ronaldo. Being away from Madeira at the time, the news was even harder to take.

Cristiano was blessed with sporting ability from a young age and he grew up in a family that encouraged this – his father followed football with great interest. Ronaldo's skinny, athletic frame ensured that he was rarely far from a ball during his early days and his family soon knew that a career in sport was going to be the likely future for him. His energy would not fit well with other professions and he lived for the thrill of competition.

Football became a driving force in his formative years. Scattered around Funchal, dusty football courts and pitches provided Ronaldo with his first sporting experiences. It was fiercely competitive, as Cristiano sought to outperform his friends. Yet the nature of the matches – informal and pressure-free – allowed the youngsters to develop their own strengths and style of play. There was no tension and no one told him what he should or shouldn't do on the pitch. Ronaldo would do whatever it took to fit in an extra game of football, whether that was skipping meals at home, sneaking out of his bedroom window or simply spending hours out in the summer sun on the football court in search of a match.

In England, talented youngsters are joining academies at increasingly young ages and the emphasis is on getting the basics right. Many have accused domestic clubs of ignoring flair in favour of a more traditional approach. Other countries certainly appear to develop more flamboyant, skilful youngsters and maybe the street football culture that Cristiano grew up with has an impact on this. Looking back a little further into the history of British football, many of the best players learned their trade in street football. After all, there are countless stories of George Best's displays in the streets of Belfast. This element has been lost since the notion of academies has emerged in Britain.

Ronaldo's neighbours were older boys who inevitably represented team-mates and opponents in informal kickabouts. Despite being younger, his fierce will to win meant he never gave an inch against bigger, stronger players. It is a familiar story among professional footballers – a childhood spent playing against much older boys – and it stood him in good stead for future challenges. Even before he joined his first youth team, he was a regular on a makeshift football court in his hometown. On the hard surface of the local court, Ronaldo experienced those initial feelings inspired by football – camaraderie, the joy of victory, the pain of defeat.

As his godfather Fernao Sousa observed, while Ronaldo was like any other youngster in terms of character, on the football pitch he was streets ahead. Sousa told the BBC, 'He was better at football than the other kids, he had better control, better kicking, better dribbling.' So often – too often – players are said to have a natural, God-given talent. In Ronaldo's case it is undeniable and he himself acknowledges that his skills are a quality that he was born with. The quickness of his feet combined with his co-ordination and balance made him a joy to watch, even as a boy on the courts of Funchal.

As is often the case with talented young footballers, Ronaldo quickly began playing for an amateur team, CF Andorinha. For him, this was the beginning of an incredible journey. His father doubled as the team kit man and was able to watch Cristiano's progress up close, full of pride – the pair were inseparable. Ronaldo learned plenty of valuable lessons there that would serve him well for the bigger stage. Working with a coach at Andorinha taught Cristiano plenty about the tactical side of the sport. He worked hard to improve the weaker areas of his game while maintaining his irrepressible desire to win and entertain at every possible opportunity.

While subconsciously he may have held ambitions for a wider audience, seeing the young Ronaldo in the green of Andorinha was to catch sight of a boy on cloud nine and in love with the game. Immediately, his dribbling and technique made him stand out and his colleagues found Ronaldo a formidable opponent. Frequently, opposition defenders were left cursing him after being humiliated by his footwork. His pace was also an asset that he developed early and it gave him an added advantage over others.

As well as his greater natural talent, his attitude to his football stood out as very different. No game was a mere kickabout to him – his desire to win at every opportunity marked him out as a future professional and would be crucial in his quick improvements. His determination was there for all to see and his first ever football coach, Sardinha Afonso, remembers him as a 'fighter'. Speaking to the BBC, Club President of Andorinha, Rui Santos, added, 'He had many qualities but mainly it was his disgust at losing a match.' Losing became harder and harder to take as Cristiano moved up the levels of youth football.

It was only a matter of time before big things happened for Ronaldo. Reflecting on what football means to him, he says, 'Football for me is synonymous with happiness and spectacle. That's what I try to show. I don't know how to explain the tricks, they're just part of me.' This approach to the sport allows Cristiano to play with a smile on his face, despite the obvious pressure that comes with a career as a professional footballer.

At the age of ten, he had attracted the attention of Madeira's top sides. His performances for Andorinha had been good and his natural talent was there for all to see. As is normal in the world of football, any star performer at a small club quickly attracts the attention of the bigger, more powerful clubs. Ronaldo's case was no different. It is reflective of the state of football today that even ten-year-olds – and plenty even younger – are coveted by top clubs hoping to unearth the next child sensation. While Ronaldo had the support of his parents, everything was moving extremely fast for him.

Both Maritimo and Nacional – the two main clubs on the island – expressed an interest in Ronaldo and he was naturally flattered by the attention. This was serious business and, even for a ten-year-old, the path towards professional football was becoming evident. Maritimo made the first move, setting up a meeting with the Andorinha manager, Rui Santos. But when the Maritimo manager missed the meeting, it was decided that Ronaldo's future lay at Nacional. Maritimo would rue missing that opportunity for years to come.

When he signed for Nacional, he could have been forgiven for thinking that he would enjoy a lengthy stint at the club, furthering his football education. His school education had long since been discarded as a lower priority. Those who knew him well advised him to follow his football dreams – he had a gift for football, not further education. But to Ronaldo's surprise, his youth career in Madeira came to an abrupt end when he was just 12 years old. After just two years with Nacional, he was on his way to the mainland, heading for Lisbon. While Porto and Boavista had also expressed admiration for Cristiano, Nacional owed money to Portuguese giants Sporting Lisbon for a player called Franco and, rather than pay the debt, the island club opted to send

Ronaldo, in whom Sporting were interested after a short trial. For the youngster, it was a big decision to make and Nacional probably thought they had only let a fairly promising player leave – there would be plenty more like him, they reasoned. But if there is one thing to say about Ronaldo, it is that there is no one like him.

This was a major transition in his life. It would have been a big moment for any player but for a 12-year-old it was monumental. He had to leave Madeira and his family behind and enter an unfamiliar city on the mainland. He told the documentary *Planeta Ronaldo* (aired on Portuguese TV), 'It was very traumatic to leave my family. I had never even been on an aeroplane before. When I saw my mother crying at the airport, it made me want to cry as well.' He could never have imagined leaving home at such a young age and it was all very hard to take in. Part of him knew it would benefit his quest to become a professional footballer, but another part feared the heart-wrenching absence of the comfort blanket that his family provided.

Alone in Lisbon, he experienced the most emotionally testing years of his life. It is a moving story of the sacrifices necessary to forge a career in sport and a reality check for those that think everything comes easily for professional footballers. Lisbon was louder, busier and more threatening than Ronaldo had anticipated, and his team-mates struggled to understand his accent, inevitably leading to teasing and the feeling of being an outsider. He struggled to understand and be understood. He lived with 10 other young hopefuls in accommodation provided by the club but it was a far from easy transition.

Lisbon presented dangers, too. It could be a scary place for a young boy, especially at night. In his documentary, Ronaldo recalls one particular incident that took place on the city's busy roads, 'A gang jumped on me and my team-mates in the street. The other players ran away but I stood up and fought – and the robbers didn't get anything.' Apparently, Cristiano was elusive and unstoppable even at that age!

With his family miles away, he suffered desperately from homesickness and recalls the anguish of watching his credit tick down in the phone box. For someone so attached to his family it was a tough beginning to his Lisbon adventure, and a period that taught him a lot about survival. His determined, ambitious streak was tested to the full when times were tough. His godfather, Sousa, recalls a time when Ronaldo came back from Lisbon and had no intention of returning. Cristiano had had enough of that lifestyle and he wanted to move back to Madeira. Sousa spoke with Ronaldo's parents and urged them to persuade him to go back to Sporting, knowing that his godson had a big future in football and could not throw in the towel yet.

Sporting did all they could to make Cristiano feel comfortable in Lisbon. Sensing that homesickness was eating away at their young player, they were as accommodating as they could be, paying for Dolores, Ronaldo's mother, to fly to visit him. His family had always played a huge role in his life and it was a tactic that succeeded for Sporting, who were close to releasing Cristiano due to his unhappiness. Dolores gave Ronaldo a huge boost, making him more cheerful, confident and settled. It was a reassuring reminder of home and the pride felt by all his family and friends.

Ronaldo explains in his documentary: 'There were a lot of tears in my first few weeks in Lisbon. Madeira is so small. I couldn't believe the traffic and noise of a capital city. I used to call my family whenever I could.' Cristiano was forced to become independent and fend for himself. While he had plenty of senior figures to turn to at the club, he was largely left to make his own decisions. It was a testing time, but it was pivotal in Ronaldo's development.

The desire to win – ingrained in him from his earliest days in football – kept him going. As he puts it in *Planeta Ronaldo*, 'No matter how bad things got, I had this burning dream.' He would not let any obstacle block his path. Having overcome the homesickness, there was a sense that he had beaten the most challenging opponent and that stardom and the Sporting senior team now beckoned. He was still physically small and very skinny but he had pace and skill – vital commodities for any winger. A former coach remembers not only Ronaldo's will to win but also the effect that he had on his team-mates. Ronaldo cried, shouted and fussed when results did not go his team's way, but this reaction appeared to energise his colleagues, getting a reaction from them and inspiring them to follow his example on the pitch.

Cristiano's competitive nature is also confirmed by Portuguese international goalkeeper Ricardo, in his book *Diary of a Dream*, 'Whether it is ping-pong, table football, darts or snooker, he does not let up. If there are people who were born for the game and for competition, Cristiano Ronaldo is one of them.' Ricardo spent a good deal of time experiencing Ronaldo's desire for victory during the Euro 2004 and World Cup 2006 campaigns, and is a good source for learning about Cristiano's character traits. With a squad spending so much time together during major tournaments, everyone becomes very familiar with each other.

The path to the first-team at Sporting had certainly not been mapped out for him, despite his obvious ball skills. A growth spurt had left Cristiano with an awkward physique, not necessary well suited to a career as a professional footballer, and he had to work hard to strengthen his body. The coaches were not sure he would survive against tough opponents who were determined to slow Ronaldo down any way they could. Cristiano knew that he had to toughen up if he wanted to win a regular role in the first team and he applied himself to this task as ably as he had to all the obstacles he had faced in life.

He was earning about the equivalent of £170 a week and the management were very impressed with his development. His rapid rise to stardom in Lisbon set a record at the club: he became the first player in Sporting's history to play for the under-16s, 17s, and 18s, B-team and first-team in a single season. It told the story of the impact Cristiano was having in training and in matches. His coaches were constantly promoting him to a higher age group because he displayed all the qualities required to progress. It forced Ronaldo to learn quickly, but also gave him the confidence to express himself freely.

But while his professional career was on the up, his personal life was not so rosy. His unhappiness at being away from home was increased by news that his older brother, Hugo, was battling drug addiction. Dolores had funded one stint of treatment with the money from her cleaning job but it had not solved the problem, and Cristiano became extremely worried.

His wage at Sporting was enough that he could offer to fund a second spell of treatment for his brother in the hope that it would straighten him out. Hugo went to a clinic in Lisbon where he made crucial progress on the road to recovery. Had Ronaldo not been a footballer, it is unlikely the family could have afforded more treatment for Hugo. It was a desperate time but Hugo's recovery gave the story a happy ending. This predicament back in Madeira made Ronaldo feel even more detached from his family and he wished he could be there more often to support Hugo. With Dinis still drinking heavily, it all had an impact on Cristiano's state of mind.

Ronaldo had supported Benfica as a boy but this had been complicated by his move to rivals Sporting – the Benfica fans would never let him forget it. The 2002/03 season saw him break into the first team at Sporting – a reward for the effort he had made to overcome his early problems. It spoke volumes for his commitment to his profession that he endured the harsh assimilation stage of his football education in Lisbon and emerged as such an immensely talented player. With Ronaldo's incredible natural talent, it is easy to assume that he did not have to work as hard to break through as a professional footballer. This is certainly not the case and anyone who has seen how hard he works on the training ground would not dare to make such an assumption. Many people made the same misjudgement over Ryan Giggs and Eric Cantona, who actually worked just as hard as anyone else.

His emergence as a first-team player for Sporting Lisbon brought him great personal joy and sent a wave of pride around the island of Madeira – nowhere more so than in his hometown of Santo Antonio. His father was overwhelmed with happiness to see his son lining up for one of the nation's top clubs. He loved to share his son's achievements with

15

others. He used to treasure newspaper articles and reports regarding Ronaldo's efforts in Lisbon and rushed around spreading the news on Mondays when the weekend games were reviewed in the newspapers. Certainly, everyone in the neighbourhood was kept well-informed about Cristiano's achievements!

He played in 25 games in the green and white of Sporting during the 2002/03 season, scored five goals, and showed why the club took the effort to nurture him through his difficult days. His first team career began with a league debut against Moreirense aged just 17. It was an incredible moment in his life and the feeling of entering the action with the crowd cheering will stay with him forever. His mood was now vastly improved in comparison with the early days in Lisbon. He really felt like a professional footballer.

He made his mark instantly by scoring twice against Moreirense, one of which was a wonderful dribble and shot into the bottom corner of the net. Cristiano raced away towards the crowd after this goal to the deserved applause. It was the perfect way to introduce himself to first-team football. He then added another goal against fellow title contenders Boavista. His exciting style of play quickly won him many fans; they would hold their breath in expectation whenever Ronaldo had the ball. His inclusion in the team was always met with cheers, though he spent a number of matches as a substitute. But it would not be long before he was plying his trade at an even higher level.

It was far from an ideal season for Sporting, who failed to live up to the expectations of their passionate supporters. The players had to endure criticism as they slipped out of title contention. Having won the Portuguese title in 2001/02 and triumphed in the domestic cup competition, Sporting were tipped for another prolific campaign, but only finished third as Porto began their period of dominance under the guidance of Jose Mourinho. The team was disappointed to lose nine matches and draw eight, finding themselves 27 points behind Porto and 16 behind second-placed Benfica. Sporting's cup campaign also ended a little prematurely as they were eliminated in the quarter-final by Naval 1º de Maio losing 1-0. Ronaldo was unfortunate to play in the side during one of the team's worst seasons. More recently, Sporting have returned to good form, reaching the 2005 UEFA Cup final – losing to CSKA Moscow – and winning the Portuguese Cup in 2007; but the Portuguese league title has eluded them since 2002.

Costinha, the Porto midfielder, echoed the thoughts of many when he reflected that Cristiano's first full season in the team could have been hard for him because Sporting had a bad campaign. It could have seriously dented his confidence. But Ronaldo still came out of it stronger. In fact, the winger was one of the main plus points for the club. He was a popular player within the dressing room and struck up friendships that he would keep for life, notably with Hugo Viana, a fellow midfielder.

Cristiano has not forgotten the influence that Sporting's 'football factory' had on his development into a world class player. When he is back in Portugal – usually on international duty – he drops in at the club to see the young players. It allows him to offer advice to the current prodigies and to re-live his days there – which, despite the uneasy beginning, had been enjoyable. Ronaldo explains, 'It is the place where I became a man and it makes me very proud to go back there and have dinner with young players who have the same dream I had.'

Ronaldo caught the eye of scouts throughout his time in Lisbon and had even come to the attention of Gerard Houllier, then manager of Liverpool. Things could have been so different had Houllier acted on his interest in the 16-year-old Ronaldo, who had starred for Portugal in the UEFA Under-17 European Championships. His Sporting Lisbon football education had earned him a place in the squad and he had dazzled scouts with his ability, albeit raw and untested in the more challenging leagues in Europe. It is at such tournaments that top clubs often spot potential superstars and there is no better audience for a youngster to perform well in front of.

For Ronaldo, it was an interesting experience. Some players had already benefited from playing in the first team of their respective clubs but he was still waiting to make the step up to the Sporting Lisbon senior side. He learned a lot about his game during the tournament and helped Portugal enjoy a good run in the competition. He could have been gracing Anfield not Old Trafford; he could have been linking up with Steven Gerrard, not Wayne Rooney. How Liverpool must be ruing that decision.

Phil Thompson, who spent time as Houllier's assistant manager at Liverpool, has since revealed the details of the club's interest. Thompson explained in the *Liverpool Daily Echo* that he had been invited by a contact, the agent Tony Henry, to watch Ronaldo play and was very impressed. He claims that Liverpool were offered Cristiano for £4 million by Sporting Lisbon, but the management were unsure of spending that much money on an untested youngster. The timing was wrong too, as Houllier had just signed Florent Sinama-Pongolle and Anthony Le Tallec, and did not think the supporters would appreciate another inexperienced signing as the team aimed for the title. While Liverpool dallied, United took pole position.

Current Chelsea manager Jose Mourinho also noticed Ronaldo's potential early on. While Ronaldo and Mourinho have not always seen eye-to-eye in more recent times, the Blues boss recalls, 'I went to watch Sporting and there was this tall, elegant kid playing up front. I had never heard of him before but my eyes were drawn to him right away. Cristiano has gone on to become a great player.' Gradually, word spread around the country and abroad that Sporting had unearthed a flair player with huge potential.

His excellent performance for the Portuguese Under-21s against England Under-21s in late March 2003 may have caught the eyes of some English supporters, and it certainly did not escape Sir Alex Ferguson's watchful eye. Ronaldo scored one of Portugal's goals in a 4-2 win. It was a rare sighting of Cristiano in under-21 action. Such was the winger's rise to the highest level that he barely had time to play alongside his fellow youngsters. England were simply unfortunate to have been one of the teams that had to face him.

Rather like his career with Nacional, his spell in Lisbon came to a sudden end. After just one season in the first team, he attracted interest from several top European clubs. With scouts regularly visiting the Portuguese capital, Ronaldo was in the shop window. His focus was on helping his team improve, but his suitors were lining up, poised to make bids. Sir Alex Ferguson admitted in the *Independent*, 'We were on the case of Cristiano when he was 15. Such was the acceleration of his career that Real Madrid, Arsenal and Barcelona were all after him, so we felt we had to act.'

Initially, though, reports varied over who would win the race for Cristiano. Some believed that Inter Milan were favourites, having agreed to pay a transfer fee but allow Ronaldo to stay in Lisbon to further his football education before later moving to Italy. But others suggested that Carlos Queiroz, United's Portuguese assistant manager, would be the deciding factor. Cristiano found all the attention very flattering but tried to remain focused on his game. A few rumours even suggested that Chelsea had made a late attempt to poach Ronaldo. Other reports linked Cristiano with a transfer to Real Madrid and Barcelona. The group of European powerhouses chasing him showed just how in demand he was.

With a tense scrap on the cards, Manchester United moved quickest to secure his signature, despite Sporting coach Fernando Santos' hopes of keeping Cristiano. It was a friendly match between United and Sporting at Alvalade XXI stadium that finally convinced Ferguson to snap up Ronaldo. The media reported that Sir Alex had told ex-United chief executive Peter Kenyon at half-time in the game that they were 'not leaving the stadium until we get the boy' and recalled, 'When we saw him play in a pre-season friendly for Sporting against us, at half-time I knew we had to get him.'

The consensus of the United players was the same. They saw Ronaldo as a very exciting prospect who could be great for the club and they urged their manager to bring him to Manchester. Ferguson realised that if Ronaldo carried his Sporting form into the Premiership, he could dominate English football for more than a decade. Cristiano had shown his appetite to progress and it was certainly a gamble worth taking, considering Ferguson's track record of getting the best out of young footballers.

Interestingly, the only other time that Ferguson had been so heavily influenced by his players was over the signing of the legendary Eric Cantona. Steve Bruce and Gary Pallister had told Ferguson that Cantona was well worth buying and convinced their manager that the Frenchman could be the missing piece in the United jigsaw. The rest, as they say, is history. Cantona went on to inspire the club to a string of Premiership and FA Cup triumphs. If Ronaldo could have the same impact that Cantona had, United would be ecstatic. Maybe he too would be the key component and he would lead the team's bid to retain the title.

A successful bid of £12.24 million saw Ronaldo moving onto the next chapter of his whirlwind story. Sir Alex Ferguson liked what he saw and knew that he had to pull out all the stops to sign him. The fee was big for someone so young and apparently Thompson and Houllier at Liverpool could not believe that United had paid such a high price for another 'potential star'. But deep down, even at this stage, they must have feared the worst and wondered whether they had made a mistake by overlooking the young winger. Thompson was unhappy that he had not been informed by Henry about the developments of the deal, as he had first offered the player to Liverpool.

Ferguson certainly made a strong impression on Ronaldo's family with his generosity and his promise to nurture the youngster's talent effectively – Dolores calls the United boss 'our friend' and the player's family felt happy with Ferguson's plans. Dinis, meanwhile, also praised the role that the United manager has played in Cristiano's life, 'Ferguson is an exceptional person. My son has a second father in Manchester who looks after him.' Without doubt, the good treatment that Ronaldo received at Old Trafford helped him to settle at the club and overcome any uneasiness. He did not suffer in the way that he had in Lisbon.

With Ferguson having sold wideman David Beckham to Real Madrid, Ronaldo had been selected as the man to take over on the right wing. Beckham's were big boots to fill, but Ronaldo would offer something very different. Rather than a succession of crosses, the United strikers could expect Ronaldo to head for the bye-line, beating his man before delivering a cross. He was a player more in the mould of a young Ryan Giggs than that of Beckham. Cristiano vowed to stamp his own identity on the United team and leave a legacy at the club.

With his transfer complete, the praise came flooding in. Eusebio, Portugal's finest ever player, announced, 'At that age, Ronaldo is not just a footballer, he is waiting to be an icon. He would enhance any team, any league anywhere. I really believe he is that good.' Luis Figo, at the time playing for Real Madrid, predicted a bright future for Cristiano in Manchester, 'He is good enough to embarrass English defenders and I think he will have too much skill for a lot of them. He can do whatever he wants as a footballer. There are some things he does with the ball that make me touch my head and wonder how he did it.' It was certainly a boost for Cristiano to hear such tributes.

Still only 18, it was the move of his dreams. Every aspiring young player hopes to make the step up to a big club and Ronaldo had done it. Now he had to justify the price tag.

While he was known to scouts of Europe's biggest clubs, Cristiano was not a household name in England and few would have selected him as a candidate to top United's summer transfer list. But at the same time, few doubted Ferguson's ability to unearth top young players. Everyone at United waited with baited breath to see Ronaldo in action, but Ferguson insisted that he would introduce Cristiano to English football carefully and gradually. Ole Gunnar Solskjaer had played so well on the right flank towards the end of the previous campaign that Ronaldo could be eased gently into the fast-paced Premiership action.

He looked shy and slight when he arrived at Old Trafford – as if he was innocent and naïve. In fact, Ronaldo had already endured some very testing times and he knew all about the dangers in life. His experiences with the problems faced by his father and his brother ensured that he was well aware of the excesses to avoid. His mother told the *Daily Mirror*, 'Cristiano has seen what drink and drugs can do to people close to him and it's part of the reason why he's become who he is today. His only addiction is football.'

Football has always been Ronaldo's chief focus and it has enabled him to avoid the pitfalls that so many young players have fallen into. When sudden wealth arrives, it is very easy to get carried away and caught up in the fame, yet he is not a man spotted out in the early hours of the night. He had not been swayed by the nightlife on offer in Lisbon, where he seemed to prefer a quiet life away from the spotlight, and it was unlikely that he would change now. It was simply not in his character to embrace the celebrity lifestyle.

There was some concern that girls would target Cristiano in a bid to get their hands on his money. But Alberto Joao

Jardim, president of Madeira, among others, had warned Ronaldo of the perils of fame and fortune. Jardim pointed out that girls would show more interest than ever in Ronaldo and that he would need to be sensible and avoid difficult situations. The president remains very proud of Cristiano and keeps a close eye on his progress.

Cristiano has never forgotten how hard his parents worked to give him a happy upbringing, and now that he has the wealth that comes with life as a footballer he has tried to show his appreciation. Nowhere is the transformation more obvious than in the case of his mother, Dolores. Having struggled to make ends meet in her cleaning job, she could not have been described as flashy with her clothes or jewellery. Now, though, she is usually seen wearing designer labels. She is set to move into a house that Ronaldo has bought for her and she is learning to drive. After the difficult years that she battled through so bravely, she deserves every bit of her new luxurious lifestyle and she looks set to enjoy it to the full.

Ronaldo still returns to Santo Antonio to see the same friends that he grew up with. Clearly, the town holds many happy memories and his friends obviously see him as the same boy they knew as youngsters. He has kept his feet on the ground and is able to renew these acquaintances with ease. Sometimes, he can be found playing pool with his best childhood friends and, when possible, he likes to return to the climate, the greenery and thriving port of his home island.

Even now that he has the celebrity status to move in any number of distinguished circles, he still prefers to spend his spare time with family and friends, eating together and playing ping pong. His fame has not changed his personality, even though his popularity has never been greater than it is now. For all the flashy confidence that he shows on the pitch, he does his best to live a quiet, 'normal' life off the field.

2003/04:
A NEW BEGINNING
IN MANCHESTER

ARRIVING IN A NEW country as a youngster is naturally a very daunting prospect. When you consider that Ronaldo moved to Manchester with limited knowledge of the English language and left the warm Lisbon climate behind, it was a big lifestyle change. Looking back, he acknowledges that his world was turned upside down, 'It was a big change in my life; the climate, the food and of course the football level. The game is a lot faster here, much more physical.' The difficulties that Cristiano experienced adjusting to life in Manchester should not be underestimated.

Additionally, he faced the intense pressure of not only replacing the departed David Beckham, but also continuing the long line of Manchester United number 7s. George Best, Steve Coppell, Bryan Robson, Eric Cantona and Beckham, amongst others, had given United supporters some of their best memories and the expectation was that Ronaldo would achieve similar feats. Despite initially requesting the number 28 shirt, the club had other ideas. Cristiano told the media that the prospect of emulating the club's great number 7s was very exciting, 'I would be very proud if one day I was held in the same esteem as Best or Beckham. It is what I am working towards. The number 7 shirt is an honour and a responsibility. I hope it brings me a lot of luck.'

When Ronaldo moved to Manchester, he arrived with his girlfriend Jordana Jardel (the younger sister of former Brazilian international Mario Jardel). Immediately, comparisons were made with David and Victoria Beckham, who had recently swapped Manchester for sunny Madrid. Jordana, however, wasted no time in dismissing these comparisons with some rather spiteful comments, telling the press, 'I wouldn't want to look like her. She is pretty but she is a bit anorexic looking and that is not so attractive, at least not to Portuguese or Brazilian men. I like music but no, I don't have anything by the Spice Girls in my collection. I don't think you should sing if you have no talent for singing.'

Jordana also made the bold claim that Cristiano was a better footballer than David Beckham. It was certainly an unusual and interesting way to introduce herself to a new country. 'Ronaldo is pure natural talent,' she explained. Meanwhile, Cristiano stayed in the background, concentrating on the season ahead and getting to know his team-mates. Somehow, his girlfriend had managed to make a bigger impact than Cristiano himself in these early moments. The newspapers were quick to take photos of the couple as Ronaldo got his first taste of the English media. He and Jordana would split up during the course of the season, but they remain good friends.

The media instantly swarmed around Cristiano. He would be seeing plenty more of them over the years. As the club's major summer signing, he hit the headlines regularly in his first few weeks in the country and, with the price tag, much was expected of him. Ronaldo tried to take it all in his stride and announced, 'I am very happy to be signing for the best team in the world, and especially proud to be the first Portuguese player to join Manchester United. I look forward to helping the team achieve even more success in the years to come.'

Yet, some feared that things would be too intimidating for Ronaldo in the early days. After all, he had arrived at one of the biggest clubs in the world. Sporting Lisbon were a top team in their own right but this was another level altogether. He joined the likes of Roy Keane, Ryan Giggs and Gary Neville, who had dominated English football and had Champions League winners' medals to their names. The weight of expectation resting on Ronaldo's shoulders was immense for a young man.

Cristiano's week got even better when, two days after signing for United, he was called up to the Portugal senior squad. Manager Luiz Felipe Scolari, or 'Big Phil' as the media liked to call him, wanted to see how the youngster fared on the big stage and decided to hand him an opportunity to impress. Ronaldo was stunned, thrilled and nervous all at the same time. He could never have imagined reaching the dizzy heights of the Portugal national team squad at such a young age. There was still a chance for Cristiano to force his way into the Euro 2004 squad too.

Like many United players, he bought an apartment in Alderley Edge – the exclusive Cheshire village where David Beckham had lived. Reports suggested that he had spent £500,000 on the ground-floor apartment. He would not have to look far for United neighbours as Sir Alex Ferguson and Rio Ferdinand both lived close by. At the time, another neighbour told the *Manchester Evening News*, 'He will be made to feel very welcome here.' It was important for Cristiano to find a property so that he could begin to settle in the area. In his favour was the fact that he had experience of arriving on his own in a new city from his days in Lisbon. He understood about adapting and finding ways to feel comfortable in his unfamiliar surroundings. He may have arrived alone but it was not long before his cousin Nuno and his brother-in-law Zé were joining him. The trio spent plenty of time together, playing ping pong and tennis.

That summer, United were linked with a number of high profile signings, ranging from Brazilian attacker Ronaldinho to Arsenal nemesis Patrick Vieira. Everyone expected the club to recruit big-name midfield players, with Roy Keane and Ryan Giggs moving into the latter stages of their careers. Harry Kewell of Leeds was thought to be on the wish list as an eventual replacement for Giggs. Certainly, few mentioned Ronaldo's name in discussions about possible transfer targets. Probably even fewer had seen him play!

But Sir Alex Ferguson had decided to focus primarily on the long-term future of the club and this was clearly reflected in his dealings in the transfer market. Along with Ronaldo, young stars such as the Brazilian World Cup winner Kleberson and the Cameroon international Eric Djemba-Djemba were brought to Old Trafford as United sought to build towards long-term domination. The previous campaign, in which the team had pipped Arsenal to the Premiership trophy, had lifted the spirits at the club and there were high hopes that United would produce more exhilarating performances with the new, young blood. Ronaldo may have arrived in England as a skinny 18-year-old with braces, but he had the determination to be a star.

Some feared that United would simply be too inexperienced to enjoy success, especially as the club would once again be chasing four trophies. But Ferguson believed that even though Cristiano was young, the winger still had enough experience. 'At 18, Ronaldo has gained the experience of playing at the highest level in Portugal, so I don't see that as a problem,' he said. Also, there were still plenty of old heads in the United dressing room – Roy Keane, Ryan Giggs and Gary Neville to name just three – so Ronaldo would have plenty of people to turn to for advice.

Unfortunately, United's Portuguese assistant manager, Carlos Queiroz, with whom Ronaldo could have spoken in his native tongue, left the club to take over as manager of Real Madrid. It was disappointing for Queiroz, too, as he had worked hard to secure Ronaldo's transfer to United. It made the start of Cristiano's time in England a little trickier not having Queiroz there to relay instructions for him in Portuguese.

But things do not always work out as expected. Despite all Ferguson's plans for United to develop a stranglehold on the Premiership, success would not come automatically, as the new signings took time to adapt to the new language, new team-mates and a new style of play. Arsenal, meanwhile, certainly felt that they had a point to prove after the heartbreaking end to the 2002/03 campaign. Having dominated the league for long periods, second place was a bitter pill to swallow and many of the team's stars returned with even greater motivation. If United wanted to retain the title, they would be in for a long, hard fight.

As for Cristiano, he was immediately in the headlines as United's most expensive signing of the summer. Beckham, for all the controversy, had been a phenomenal player for United and Cristiano was stepping into big shoes. But, even in his early days, nothing seemed to faze the Portuguese winger. He did not feature in the FA Community Shield against Arsenal at the Millennium Stadium, a game that United won 4-3 on penalties, but made his mark on his Premiership debut. Bolton were the visitors on the opening day of the season and, with United only leading 1-0 with half an hour to go, Ferguson turned to Ronaldo in a bid to seal the three points. He did not disappoint. For many, this was the first sight of the new man in action and his spellbinding cameo inspired United to a 4-0 victory. He gave the Bolton back four no end of problems, winning a penalty which Ruud van Nistelrooy failed to convert.

Old Trafford was on its feet. Ferguson said, 'It looks like the fans have a new hero. It was a marvellous debut, almost unbelievable. I felt his penetration could make a difference for us.' But he ended with a note of caution, 'We have to be careful with the boy. You must remember he is only 18. We are going to have to gauge when we use him.'

Cristiano had introduced himself to English football fans in the most mesmerising way possible and had whetted their appetite for more. It left everyone wondering just how good the 18-year-old could become. Paul Scholes was certainly impressed. Referring to Ronaldo's debut, he said, 'He came from Portugal with a bit of a reputation and last week he lived up to it.'

Francesco Filho, the Brazilian whom Carlos Queiroz recommended to Ferguson as a youth coach, was also excited about Cristiano's capabilities. Filho claimed, 'Ronaldo is an exceptional case.'

Ronaldo's whirlwind adventure continued apace as he joined up with the Portuguese national team; he was now linking up with the same players he had been idolising only years earlier – the likes of Figo and Rui Costa. It was an amazing story. His displays for the Portugal international youth teams were the first indications of his qualities for a worldwide audience. The Portuguese tend to enjoy plenty of success at youth level and Ronaldo was the latest on a long conveyor belt to burst onto the scene.

He made his international debut in a friendly against Kazakhstan on 20 August 2003, just four days after his United debut. It was a routine match against weak opposition, perfect for introducing a new player to the world stage. He came on as a half-time substitute and gave glimpses of his talent, as he savoured every moment in the Portugal shirt. Despite their clear superiority, Cristiano and his team-mates only managed a 1-0 victory. It had given him a taste of international football and he was desperate to cement a place in the squad ahead of Euro 2004, which would be held in Portugal. The prospect of playing a major tournament in front of his home fans greatly excited him and it gave him added motivation to impress at United.

Ferguson helped to keep Ronaldo's feet on the ground as he was selected as a substitute for two of the next three games. A trip to St. James' Park to face Newcastle United gave Ronaldo the chance to meet up with his old friend Hugo Viana, whom the Magpies had signed over the summer for £8.5 million. The two had played together for several years at Sporting Lisbon. Viana had only good things to say about

Cristiano, 'He is quick and strong and has great technique. I've known Ronaldo since I was 12 years old. He is my closest friend and we used to do everything together. We dreamed we would play for Sporting and for Portugal.'

Young Portuguese players were clearly in demand across Europe as, along with the transfers of Ronaldo and Viana, exciting winger Ricardo Quaresma completed a move from Sporting to Barcelona.

It was Cristiano who had the last laugh against Newcastle, as United produced a strong second half fightback to win 2-1, through two goals from Paul Scholes. Referee Jeff Winter ought to have shown a red card to Andy O'Brien for a blatant professional foul on Ryan Giggs, but the Reds still had enough quality to break down a stubborn Newcastle team. The players would have to get used to unlocking determined defences as opponents often opted for a 4-5-1 formation, particularly when facing United at Old Trafford. It put more pressure on Ronaldo to perform.

He started the home game against Wolves, but this time his trickery did not have the same effect as in his debut against Bolton. Cristiano tried too many fancy flicks and overcomplicated the team's build-up, but it was all part of the learning process. It was a disappointing performance against the newly promoted side yet United got a 1-0 win. The other new arrivals, Kleberson and Djemba-Djemba, were having bigger problems with the transition to the English style of play and many were questioning whether they could really be the future for United. Defeat away to Southampton brought an end to the team's 100 per cent record in the league but, more significantly, it was another inexcusably below-par United performance, even in the absence of Paul Scholes and Rio Ferdinand. Ronaldo quickly learned that the English media were ruthless when the top sides lost.

The United squad, though, was still brimming with both quality and experience. They responded to the defeat at St. Mary's by taking 13 points from a possible 15 in their next five Premiership games. Firstly, United travelled to The Valley where Ronaldo instantly upset the home supporters with a couple of theatrical tumbles to earn his side free-kicks. But he was constantly involved and he rose above some of the harsh treatment he received from Charlton defenders to prove United's main threat.

It was van Nistelrooy's predatory instincts that settled the game, scoring twice to claim a 2-0 win in a match that had come to life in the final half hour. After the match, Cristiano was the topic of conversation. Chris Perry, the Charlton centre half, showed his frustration when he spoke to the media. He was very unhappy with Ronaldo's inability to stay on his feet, 'Once or twice when you go down, it's legitimate. But he went down five or six times in the game and he certainly was not caught for every single one. It's a foreign thing but if the press and fans keep on him, he will change,' he fumed. Perry's disgust was mirrored by his team-mates, and they all refused to shake hands with Ronaldo at the final whistle to make their point.

Ferguson backed his player, telling the media, 'I have watched the video again and Cristiano would have needed the strength of Atlas not to go down. We have seen evidence over the weekend that diving is a problem in our game and I believe the introduction of foreign players has brought that part. But I don't think Ronaldo dived.'

The diving allegations would follow Ronaldo around all season. Former United great George Best chose to focus on the quality of Cristiano's performance: 'He was definitely man of the match. He was a magician and, at times, it looked like he had three legs as he was doing so many step-overs.'

The controversy was a major part of Ronaldo's first season in English football. He quickly noticed the differences between the Premiership and the Portuguese league, feeling that defenders escaped punishment more frequently in England and that referees tended to favour defenders. He was accustomed to seeing a defender booked immediately for a bad challenge, but in the Premiership he thought his markers got away with several fouls before receiving a yellow card. A common sight during Cristiano's early days was a frustrated, exasperated and quizzical expression on his face as he struggled to accept the referees' decisions.

Ronaldo was admittedly a very slight young man but he could handle the rough treatment. His days playing street football against older boys had stood him in good stead. Back then, he would be fouled or even beaten up for outwitting his stronger but less skilful opponents. That was not the issue. Cristiano was simply used to flair players being better protected by officials. He had already noticed that referees in Champions League matches were stricter over fouls.

The situation was very delicate and many players' tendencies to fall easily was a growing trend in world football. As a skilful attacker, Ronaldo felt that he had the right to fall if he was fouled. This continues to be a problem. The difficulty comes from the fact that often minor, more subtle fouls – shirt tugs, nudges, obstructions – are only awarded by referees if a player falls to the ground. When he tries to stay on his feet, a player is rarely awarded a free-kick. The same is true of football all over the world.

In midweek, United began their European campaign with a 5-0 win over Greek side Panathinaikos. Ronaldo was pleased with the Champions League group stage draw, as the Reds received three very beatable opponents. As well as Panathinaikos, United would face Stuttgart of Germany and Glasgow Rangers. Facing Rangers at Ibrox was a match that excited Ronaldo greatly, and his team-mates told him all about the kind of atmosphere to expect when the team travelled to Glasgow.

Ferguson opted to rest Ronaldo against the Greeks in order to keep the winger fresh and, in fairness, he was not required on a night when United overpowered their opponents. Five different scorers showed good squad depth and everyone was pleased with a winning start in the competition. Part of the incentive for Cristiano in joining United was the chance to compete and challenge for the Champions League trophy. But he would have to wait before he got his first appearance in the competition.

By leaving Ronaldo and captain Roy Keane on the bench, Ferguson ensured that they were raring to go for the home fixture against Arsenal on 21 September. A tight battle ended in a 0-0 draw, but it was not lacking in controversy. The first 80 minutes were rather uneventful, but the contest truly sparked into life when Patrick Vieira was sent off late-on. Diego Forlan then won a dubious penalty, van Nistelrooy smashed it against the underside of the crossbar and a mêlée broke out between United and Arsenal players. The Gunners, having put in a very good performance, behaved disgracefully in taunting and shoving van Nistelrooy over his penalty miss, and it all left a sour taste in the mouth.

It certainly was not a happy first experience of the United–Arsenal rivalry for Ronaldo, whose willing runs were well-marshalled by Ashley Cole. The winger also found himself involved in the chaotic aftermath as tempers flared on both sides, clashing with Martin Keown and earning himself an improper conduct charge. The FA took firm action, particularly against the Arsenal players, handing out fines and bans to Lauren (four games), Keown (three games) and Ray Parlour (one game). For United, Ronaldo and Giggs received fines. Predictably, a poll in the *Manchester Evening News* showed that 90 per cent of people felt that the punishments given to the United players were unfair.

A van Nistelrooy hat-trick sealed a 4-1 win away to Leicester on 27 September, putting United back on track. Ronaldo was an unused substitute as Ferguson looked to prevent his young star from tiring. With the team competing for four trophies, the manager knew he had to keep shuffling his pack in order to get the best from his players. Ronaldo returned to the starting line-up for the Champions League match away to Stuttgart. Despite playing well in patches, it was a bad night for United as the Germans took advantage of a few sloppy moments to go 2-0 up. It was Ronaldo who pulled United back into the game when he was fouled in the area and van Nistelrooy despatched the resulting penalty. At the other end, Tim Howard saved a Stuttgart penalty to keep United in the hunt for a point, but it was not to be – and the Reds could have few complaints.

The Germans, however, had one particular complaint to make. Stuttgart goalkeeper Timo Hildebrand made it clear that he was unhappy with Ronaldo's role in earning United their penalty, 'I had been told that Ronaldo had a reputation in England for diving and I have to say that after this game I can see why that is. He definitely dived for his penalty. I was behind him and the next minute he was on the floor. The referee was fooled.'

This outburst was the second time that Cristiano had been accused of diving by opponents and he had only been at the club a matter of months. He struggled to understand what all the fuss was about.

Birmingham arrived at Old Trafford fearing a backlash after United's European defeat. Their worst fears were confirmed when the Reds put in a fluent performance to win 3-0. Ferguson left Ronaldo on the bench and the winger sat comfortably as his team-mates turned on the style. It was a little reminder for Cristiano that there was plenty of work ahead of him if he wanted to be a regular in the United first team. There were a number of other players ready to snatch the winger's place if his standards dropped.

Hungry though he was for more international experience, Ronaldo had to wait until October for his next appearance, having missed out on the friendlies against Spain (a 3-0 defeat) and Norway (a 1-0 victory). A home game against Albania gave him another opportunity to impress and this time Scolari named Ronaldo in the starting line-up. The winger experienced walking out to a packed stadium and singing the national anthem with his team-mates for the first time. It was reassuring to look around the team and see so many veterans of international football. Captain Luis Figo, playmaker Rui Costa and striker Pedro Pauleta had all collected knowledge through years of playing at the highest level – both at club and international level. They helped to ease Cristiano into the set up and it was important that he had players to turn to for advice.

The game against Albania proved to be a thrilling contest, with Portugal eventual 5-3 winners. Ronaldo thoroughly enjoyed the atmosphere of the occasion, but he was substituted at half-time to allow others to stake their claims for a place in the Euro 2004 squad. As hosts, Portugal had qualified automatically for the competition and so played friendlies in the build-up to the tournament rather than qualifiers. These friendlies were the only chances to impress the manager and Cristiano was anxious to know whether he had shown enough potential to earn a place in Scolari's plans. Albania were far from a strong side but to score five goals was a positive sign nonetheless, and Ronaldo was well aware that he faced stiff competition for a spot in the Euro 2004 squad. But every now and again he had to pinch himself – he still found his progress from the Sporting youth teams to the Portuguese national team unbelievable. Now a major international tournament beckoned for the young winger, if he got the nod from Scolari.

At Elland Road against Leeds on 18 October, the Portuguese star was restored to the line-up and was never far from the action. Rio Ferdinand, returning to his former club, received a hostile reception, but Ronaldo did not escape their abuse either. One tumble earned him a yellow card for diving and an earful from the Elland Road crowd. The exciting aspect for Ferguson was that Ronaldo did not hide in such situations and continued to seek the ball in the final third of the pitch. He struck the angle of bar and post with a long-range strike and kept the Leeds back four on their toes. United left it late to grab the three points, as

Roy Keane headed home Gary Neville's cross with nine minutes remaining. It was a valuable 1-0 win, which the players had deserved.

In the build up to the midweek Champions League fixtures, Portugal international Costinha warned Rangers that they were in for a tough night when facing Cristiano. 'I think the Rangers left back will need an awful lot of luck when he comes up against Ronaldo in his current form. I believe the kid is now ready to make a real impact in the Champions League. He has a strong mentality and the challenge won't scare him,' he said. As chance would have it, United would see Costinha and his Porto team-mates later in the season.

But, as was becoming typical with Ferguson, he gave Ronaldo a place on the bench again for the European match with Rangers after his display against Leeds. Sir Alex was determined not to overuse Cristiano so early in his career. Phil Neville was United's hero as they put in a very professional team performance to win 1-0 at Ibrox. Cristiano was just disappointed not to experience the atmosphere himself. With a home game against Rangers to come, United felt confident of making the next round of the competition.

Domestically, though, Ronaldo and his team-mates played poorly at home to Fulham and suffered an embarrassing 3-1 defeat. It was one of the winger's worst displays of the season, as he struggled to make an impact on the match and wasted the ball too often. With a style of play like his, there were bound to be off days and Cristiano tried to remember this in his disappointment. Ferguson was left to rue his decision to rest Roy Keane, as Steed Malbranque weaved his magic in Fulham's midfield. It was the kind of result that United could do without if they were to match Arsenal's strong start.

Despite not producing their best form, United continued to pick up points both domestically and in the Champions League. After losing against Fulham, the team won six consecutive games in all competitions. November began well with a 3-0 home win over Portsmouth. Ronaldo and Keane came off the bench for brief cameos and turned a nervy 1-0 lead into an emphatic victory; Ronaldo scored United's second goal with a fizzing free-kick from the left touchline that evaded everyone and curled into the corner of the net and Keane grabbed the third. Cristiano's relationship with Keane was an intriguing one. His captain was as vocal as anyone in letting Ronaldo know when he had made the wrong decision, yet significantly, his words seemed to inspire Cristiano rather than leave him dejected.

Ronaldo's display against Portsmouth was further evidence of the impact that he could have on a game and he was relishing playing in front of 75,000 people inside Old Trafford. Ferguson was pleased with the result, but he was well aware that Arsenal had flown out of the blocks at the start of the season and were yet to be beaten. Arsène Wenger's players seemed extremely focused on bringing the trophy back to London. Having lost two Premiership games already, United were playing catch-up.

Victory over Rangers in the Champions League pushed United towards the next stage of the competition. Cristiano returned to the starting line-up as Ferguson revealed his tactics regarding keeping the youngster fresh, 'What we realised after the game we lost in Stuttgart is maybe we asked too much of him. We keep forgetting he is only 18. We can't ask him to play every game.' A 3-0 scoreline reflected the team's dominance and Ronaldo played a key role in the team's second goal, scored by van Nistelrooy. Cristiano's energetic display made it harder for Ferguson to leave him out of the team.

One of the grittiest performances of United's season came in the cauldron of Anfield on 9 November, as Liverpool were beaten 2-1. Ferguson chose to leave Ronaldo on the bench, selecting a more defensive line-up and perhaps thinking that the tension of the occasion might affect the youngster. Keane had a phenomenal game and United took plenty of positives from the match. It was a major boost for an injury-hit squad and Cristiano savoured the jubilant mood in the dressing room. Seeing the reactions of club stalwarts Gary Neville and Ryan Giggs, Ronaldo quickly understood the passion involved in matches against Liverpool. The team won again two weeks later against Blackburn, with Ronaldo providing a cameo off the bench.

Ronaldo was selected in a very young United team for the away Champions League fixture against Panathinaikos on 26 November, and he seemed to relish the responsibility of being one of the few regular first-team players. He enjoyed the weight of expectation. It was a narrow 1-0 win, through a late Diego Forlan goal, but there was little to praise in the team performance apart from Ronaldo's contribution. He constantly eluded his marker and tried his best to craft chances for his team-mates, almost finding Giggs on one occasion. The result meant that United cruised into the Champions League second round and there was plenty of belief in the squad that they could go all the way to the final.

But in the league, Arsenal were proving untouchable and seemed intent on exacting revenge on United for the previous season's disappointments. When United lost 1-0 away to Chelsea on 30 November, their title chances were already looking bleak. On the bright side, with every game, Ronaldo was learning more about his team-mates and about the team's style of play. It was a tough learning curve, with every move monitored so closely, but signs of development were evident. His grasp of the English language was slowly improving and the more he learned, the more comfortable he felt in the dressing room with his team-mates, who had given him the fairly unoriginal nickname 'Ronny'.

However, the big criticism levelled at the winger was the lack of an end product. His skills regularly left defenders flummoxed and he would find himself in excellent positions, but he would then let himself down with a poor cross or a weak shot. This seemed not to concern Ferguson, but his boss must surely have hoped Ronaldo would contribute more goals to the team. In these early months of his career in England, it was easy to forget that Ronaldo was still so young and the United supporters needed to be patient with him. Ferguson rarely misjudges young footballers and he certainly did not on this occasion. His main concern was that Ronaldo did not burn out, but with the United squad so badly hit by injuries, the heavy fixture list left Sir Alex with little choice.

The United manager explained to the media that he wanted to give his winger a rest, once the congested Christmas fixture list had finished, to prevent Cristiano from suffering with exhaustion, 'He is only 18 and we have to be careful how we use him. The secret will be giving him a good long rest, maybe for about three weeks, which will allow him to come on again later in the season.'

It is always a delicate situation for a manager – the dilemma of whether to rest a young player with a view to the future or to play him regularly to aim for short-term success. Ferguson was lucky enough to have able deputies, and this made his choice easier.

It was strange for Ronaldo not to have the luxury of a winter break. He had been accustomed to a rest over the Christmas period back in Portugal, but found that in England the fixture list actually became more congested at that time of year. It made little sense and came as a bit of shock to Cristiano, but he put his gloves on and faced the worst of the English winter. It was all part of the learning experience, and it was something that he had to get used to because there was no sign of the FA adopting the winter break any time soon.

Bad news arrived for United in December, in the shape of Rio Ferdinand's eight-month suspension for missing a drugs test. Ferdinand received a £50,000 fine, along with the ban, after the verdict of a three-man FA disciplinary panel. The ban was due to begin on 12 January. The club made it clear that they would appeal and, if an appeal was lodged, the defender would be able to keep playing until the issue was resolved. It was a bitter blow for the team, but Ronaldo tried to think positively about Rio's absence. The two had struck up a good friendship and got on very well. Of his new team-mate, Cristiano said, 'Ferdinand is a great player, one of the best defenders in the world, and an athlete of his quality is always needed. Still, Manchester United has many good players and there will be valid alternatives to fill his spot.' Speaking at the time of year when presents are traditionally handed out, he also mentioned his own aim for the season, 'The best gift for me this season would be to be selected for

Portugal's squad in Euro 2004. That is the big objective of any player.'

Though United trailed in the title race, the players proved that they were still capable of some stunning performances. After a weakened side lost to West Brom in the Carling Cup, the team won eight games in a row in all competitions to hit back at the critics. Ronaldo, who may have expected to be used mainly as a substitute in his first season in England, was regularly playing the full 90 minutes and entertaining crowds up and down the country with his footwork. As usual with United, the Christmas period had brought out their best displays, with the team taking maximum points. Yet there still remained a feeling that the club's weaknesses could be exploited, and Arsenal's exceptional form showed no signs of fading as they stretched their unbeaten run.

Further disappointment for Ronaldo came from the fact that some were critical of Ferguson's new signings because they had not had an instant, brilliant impact. While Djemba-Djemba and Kleberson had failed to live up to expectations, Cristiano had shown patches of excellent football. Yet he still seemed to be carrying some blame for the side's inability to reach the heights of the previous season. This view, though it may have had some merit, appeared to overlook the injury problems at the club and the need for the younger players to settle at Old Trafford. To expect Ronaldo to lead United's title charge in his first Premiership season, and at such a young age, was massively unrealistic.

Cristiano put in one of his most gutsy performances of the season away to Everton on Boxing Day. United desperately needed the points and Ronaldo showed great resilience to overcome some very physical marking. Gary Neville praised

46

the winger's courage, 'Cristiano Ronaldo was brilliant. He was a constant danger. He takes the ball all the time. No matter if he loses, or he gets fouled, he comes back for more. He is a really brave player. He had a few lumps kicked out of him but people can never question his bravery.' Neville even admitted that he would be tempted to put a few kicks in on Ronaldo if he was facing him because the youngster's skills were so dazzling.

Ronaldo had always taken the physical challenges as a compliment to the threat that he poses to opposition sides. It was an extra challenge for him to overcome to prove his quality. He explained his point in the media, 'When defenders think there is a player capable of creating danger, they try to stop him no matter what, and often that means fouling him. When defenders get so aggressive, it just proves that they are worried about a player because he is quick and skilful.' While such tussles left Cristiano with cuts and bruises, he enjoyed the satisfaction of knowing that the opposition had been afraid of his ability.

The New Year saw the continuation of Sir Alex's on-going row with John Magnier and JP McManus, whose company, Cubic Expression, owned over 25 per cent of United. The quarrel escalated due to disagreements over the ownership of the racehorse Rock of Gibraltar. Ferguson claimed he had been offered a half-share in the horse, which went on to achieve great success and earn in the region of £150 million. The dispute became rather nasty, and it was an unwanted distraction for Sir Alex. He had enough problems on his plate.

January and February ended any realistic hope of United catching Arsenal at the top of the Premiership, much to Ronaldo's frustration. January began well for the team with a 2-1 win away to Aston Villa in the FA Cup – Villa Park has often been a happy hunting ground for the Reds – and United were hopeful of enjoying a long run in the competition. Another good win, again away from home, in the Premiership against Bolton suggested that the players had carried their Christmas form into the New Year. Ronaldo felt that United could at the very least apply pressure to Arsenal in the hope that they could claw themselves back into contention.

But their Premiership form soon fell away again. A disappointing 0-0 draw at home to Newcastle was followed by a devastating 1-0 loss to lowly Wolves at Molineux on 17 January, where Ronaldo toiled to produce chances that were not converted. It seemed that at times he was on a different wavelength to the team's strikers, and this explained some of the side's scoring problems. Louis Saha arrived from Fulham for around £13 million in the January transfer window, and it would take time for him to settle at the club. His form so far during the campaign suggested he would score plenty of goals at the Theatre of Dreams. But he had come in at a tricky time with United's form wobbling badly.

The gap at the top increased further due to these slip-ups, and Arsenal must have been laughing at United's inconsistency. It frustrated everybody at Old Trafford that the players were not putting Arsenal under any pressure – if anything they were gifting the Gunners an advantage. The defeat away to Wolves had been an initial sign of trouble before United conceded eight goals in their next three league matches, winning two and losing at home to Middlesbrough.

On a more positive note, Ronaldo and his team-mates kept up their pursuit of the FA Cup with a 3-0 win over

Northampton on 25 January and it seemed as though this was the only competition in which United could play consistently well. In a second-string line-up, Ronaldo was the star of the show. He relished taking on the Northampton defenders and tied them in knots with his skills. His threat led to him being fouled in the area – though contact was minimal – but Forlan missed the spot-kick. Ronaldo did not end up on the scoresheet, yet he was seemingly everywhere, crafting United's best moments and exploiting the tiring legs of the opposition. Against the same team that George Best had fired six goals in a single afternoon, the current United number 7 was fittingly the key man.

United were involved in some thrilling contests. Defensively, though, they were stretched by an injury to Gary Neville and the suspension of Rio Ferdinand. It led to some confusion in the back four, and the team found themselves having to score more goals to win games. At home to Southampton, United conceded two but scored three to seal a less than convincing win. Louis Saha scored on his United debut, but Old Trafford was somewhat stunned by the side's current vulnerability. The untried back four of O'Shea, Brown, Silvestre and Fortune struggled to deal with an energetic Southampton attack as Kevin Phillips struck twice.

Away to Everton on 7 February, United's defensive problems were highlighted once more. With Ronaldo only a substitute, United still had the creativity to destroy the Toffees in a sweeping first half display that seemed to have clinched the points for the Reds. But a 3-0 lead was quickly squandered as the team wilted under pressure. Confidence in the defence looked minimal and Everton exploited it.

Cristiano could only warm-up and hope that Ferguson sent him on to remedy the situation. Just when it looked like United were heading for a disappointing draw, substitute Ronaldo burst down the right, his cross found van Nistelrooy at the far post and the Dutchman headed in a dramatic winner. Ferguson was thrilled with the win and Ronaldo's impact during his brief cameo. It was the type of flowing football that the team was clearly capable of producing, but for some reason it had been missing for parts of the season. Cristiano left the field delighted with his brief contribution, especially in the face of some of the criticism of his end product.

The FA Cup Fifth Round served up a treat, as United were drawn against neighbours Manchester City at Old Trafford on 14 February. This Manchester derby, like so many before it, was a bad tempered affair and Cristiano would be called upon to make a difference. When Gary Neville was sent off in the first half for a head-butt on Steve McManaman, United had to resort to counter-attacks, and this played into Ronaldo's hands. City left-back Michael Tarnat endured a torrid time, as Ronaldo danced past him and set up wave after wave of United attacks. The fact that the Reds had only ten players did not allow City into the game as expected but only exposed them to the ruthless pace and skill of United's attackers. Ronaldo got on the scoresheet with the team's third goal in a solid 4-2 win, and his popularity rose even higher in the estimations of the United fans – after all, a win over City is always a season highlight, and the Old Trafford fans certainly needed something to cheer about.

Cristiano was back with the Portugal squad again in mid-February for another friendly – this time against England.

Having sat out of two friendlies in November, one of which was an emphatic 8-0 win over Kuwait, Ronaldo was itching to take on the English and impress Scolari. Not only was it a chance to pit his wits against club colleagues, but it was the type of exciting game that brings the best out of him. He was also anxious not to lose any ground in the race for a place in the Euro 2004 squad.

Scolari chose to leave Ronaldo on the bench for the first half, but he came on for the second period. England took the lead through Ledley King, but Ronaldo helped his team claw their way back into the game. The equaliser arrived after 70 minutes through an excellent strike from Pauleta. It was a good result all round, and Ronaldo was able to laugh and joke with his United colleagues after the game. Nights like this were important building blocks for Ronaldo's international career as he showed his strong character. Every international match that Cristiano played served as good experience and helped him learn more about other European sides. This information would be useful in case Portugal met these sides in major international tournaments, where it would be vital to know opponents' strengths and weaknesses.

If January and February had been below-par for United, worse was to follow in a forgettable March. As well as a busy domestic programme, the Champions League second round awaited against Jose Mourinho's Porto, and gradually attention turned to the club's bid for European glory. Few really rated Porto's chances, but they had looked solid during the group stage. Everyone was a little edgy, but few could have anticipated what was to come.

United arrived in Portugal with plenty of confidence in their ability to score away goals but, with only one clean sheet in their last seven league games, there were defensive problems to worry about. Porto duly recovered from Quinton Fortune's early goal to win 2-1, and a frustrating night ended with captain Roy Keane being sent off for stepping on the grounded Porto goalkeeper Vitor Baia. Ferguson so desperately craved another European triumph, but the current squad simply did not have the talent of the 1999 team. There were too many inexperienced players and, for all Ronaldo's improvements, he had plenty to learn at the highest level. But he was disappointed that he was only given 14 minutes to impress as a substitute.

This match marked the beginning of the Ferguson–Mourinho relationship. The United manager was unhappy about Baia's part in Keane's dismissal, suggesting the goalkeeper over-exaggerated the contact. In the wake of the game, it was the red card that overshadowed a below-par display from Ronaldo and his team-mates. Mourinho was quick to remind United of their shortcomings, proudly declaring, 'You would be sad if your team gets as clearly dominated by opponents who have been built on 10 per cent of the budget.' It was a confident and brave statement from the Porto boss, considering that the tie was only halfway through.

Ronaldo still felt sure that United could fight back at Old Trafford, willed on by a raucous home crowd. It was sure to be an intimidating atmosphere for the Porto players to endure. The first leg had not gone to plan for Cristiano, but the team was still well placed.

In the Premiership, a 1-1 draw away to Fulham was followed by a 2-1 FA Cup victory over the same opposition. A van Nistelrooy double was enough to clinch a place in the next round. Cristiano hit the crossbar with a free-kick and lit up the match several times with his trickery. After sitting out of the majority of the first leg against Porto, Ronaldo was doing his best to persuade Ferguson to give him the chance to start in the return match.

When Porto came to Old Trafford for the second leg on March 9, United still seemed a good bet to overturn the first-leg scoreline. A large crowd and a passionate performance was called for. The Reds appeared to be cruising into the quarter-finals, leading 1-0 through Paul Scholes and handling the visitors with some ease. Ronaldo was frustrated only to be on the substitutes bench but willed on his colleagues. It certainly seemed an odd decision to prefer the more defensive-minded Darren Fletcher on the right flank when the team needed to score goals to get back in the tie.

Ferguson introduced Ronaldo to the action in the 75th minute, with United still 1-0 ahead and set to go through to the quarter-finals on away goals. But his role in the action ended early as he left the field on a stretcher just nine minutes later, following a challenge from Dmitri Alenitchev. The foul had obviously been a lot more painful that it had first appeared. Sadly for Cristiano, his evening got considerably worse as he could only watch on from the sidelines. United were made to pay a heavy price for not taking their chances when goalkeeper Tim Howard fumbled a Benni McCarthy free-kick late in the game, and defensive midfielder Costinha slammed in an equaliser that put Porto through to the next round. Old Trafford fell silent in shock and dismay.

It was the most devastating moment of Cristiano's first season in English football, and it was delivered by a team from his native Portugal. Having left Portugal to further his career, Cristiano now faced the embarrassment of being eliminated by a Portuguese club side. It was an unhappy time at Old Trafford, and Ronaldo would have to wait to sample the latter stages of a European competition. The team was having no difficulties finding the net, but the defence was proving very leaky, creating a feeling of vulnerability throughout the team. For so much of the match he had felt that United would reach the quarter-finals, but there was a sting in the tail. Ronaldo rued the assistant referee's incorrect decision to disallow a second goal from Scholes that ought to have sealed the tie. Ferguson was stunned, 'You get shocked in life and I suppose you couldn't see that one coming. Porto had a lot of possession of the ball but I felt that we were in complete control.'

The season had only reached March, but Ronaldo and United were now realistically out of contention in the Premiership and had been eliminated from the Champions League. It was a bizarre feeling, especially after the stylish end to the previous season. There was no choice now for Cristiano but to focus on reducing Arsenal's lead at the summit of the Premiership table and ensuring a respectable finish. The club's pride needed to be restored, and the fans required something to cheer about.

In March, Ronaldo turned his attention away from football temporarily to promote his home island of Madeira. He was a special guest when tourism chiefs arrived in Manchester and, with his celebrity status, he hoped to be able to increase the number of British visitors to the island. Having won the European Region of the Year in 2004, the island seemed to be becoming a very popular destination for tourists. As a proud product of Madeira, Ronaldo was naturally happy to offer his support to the cause.

Inconsistency marred the remainder of the Premiership season, but every day was a valuable chance to learn for the Portuguese star. He would be a stronger player as a result of his experiences in his first season and, after all, it was still such an early stage of his career. His third Manchester derby of the season was instantly forgettable, as the team crashed to a 4-1 loss at the City of Manchester Stadium in one of Sir Alex's most humiliating afternoons as United manager. The result reflected the hangover from the European nightmare and the greater passion that City had shown. Ronaldo, though, was quick to bounce back, as he scored United's second in a 3-0 win over Tottenham on March 20, coming off the bench for the final 15 minutes. His run, starting in his own half, ended with a powerful strike that flew into the net, via the post. Sadly, these glimpses of good United form were all too brief during the campaign, though it was pleasing to see Ryan Giggs back to his splendid best as he tormented the Tottenham defence.

Ferguson worked hard to get his players back on track and he wrote defiantly in his programme notes, dismissing the criticism his team had faced, 'There are people dancing on what they perceive to be our grave but I am not cracking up and neither am I feeling the pressure. People cast around for reasons for our setbacks, which range from my supposed preoccupation with a racehorse to my transfer signings. We will come out of this and we look to our supporters to stand firm and help us through a rough ride.'

Back-to-back fixtures against Arsenal gave United the opportunity to address some of the season's frustrations. The Gunners had shown the type of consistency that Ronaldo and his team-mates had been lacking, but this was United's chance to hit back. Cristiano had been in the thick of the action in the 0-0 draw earlier in the season, which was remembered for all the wrong reasons. He insisted, though, that the quarrels were in the past, 'I was a little surprised by what I saw but it is water under the bridge now. Arsenal are a strong team, they have got some good players, so I am sure it is going to be an interesting battle.' With the Gunners still unbeaten in the league, United had the opportunity to end that run, but Arsenal would be determined not to throw it away, especially against Ronaldo and co.

The first match on 28 March, in the Premiership, was a relatively dull affair and United required a late Louis Saha goal to come away with a point. However, the teams had appeared well-matched, suggesting that the upcoming FA Cup semi-final would be a tight contest. For United, the FA Cup was the sole remaining target and, as Gary Neville pointed out before the game, this was the most important match of the team's campaign. Neville was adamant when he wrote in his column in *The Times*, 'There is no point trying to play down the importance [of this game] for United. It is the most important match of our season. It is our season.'

The players responded with a display full of passion and belief, determinedly repelling Arsenal attacks. Arsène Wenger had surprisingly elected to leave talisman Thierry Henry on the bench for this game and United took advantage, going ahead after 32 minutes, through Paul Scholes. From then onwards, United's desire not to end the season empty-handed carried them to victory, and some of the resilience that had been missing in the Premiership returned to the side. They defended manfully and by the time Wenger introduced Henry, United were comfortable. 1-0 proved to be enough, and United advanced to face

Millwall in the final. For Ronaldo it would be his first showpiece final and the chance to win some silverware in his first season at United.

Boosted by reaching the final, Cristiano came off the bench away to Birmingham in the league and turned the match in United's favour. Trailing to a Martin Grainger goal, Ronaldo sparked his team into life as he headed home Giggs' cross to equalise. Giggs then crafted a chance for Saha, who sealed the three points. The energy that Ronaldo had brought to the side had been crucial, and Birmingham's weary legs had no answer. Frustratingly, United seemed to have waited until the title had slipped away before producing their best displays.

On 13 April, Ronaldo collected his first Sky Sports Man of the Match award in the 1-0 home win over Leicester. He terrorised the Foxes' defenders, forced good saves from goalkeeper Ian Walker, and it was his shot that deflected into the path of unlikely goalscorer Gary Neville. Ronaldo, still only 18, struggled with the language during the post-match interview but Neville was there, just like earlier on the pitch, to pick up the pieces. 'He's very confident. He's only 18 years of age and to come to a foreign country and adapt the way he has, it's been incredible and he's a very good player,' Neville enthused.

The interview showed that Ronaldo had settled well in the dressing room and was certainly a popular member of the squad. He laughed and joked with Neville and was clearly enjoying life at Old Trafford. It was a rare sighting of Ronaldo in front of the camera during his opening season at United – he would be more and more in demand as the years rolled on and his grasp of the language improved markedly.

It had not been the fairytale start that Ronaldo might have imagined, but he had cemented a place in the team and would now have the chance to cap it all with an FA Cup winners' medal. The remainder of the season was fairly uneventful as United went through the motions in the league with the FA Cup final in all the players' minds. Back home in Madeira, the excitement was growing as everyone looked forward to seeing Cristiano play in such a major final. The closing weeks summed up the whole season as United moved from victory to defeat on a weekly basis, including a painful 1-0 loss at home to Liverpool on 24 April. The fans were far from happy about surrendering points at Old Trafford against their fierce rivals, but the energy had gone from United's play. Minds had started to wander towards the end of the campaign.

An international friendly offered a welcome change of scene for Ronaldo, as Portugal drew 2-2 with Sweden on 28 April. Once again, Ronaldo only played a part of the game – but this is often the way with friendly matches. He came off the bench after 63 minutes and gave further evidence of his potential. A draw with Sweden was a solid result as the Swedes were expected to have a decent run in the competition. With Euro 2004 nearing, Ronaldo was determined to secure his place in the squad and make his family proud. The little boy from Funchal had come a long way.

It seemed likely that Sir Alex Ferguson had instructed Scolari not to play Ronaldo for full games in friendlies, especially considering that he was still so young. Earlier in the year, against Italy at the end of March, Ronaldo had again played only a part of the game. Italy had won 2-1 and, while it was a valuable lesson to witness the quality of the Italian defenders up close, Portugal would doubtless have preferred to use Cristiano for the full 90 minutes.

Back with United, the team continued to limp towards the finishing line. When Ronaldo and his team-mates succumbed to a 1-0 defeat away to Blackburn on 1 May, the team had lost three of their last four Premiership matches, failing to score in any of the defeats. A 2-0 win over Aston Villa at Villa Park on the final day of the league season meant that the players had at least ended on a high. Ronaldo was amongst the goals, opening the scoring with a fine curling shot that beat Thomas Sorensen at the near post. Van Nistelrooy doubled the advantage six minutes later and Villa never recovered, their UEFA Cup hopes dashed.

With the clock running down and United already down to 10 men after Darren Fletcher's dismissal, it seemed that the match would just peter out. But nobody told Ronaldo. Having been booked for diving earlier in the game, he then kicked the ball away in frustration with five minutes remaining to collect a totally unnecessary red card. He had been the star of the show, but now he had ended his first league campaign in England on a bitter note. Ferguson was not amused, but seemed to blame the referee rather than his players. He told the press, 'You can't even comment on those decisions – it's bizarre. But the seriousness of it is that those players will miss the first game of next season which is disappointing. Otherwise, I think our performance was very good. That was our best performance since our away win at Everton in February.'

But by now all eyes had turned to the final and, although Millwall were vastly inferior opponents, everyone was wary of the scope for the competition's biggest ever upset. Dennis

Wise, the Millwall manager, had done an excellent job and his players knew that they had nothing to lose. The Lions were quoted as 8-1 outsiders by the bookmakers. Even though United were expected to win, it would be a tricky game. To put it into context, even the experienced Ryan Giggs admitted that he was feeling nervous on the eve of the match. Unsurprisingly, Cristiano was overwhelmed with a combination of anxiety and excitement as he prepared for the game.

The final, played in front of 71,350 at the Millennium Stadium in Cardiff, belonged to Ronaldo. It was undoubtedly his finest performance of the season, and he had produced it on the biggest stage. Some experts even likened it to the great Sir Stanley Matthews' display for Blackpool in the 1953 FA Cup final – perhaps the 2004 final would be dubbed the 'Ronaldo final'. It quickly became clear that, for all Millwall's efforts, there was a gulf in class between the two sides, yet United struggled to make it count. It was Ronaldo himself who eventually opened the scoring just before half-time, heading home from Gary Neville's cross. Ruud van Nistelrooy grabbed the other two goals – one from the penalty spot – but it was the Portuguese winger who was at the heart of all of United's best moves. Incredibly, Cristiano was not awarded the man of the match trophy, as Sven-Goran Eriksson chose van Nistelrooy for that honour. The Dutchman, like everyone else, could scarcely believe that Ronaldo had not been rewarded for his performance. The critics suggested that it summed up Eriksson's powers of judgement.

All the talk after the game centred around Ronaldo. In front of millions of viewers worldwide, he had delivered a match-winning display, worthy of gracing any game. Ferguson was delighted, 'Ronaldo was outstanding. We need to look after him in the right way because he is going to be an outstanding footballer.' For Ferguson, it was also a relief that one of his young signings had played so spectacularly; Sir Alex had received plenty of criticism for the fact that a couple of his other signings had flopped in the fast pace of English football.

Gary Neville echoed his manager's sentiments, 'To come with the price tag on his head and at his age, he has been outstanding for us this season.' His family watched the match with immense pride and his father, Dinis, was overjoyed with Cristiano's achievements. One of Madeira's home grown youngsters had gone to England and won the FA Cup. Word soon spread around the island as Ronaldo's relatives celebrated his success.

As he stepped up to receive his medal, it was a tremendously proud moment. The whole squad wore shirts with 'Davis 32' on the back in memory of Jimmy Davis, the United youngster who had died tragically in a car accident. It was a moving act and made the success more special because it was dedicated to Davis. The idea for the shirts came from Roy Keane, while Gary Neville spoke for everyone at the club when he said, 'We still think about him [Davis] and we mention him regularly. Hopefully, what we did today will make Jimmy's parents smile for a moment.'

The Premiership had been the main aim, but the United players were visibly delighted to lift the FA Cup. Ronaldo basked in the glory of his starring role and savoured the compliments of his manager, his team-mates and the pundits, although Alan Hansen still maintained that he would rather play against Ronaldo than in the same team as him. It was impossible not to think about Ronaldo's promising future. The only concern was that the positive words might go to his head. As James Lawton observed in the *Independent*, Cristiano had to be careful not to listen too carefully to the praise of others. Lawton felt that there was still plenty of vanity in the winger's game and that he ought to look more closely at the manner in which Ryan Giggs has acted throughout his lengthy career at Old Trafford. The fact that Ronaldo had dazzled Millwall, not AC Milan or Real Madrid, was a valid point and was a warning against getting carried away by the hype.

It had been a season full of ups and downs for Cristiano, but he had ended it on a high. He had gained experience and maturity in abundance and would look to continue his improvements when the new campaign began. In the meantime, he was focusing on Euro 2004.

EURO 2004:
LIVING THE DREAM

CRISTIANO PLAYED A part in both remaining warm-up friendlies prior to Euro 2004 – the last chances to impress the manager and show his quality. He came on for the second half against Luxembourg on 28 May, replacing Luis Figo, but by then the game was over as a contest – Portugal led 3-0 at half-time and did not add to their score in the second period. A final friendly followed on 5 June as Portugal hammered Lithuania 4-1, and Ronaldo produced a short cameo in the final 20 minutes. The team was hitting good form as the competition approached, and Scolari seemed content with the build-up. He had an abundance of quality players to choose from.

Ronaldo was thrilled and relieved in equal measure when it was announced that he had been selected in the Portuguese squad for the tournament. Scolari obviously felt he had a role to play, and it was destined to be the most intense month of the winger's career to date. Cristiano had held high hopes of making the squad, though there had been a few anxious moments, none more so than when Scolari reacted angrily to United's attempts to pull him out of the match with Sweden. The Portugal manager had raged, 'Cristiano Ronaldo is an unknown for me. I've seen him play more for Manchester United than here. I want players who are as keen to play for their country as their club. If you can play with a knock for your club, you can do it for your country.' Scolari had also referred to Ronaldo as a 'doi-doi' or 'fancy dan' in the build up to the tournament, so doubts had understandably been raised in Cristiano's mind over whether he would make the squad.

But he had made it. However, it looked increasingly likely that Cristiano would be used as a substitute during the tournament to exploit tired legs in the latter stages of games. Scolari reasoned that there would be nothing worse for weary defenders than the sight of Ronaldo's pace and trickery entering the game in the closing stages. With a midfield boasting talented players like Figo, Rui Costa and Brazilian-turned-Portuguese Deco, there was no room in the starting line-up for another flair player. Ronaldo had to be patient and wait for his opportunity. He was naturally thrilled to be in the national squad but his ambitious streak would not allow him to settle for being a squad player. Ronaldo believed he could break into the side and was always working hard in training to prove to Scolari that he deserved a chance. As the squad gathered for the tournament, there was great excitement and a steely determination to deliver success in front of the Portuguese nation.

For Ronaldo, a young footballer still learning the game, the feeling of playing an international tournament in Portugal in front of his own fans was a dream come true. His late surge into contention for the squad reflected the speed of his development. He had only made his international debut in August 2003, yet here he was in a major competition less than 10 months later. His family were over the moon with excitement.

Despite his young age, much was expected from Cristiano. Former Portuguese international midfielder Paulo Sousa certainly believed him to be an integral part of the new guard, 'The team is going through a transitional period. I think Cristiano Ronaldo will be the sensation of the European Championship Finals. He has the potential to be the best player. He went to the right club. Manchester United will enable him to develop and do exciting things.'

Able to stop and take in his achievements over the past season, Cristiano could scarcely believe his journey to the top. He recalled sitting in the Sporting dressing room prior to the friendly with United in 2003, unaware of the direction that his career was about to take. It had all happened so quickly. A few years earlier he could not have imagined that he would have moved to England, lifted the FA Cup and played in the European Championships so soon. Winning the tournament in his home country would be a dream come true for him – something he longed for as a boy in Funchal.

Asked about his first season in England, he said, 'We were disappointed not to win the title, but the FA Cup final was a great day – and one I will never forget. Now, I have Euro 2004 to look forward to.'

The country was buzzing and the preparations for the tournament had been completed successfully. Now everyone simply wanted the action to begin. Fans from the nations involved flocked into Portugal, as football brought the country to a standstill. Supporters from all over Europe mingled in the big cities, which were awash with colour.

Portugal received a massive boost as hosts of such a major event and optimism swept the nation. Having qualified automatically, the team was drawn alongside Greece, Spain and Russia in Group A. It was a very tough group, yet Ronaldo and his team-mates still held high hopes of reaching the quarter-finals. Scolari had great expectations for his side. After all, they did not want to disappoint their own supporters, who had fallen in love with Euro 2004 even before it had begun.

With their home fans behind them, many pundits saw Portugal springing a surprise or two along the way – maybe even as dark horses to win the competition. There were plenty of other top sides challenging for glory, but the crowd support could be a key factor. The stadiums selected for the tournament all had relatively large capacities, especially those of Sporting Lisbon, Porto and Benfica. They ensured that Portugal's matches, in particular, would be very noisy indeed.

The spirit within the squad was generally very good. But the one issue that caused some friction in the camp came from tension between captain Luis Figo and fellow midfielder Deco. Deco was originally Brazilian by nationality but changed to make himself eligible for Portugal. Figo found it insulting that this had been tolerated by the Portuguese Football Federation. The media discovered the uneasiness and it quickly became public knowledge. With Scolari being Brazilian himself, the dispute became all the more intriguing. However, the two players appeared to have let the matter drop – there were more important issues to concentrate on. The duo needed to be on the same wavelength once the tournament got under way.

Portugal's opening match was against Greece on 12 June, a useful team but not expected to cause too many problems in Group A. Yet the occasion seemed to get to the hosts and Greece flew out of the traps with nothing to lose, taking Portugal by surprise. Ronaldo was not selected in the starting line-up and watched on nervously from the touchline as his team-mates made a poor start. The difficulty for Scolari was in fitting all the attacking players into the starting 11. As well as Cristiano's obvious creative flair, the Portugal manager had captain Luis Figo, Rui Costa, Deco and Simao to accommodate – all of whom possessed immense talent. Ronaldo's inexperience meant that was one of the unlucky ones who missed out at the start of the tournament. He would, though, get chances to impress as a substitute.

Greece took a shock lead through a 25-yard strike from Georgios Karagounis, following a mistake by Paulo Ferreira, and held firm against Portugal's attempts to equalise. Some stinging words at half-time and the second half arrival of Ronaldo were designed to spark life into Portugal, but it was the Greeks who started the brightest. Unfortunately for Ronaldo, one of his first contributions was to foul defender Giourkas Seitaridis in the penalty area. Angelos Basinas stepped up to double Greece's advantage and Cristiano hung his head in dismay. He had dreamt of many Euro 2004 scenarios, but this was most definitely not one of them.

Portugal did their best to claw themselves back from the abyss. Ronaldo teased defenders and conjured good opportunities for his colleagues, but they had left themselves too big a mountain to climb. Greece sensed their chance to throw the group wide open and defended heroically. Ronaldo was the man who finally provided the breakthrough, but it came in injury-time and left no chance of a comeback. He took some comfort from his goal – a header from a Luis Figo cross – but the loss was painful. Naturally, the 2-1 defeat was not well-received locally; suddenly qualification looked in jeopardy with tough games against Russia and Spain ahead. This sluggish start was definitely not in the script.

Scolari told the media about the mood in the camp, 'I'm beaten down and sad. But these results happen. The players are really depressed and myself too. The next game is crucial for us. The next game is life or death.' His intensity spoke volumes for the pressure that he was under.

Captain Figo was also downcast, reflecting the way that Ronaldo and his team-mates were feeling, 'We didn't deserve to lose this game, Greece created two chances and scored two goals. We're all disappointed. It's a big disappointment for the supporters.' There was nothing more to be said, and Cristiano notably made it obvious that he did not want to discuss the game or his own performance with any of the reporters present – such was his bitter disappointment. He just headed straight down the tunnel and back to the dressing room.

The result temporarily dented morale, but Ronaldo knew that the team were far from out of the competition. Two wins from their last two games would be enough to reach the quarter-finals. The big frustration was the enforced wait before their next game. The Portugal players were desperate to make amends but could only sit and watch as the other nations kicked off their Euro 2004 campaigns. Cristiano and his team-mates did not want to be out training or restlessly passing time in the hotel. They wanted to be in action again. Their chance would come again, and they simply had to grab it with both hands.

No team stood out as a clear favourite after the first round of fixtures. A below-par French side had sneaked past England, thanks to the magic of Zinedine Zidane, while Italy also looked out of sync. Portugal felt capable of competing with anyone on their day, and the opening round of matches had not dispelled that feeling. They were itching to get back out and restore some pride for their supporters. Tournaments always tend to go a little flat once the host nation has been eliminated so many neutrals hoped that the Portuguese players would get back to winning ways.

Ronaldo was soaking up every bit of the atmosphere. The passion of the crowds and the non-stop attention of the media made it a very special time. The game against Russia on 16 June was an absolute must-win match, with Spain having beaten the Russians 1-0 in their first fixture. Cristiano again found himself amongst the substitutes but knew that he would probably play some part in the action, especially if the team was struggling. Scolari at least had the benefit of knowing that he had a few aces up his sleeve on the bench.

Portugal's major weakness was their lack of a razor-sharp centre forward, meaning that Ronaldo's eye for goal might well be required. PSG front man Pauleta was a good option but did not have the attributes to be a clinical lone striker. Russia proved stubborn opponents, but goals from Maniche and Rui Costa took Portugal to a vital 2-0 victory. As expected, Ronaldo came off the bench and exploited weary Russian legs. It was his cross that set up Rui Costa's match-clinching goal. Cristiano had staked his claim to start the critical match with Spain.

So everything was perfectly balanced going into the final group match. Portugal's fate was still in their own hands. Spain had managed just a 1-1 draw with surprise package Greece so Portugal needed a win to be sure of reaching the quarter-finals. In some respects, it simplified the situation. Ronaldo and his team-mates knew exactly what was required and would be firing on all cylinders. It would the Spanish players who would have to decide how aggressively to approach the match. A number of experts were adamant that Cristiano had to start the match against Spain. Bobby Robson claimed, 'The Portugal coach should pick Cristiano Ronaldo from the start. He has done well in the two games, making a goal and scoring one.'

Terry Venables, who, like Robson, was a former England manager, agreed that Ronaldo deserved to be in the team. Cristiano's compatriot Jose Mourinho added his weight to the argument while working on Portuguese TV during the competition, 'Cristiano Ronaldo is Portugal's best forward and he should have started for Portugal since the beginning of the tournament.' All eyes were on Scolari's teamsheet. Would he heed the advice of others or stick to his original plans?

With the form Greece had shown, many expected them to beat Russia and take top spot in the table. So Portugal and Spain would probably be scrapping for second place in the group. Ronaldo's reward for his fine cameos as a substitute was a place in the starting line-up – perhaps the calls from experts had finally worn Scolari down. Cristiano remained calm, despite the high stakes resting on the outcome of the match, and felt assured by the unity and spirit that he saw in the dressing room. He had great confidence in his ability and was ready for this chance.

Lisbon was full of tension on a night that would make or break Portugal's Euro 2004 bid. Nobody wanted to think the unthinkable – least of all Ronaldo. History was not on Portugal's side as they had not beaten Spain in 23 years of football, but this Portugal team was determined not to go out early in front of their own supporters. The reception that the players received from their fans as they went out to warm up was a big boost. Back in the dressing room there were the usual sounds: the clattering of studs; the bouncing of footballs. But there was something different about this night. The Portugal squad felt it, and so did the fans.

The match was not a classic, but it was certainly cherished in Lisbon that night. A 1-0 victory, courtesy of a Nuno Gomes goal, saw Portugal take top spot in the group (Greece lost to Russia) and Spain pack their bags for home. There had been an element of arrogance in the way that the Spanish side had approached the group stage, and they had paid a high price for their over-confidence. Having beaten Portugal comfortably in a recent friendly, the Spanish players and management may well have taken their opponents lightly. The Spanish media prepared to evaluate a remarkably familiar story, all the more frustrating considering the immense talent in the squad.

Ronaldo's unpredictability and Figo's cunning were major threats, and as Kevin McCarra of the *Guardian* suggested, 'The promotion of Ronaldo spoke of Scolari's recognition that bravado was no longer viewed as a flaw.' The Portuguese knew that a win was needed and they showed more desire than the Spanish players, feeding off the wonderful support that came from the crowd. Cristiano loved every minute of the contest as he played his part in a great victory. Celebrations in the capital went on well into the night. It was crucial for the success of the competition that the hosts made the quarter-finals because as a result the nation continued to buzz with excitement.

Portugal had reached the quarter-finals and now had their sights set on the big prize. Their opponents would be England, whose progress in Group B ensured that they qualified in second place behind France. Ronaldo would go head-to-head with his United colleagues Gary Neville, Paul Scholes and Rio Ferdinand, knowing that he would never hear the end of it in the dressing room if Portugal were beaten. Wayne Rooney's excellent performances for England had grabbed plenty of headlines, but Ronaldo gave the rallying cry from the Portuguese camp: 'We're not afraid of England or Wayne Rooney.' The media thrived on the idea that with some of the more established stars looking below-par in the tournament, it was a chance for younger players to stake their claim. Thus, Portugal against England became Ronaldo against Rooney.

Club colleague Gary Neville lavished praise on Cristiano and said at the pre-match press conference, 'I know that Cristiano Ronaldo isn't going to give me a minute's rest on Thursday night.' But Ashley Cole did his best to unsettle Cristiano in the days leading up to the game by suggesting that a few strong challenges would be enough to put him off. The winger did not rise to the bait but simply prepared himself for the biggest game in his international career. He was pleased that Portugal had avoided a quarter-final with

France and was quietly confident of his team's chances. He hoped his performance against Spain was enough to clinch a starting role again.

The quarter-finals consisted of Portugal, England, France, Greece, Sweden, Czech Republic, Denmark and Holland. France were still most people's favourites, but the Czech Republic had been impressive and were the only team to qualify with maximum points. In turn, with the whole country behind them, Ronaldo and his international colleagues were full of hope. There had been many twists and turns already and few would bet against there being several more as the tournament progressed. Everyone was on tenterhooks.

On 24 June, Ronaldo made the starting line-up again for the quarter-final clash at the Estadio da Luz, home of Benfica. The two sides seemed well matched and everyone predicted that it was going to be a very tight contest. Portugal got off to a bad start when Michael Owen burst through and lobbed the ball over goalkeeper Ricardo, silencing the crowd in the process. The turning point in the match came when Rooney, who had started very brightly, went off with a metatarsal injury. Portugal gradually took control of the match but met firm resistance from the England defence, with Ashley Cole doing a good job of stopping Ronaldo. Cristiano kept trying to make the breakthrough and forced Cole to stay deep in his own half. But England's central defenders were coping easily with Portugal's lone striker and the longer the game wore on, the more likely it looked that Ronaldo and Portugal's bid for glory would end in tears.

But England's brave rearguard was beaten in the 83rd minute by a Helder Postiga header. Manager Phil Scolari had been brave enough to take off Luis Figo in the bid for an equaliser, and it had paid off as substitute Postiga, who had been a flop at Tottenham, threw his team a lifeline. 90 minutes could not separate the sides so the game headed for extra-time. The Portuguese fans were up in celebration again when Rui Costa fired Portugal ahead in the 110th minute. Ronaldo and his team-mates just had to hold on to claim a semi-final slot. But England came roaring back, and Frank Lampard made it 2-2 with five minutes remaining, breaking Portuguese hearts in the process. The game would be decided by the dreaded penalty shootout. It was now all about who held their nerve better.

In Ricardo, though, Portugal had an ace up their sleeve. His excellent track record of saving penalties gave the side a boost heading into the shootout. Ronaldo's confidence in his own ability was such that he was happy to take one of the team's five penalties. The adrenaline rush of the shootout appealed to him, and he relished the head-to-head battle with the goalkeeper in much the same way that Gary Lineker used to during his international career. How England would have loved to have a Lineker-like player to turn to here. To put it simply, the team with the greater nerve would earn a place in the European Championships semi-final. It was too good a chance to waste.

Ronaldo and Portugal were handed a great start as David Beckham missed England's first penalty. But a Rui Costa miss made it 2-2 in the shootout, with three kicks taken each. John Terry put England ahead 3-2 and then Ronaldo stepped forward to face the pressure of the situation. If he missed, England could win with their next penalty. But missing was never a consideration for Ronaldo and, even though he was still so young, he tucked away his kick with aplomb. Back home in Madeira, the family were gathered around the television. His father could not bear to watch his son's penalty and relied on the reaction of the crowd in the stadium to hear whether Cristiano had been successful. Dinis told reporters, 'They are proud of him [Cristiano] coming from a place like Santo Antonio and going to the biggest club in the world. Not everyone born in a village like this can play for such a big club.' Dinis missed seeing his son on a regular basis but the two spoke regularly on the telephone to make amends.

The teams were so inseparable that they remained locked at 4-4 after the five penalties, and the shootout went into sudden death. Then 5-4, 5-5. Darius Vassell stepped forward next to take England's seventh attempt, but Ricardo sprung to his left and saved his spot-kick. Remarkably, as Ronaldo and his team-mates wished Nuno Valente luck on his walk from the halfway-line, Ricardo snatched the ball and decided that he would be taking the potentially match-winning kick. He wanted to be the hero. Nobody argued and Ricardo smashed the penalty into the bottom corner, sparking wild celebrations in the stadium as Cristiano and his team-mates converged on their jubilant goalkeeper. Portugal had outlasted England in a titanic struggle, and Ronaldo was heading to the semi-finals. He offered a few words of consolation to his devastated United colleagues in the England team, but there was nothing that could numb the pain that they were feeling.

England were left to rue the fact that referee Urs Meier had dubiously chosen to disallow them a goal late on in normal time, for a foul by John Terry. Sol Campbell had scrambled the ball into the net, but he was to be denied, just as he was in St. Etienne in 1998. Contact seemed minimal. It was a real let-off for the host nation. The English supporters and media were furious, and a bitter reaction followed in the press. Meier received some unsavoury threats as the incident spilled out of control. Ronaldo was certainly relieved to hear the referee blow the whistle for a free-kick – a goal then would have left Portugal no time to respond.

Cristiano and his colleagues now had a massive semi-final to prepare for against Holland as their adventure continued. The quarter-finals had thrown up one monumental shock, as Greece continued their own incredible journey by beating much-fancied France 1-0. So Portugal would face either the Czech Republic or Greece in the final, if they could overcome a Dutch side that had needed a penalty shootout to eliminate Sweden. With a number of the glamour names now eliminated, it presented a chance for someone new to stake a claim for stardom. Everywhere Ronaldo went now, he drew attention from adoring fans and he was quickly replacing some of the nation's older icons. Arsenal manager Arsène Wenger even noted that Cristiano's direct style of play was a key factor in Portugal's progress thus far in the competition.

The Portuguese supporters were full of hope. There was now no question of whether or not Ronaldo would make the starting 11. He was not only a regular but a key man, to whom Portugal looked for inspiration and creativity. Boasting Ruud van Nistelrooy, Arjen Robben and Clarence Seedorf, Holland would be strong opponents, but with Ronaldo, Figo and Maniche pulling the strings in midfield, Scolari was confident of plotting victory. The bookmakers expected a tight contest, while some pundits, including Spaniard Guillem Balague, felt Portugal had the edge. Just 50 days after they had linked up to win the FA Cup for Manchester United in Cardiff, Ronaldo and van Nistelrooy found themselves on opposite sides in a Euro 2004 semi-final.

Playing in Lisbon again, Ronaldo was back at Sporting Lisbon's Estadio Jose Alvalade, where he had enjoyed a great football education. It was to be another very special night for him. Willed on by passionate Portuguese support, Ronaldo and his team-mates began quickly, trying to take a firm grip on the match. Cristiano's dream moment arrived after 26 minutes when he gave his team the lead. Luis Figo delivered a corner and Ronaldo escaped his marker to power a downward header past Dutch goalkeeper Edwin van der Sar. Scoring in a European Championships semi-final was pure ecstasy for the winger, and his goal celebration showed his joy.

Maniche doubled the lead with a wonderful shot that found the top corner, but Figo was the star of the show, proving his critics wrong by re-capturing his best form. Jorge Andrade's own goal gave Holland hope with just under half an hour remaining, but Portugal held out with ease. Cristiano and his colleagues had played very well, but the Dutch had been disappointing in equal measure, leaving danger man van Nistelrooy isolated too often in attack. The crowd had played a key role for Portugal, lifting the players whenever they seemed to be running out of steam.

Ronaldo could not contain his joy after the game, telling the hoards of journalists gathered, 'It's an incredible sensation, something unique. We will do everything in our power to finish the job now on Sunday. It will be a spectacular encounter. But we must be aware that in 20, 30 or 40 years' time people will only talk about who won, not who came second.' Figo was equally delighted after his own display, 'It's difficult to explain in one word the emotion I feel right now. We've suffered a lot to reach the final in our own country. I'd trade everything I've ever won for this one moment.'

Meanwhile, van Nistelrooy was unhappy with referee Anders Frisk. 'It's unbelievable how the referee ruled everything in favour of Portugal,' he told the media. But the Dutchman did admit that Portugal had deserved to win the match.

Portugal's great run had continued and now only one match stood between them and the trophy. The following day, Greece sprung yet another surprise by dumping the Czech Republic out of the tournament in extra-time. The Czechs had been so impressive during the competition, dominating a group including Germany and Holland, but their journey was over. So, it would be a final that few could have predicted. Portugal would be the favourites but they were taking nothing for granted. Ronaldo knew that it would require another strong performance to clinch the trophy and, having lost 2-1 to Greece in the opening match of the tournament, he would not be taking the opposition lightly.

Midfielder Maniche stressed the fact that this match was not about revenge for the earlier defeat – it was bigger than that. Scolari spoke cautiously to the press, 'It will be very, very difficult. It's 50-50. One strike – a free-kick or a lapse in concentration – could decide the outcome.'

The bookmakers were in no doubt over the outcome, making Portugal massive favourites and Greece clear underdogs at odds of 2-1. But it was unfamiliar territory for both nations, and there would be lots of nerves on show as the sides walked out onto the pitch for the final.

Cristiano tried to prepare for the Euro 2004 final as if it was just another match for him. There was nothing to be gained by getting overawed by the prospect. Scolari ensured that the players stayed calm and, while the whole country was on the crest of a wave, Ronaldo and his team-mates quietly got on with their training sessions and discussed the tactics for the big game. At least they were familiar with their opponents. Having played Greece in the first fixture of the tournament, Portugal would now face the Greeks in the last fixture too. It was very rare to play the same team twice in a major competition, but Cristiano and his team-mates hoped that it could have its advantages.

On 4 July, back at the home of Benfica, it was fitting that Ronaldo should play in the stadium of his childhood team for this massive occasion. Though he was disliked by Benfica fans due to his spell at Sporting, Ronaldo still held Benfica close to his heart. The match itself had a cat-and-mouse feel to it. Greece, well organised and full of energy, kept Portugal's array of stars at bay despite the best of efforts of Ronaldo, who was determined to put in a good performance. The game remained goalless until just before the hour mark, when Portuguese hopes were dashed. Greece, having defended for much of the contest, won their first corner and promptly took the lead through a header by Angelos Charisteas. Few could believe what they were seeing. A stunned silence followed, except for the Greeks in the crowd who celebrated jubilantly.

Portugal tried valiantly to rescue the game and had chances to pull level. Ronaldo had probably the best chance but blazed his shot over the crossbar. Scolari threw on attacking substitutes and shouted directions desperately to his players, yet the Greek defence held firm. For all the good build-up play, Portugal were once more left ruing the lack of a van Nistelrooy figure to finish off attacks. Pauleta was not the striker suited to the team's style of play, but he was not alone in spurning chances. When Figo's shot deflected wide, it proved to be Portugal's last opportunity. The final whistle blew and Greece, not Portugal, were crowned tournament winners.

For the second time in the competition, Greece had ruined Portugal's big party, and the Greek players and manager Otto Rehhagel broke down crying with joy. Ronaldo was absolutely inconsolable. The magnitude and emotion of the moment overwhelmed him and the tears flowed – he was devastated by the defeat, having so desperately wanted to lift the trophy in front of his home fans. In that moment, viewers saw just how far a young man had come and how committed he was to his country. There were, however, some Premiership supporters in England who enjoyed seeing Cristiano in tears – the anger over his theatrics had still not died down entirely.

He hoped that somewhere in the future he would experience winning a major international tournament to erase the pain of losing a final. The runners-up medal was scant consolation for Ronaldo as he had to walk past the main prize on the podium. Figo immediately took his medal off in disgust. Then the Portuguese squad endured the agony of watching on as the Greeks lifted the trophy. While it was an amazing triumph for the underdogs, it was a flat note on which to end such an action-packed competition. Euro 2004 will be remembered as the tournament of shocks – Germany, Spain and Italy crashed out in the group stages, and reigning champions France fell to Greece in the quarter-finals. Portugal had been one of the few sides who had played plenty of good attacking football.

Greece captain Theo Zagorakis spoke proudly about his team's success, 'We have given the Greek people a great pride which they will be able to carry with them for the rest of their lives.' The same, though, could be said for Portugal's tournament efforts. Yes, they had come up short, but they had captivated the country, brought the Portuguese people together and played some excellent football. There were plenty of positives to be taken, as Michael Walker wrote in the *Guardian* on 5 July, 'The journey has fascinated Portugal and they gazed on again yesterday. Fans followed the route of the team coach jumping, shouting and waving. Hysteria might be too strong a word for it but frenzy is not.' Such was the expectancy of the supporters that, after the defeat, Scolari felt the need to issue an apology to the supporters, 'We ask forgiveness from all the Portuguese because we weren't able to achieve the goal that we all wanted.'

But the feeling in the Portuguese camp reflected the attitude that the runners-up are hardly ever remembered in years to come. They had earned themselves a tremendous opportunity but had fallen short at the crucial moment, and the disappointment would stay with Ronaldo for a long time. To come so close and miss out in a game that they had dominated was incredibly upsetting. But another season at Old Trafford beckoned, and Cristiano focused on building on the positive impression that he had made during his first season in England. He was able to fit in a short break before pre-season training began and savour the prospect of representing Portugal at the 2004 Olympics – ironically in

Athens, Greece. It had been another unbelievable, character-building period in Ronaldo's short career and, if he was not already a household name, he was now.

His performances were a reminder of the potential he possessed, and he had shown signs of the player he would go on to be. He had won over many new fans and, in time, he would look back on the happy times that he enjoyed whilst playing in a tournament in front of his home supporters. After all, many international footballers never have that opportunity. Some consolation for Cristiano came in the form of his inclusion in the 23-man UEFA all-star Euro 2004 squad, based on his superb displays in the tournament. It was the very least that his performances deserved.

Unfortunately for Ronaldo, the next 12 months would bring more heartache for him. It would not be a memorable season for United, and his dream of a Premiership title triumph would have to wait.

2004/05:
SECOND SEASON
BLUES

RONALDO'S SECOND SEASON in English football offered the chance to add to his FA Cup winners' medal. That success had given him a taste for silverware and it was the Premiership title that he had his sights on next. The rest of the squad were equally determined that the league trophy should return to Old Trafford. The joy of the comeback in 2002/03 had disappeared after the poor Premiership campaign in 2003/04, but a new season represented a fresh start and a clean slate.

The downside was that Cristiano was now a known commodity and would receive closer attention from markers. Many players in the past had struggled with their second season at a top club, finding the success of their first campaign difficult to replicate. Ronaldo's tricks would have been scrutinised in the close season, and defenders would be better prepared to face him. But it was just another challenge for the winger to overcome. He was used to facing adversity.

After the Euro 2004 tournament, Ronaldo had the bragging

rights in the dressing room. Portugal's shootout win over England had been a special night for him. The competition had showcased the talent of Wayne Rooney, whose injury against Portugal was the turning point in the contest, and Rooney was the subject of most of the pre-season transfer speculation around Old Trafford. He had progressed superbly at Everton but many felt he now needed a bigger stage to display his ability. David Moyes had managed Rooney's career very well thus far, but with the Toffees not competing in any European competitions the speculation over their teenage star was inevitable. The increased profile and earnings that a club like United offered would be irresistible for any player, and Rooney was an ambitious youngster. The chance to pair Cristiano with a fellow fledgling was irresistible for Ferguson.

United soon declared their interest and spent much of the summer chasing Rooney's signature. Everton did their best to hold on to their star youngster, but eventually Ferguson wore them down, securing a deal that could eventually reach up to £27 million. Everton would receive a guaranteed payment of £20 million, and then a further £7 million was based on achievements and appearances. Alan Smith arrived from relegated Leeds United and Gabriel Heinze, the Argentine left back, completed Ferguson's summer shopping. United had signalled their intent by spending around £40 million on new options, and an attack boasting Ronaldo, Giggs, van Nistelrooy, Smith and Rooney spelt trouble for the rest of the league. There would be no excuses for a lack of goals.

An additional bonus for United and Ronaldo was the return of Carlos Queiroz to Old Trafford. His one season as manager of Real Madrid had been unsuccessful and, as tends to be the way at the Bernabeu, he was consequently sacked. Ferguson did not hesitate to bring him back to United. David Gill, the club's chief executive, explained that this move was great news for the club and particularly for Cristiano, 'We're delighted with the return of Carlos Queiroz. If you speak to Alex he is over the moon. He will particularly help Ronaldo. Look at him, he's 19, he's had a fantastic first season, but I'm sure he will benefit from having a Portuguese assistant manager working with him.' Having worked hard to set up Ronaldo's transfer to United, Queiroz was excited to have the opportunity to work with him.

Somehow, though, United's transfer coups were over-shadowed by the appointment of Jose Mourinho as Chelsea manager. Claudio Ranieri had not produced the success that owner Roman Abramovich craved so he was sacked, leaving the door open for a new boss. Mourinho began his career in football as assistant coach and interpreter at Sporting Lisbon and then Porto, working alongside Englishman Bobby Robson. The pair moved to Barcelona in 1996 where they enjoyed immediate success, winning the UEFA Cup in 1996/97. After his stints with Barcelona B and Benfica, Mourinho returned to Porto in January 2002, this time as manager. It was the making of him, as he dominated the domestic and European scenes, securing back-to-back league titles as well as the 2003 UEFA Cup and the 2004 Champions League. He had taken a relatively average team and turned them into a functional, wily outfit. Having changed Porto's fortunes on a shoe-string budget, the mind boggled at what he might achieve with Roman Abramovich's wealth. Abramovich appeared prepared to give his new manager a blank cheque in a bid for domestic and European domination.

Mourinho's tremendous achievements with Porto, capped off with the 2004 Champions League triumph, had brought him to everyone's attention. He strolled into the country and promptly announced himself to the media in an incredibly assured press conference. Mourinho said, 'We have top players and, sorry if I'm arrogant, but we now have a top manager. I am really excited at the prospect of competing week in, week out at the highest level in England as well as in Europe. I think I am a special manager because I have won the Champions League.'

Thus, Mourinho's nickname the 'Special One' was born. It was not long before everyone could see the greater steel that he brought to the Blues – a resilience and belief that was not always evident under Ranieri. The Chelsea players seemed very happy with the fresh ideas that Mourinho brought in.

Mourinho knew Ronaldo better than most. After all, he had been to watch Ronaldo play for Sporting Lisbon when he was manager of Porto, and Mourinho's profile was very high in Portugal. Mourinho had worked alongside Bobby Robson at Sporting as assistant coach and interpreter, and no doubt still had contacts at the club with whom he could discuss Cristiano's progress. The two could not be described as friends, though, and being involved at rival clubs, they were destined to clash at some stage over the next few years.

The new Chelsea manager brought several Porto players with him to Stamford Bridge – defenders Paulo Ferreira and Ricardo Carvalho – along with Czech goalkeeper Petr Cech and Dutch winger Arjen Robben, who Ferguson himself had been chasing. Ivory Coast international striker Didier Drogba arrived from Olympique Marseille, and controversial forward Mateja Kezman completed a move from PSV

Eindhoven. Both had been prolific in their respective leagues but the Premiership would be a big step up in quality. Suddenly, United's transfer activity paled in comparison. The title race now looked destined to be a three horse race, as Chelsea aimed to gatecrash United and Arsenal's party.

For obvious reasons, United were keen to protect Cristiano as the new season approached. Ronaldo's inclusion in the Portugal squad for the 2004 Olympics in Athens was an issue that particularly troubled Sir Alex Ferguson. United were paying Ronaldo's wages yet they were obliged to allow him to miss vital domestic games at the start of a long Premiership campaign. It did not seem fair to those at United. Gabriel Heinze, was playing for Argentina in the tournament and so United were forced to struggle on without two first-team players. Heinze had not even seen Old Trafford yet, despite signing for the club several months earlier.

Ferguson spoke bitterly about the situation to the media, 'We'd have to give Ronaldo two months off when he returns so we wouldn't have him until November. It's ridiculous. I just don't even think they'd be that interested after playing in Euro 2004 (Ronaldo) and the Copa America (Heinze).' But Ronaldo made it clear to his manager that he wanted to sample the experience of playing at the Olympics, 'Being in the Olympics is a unique opportunity in anyone's career. I am very pleased to represent Portugal and I intend to play.' The winger understood Ferguson's reluctance to let him depart, but at 19 he wanted to seize the opportunity to play at such a famous, worldwide event.

The issue did not end there though. Ferguson's suggestion that players going to the Olympics risked losing their place in the United team was met with an angry reply from FIFA

President Sepp Blatter, who argued, 'To tell players like Heinze and Ronaldo to not go to the Olympics because they could lose their job when they come back is definitely not in the spirit of solidarity. This is not fair.' Sir Alex dismissed these words but eventually decided to let the matter go. Ferguson just hoped that Ronaldo and Heinze returned to Old Trafford without any injuries. He was planning for a long season. As it happened, Cristiano was back sooner than anticipated after Portugal's disappointing showing in Athens.

Ronaldo was clearly excited about building on the start that he had made at United. Overall, he felt pleased with his progress in his first season but had identified plenty of areas in which he hoped to improve. Buoyed by the way he had performed at Euro 2004, he was ready to transfer that form to the Premiership campaign and add to his trophy cabinet. Once the Olympic football competition was finished, he would be match fit and ready to torment English defences.

The Community Shield match against Arsenal, though, did not bode well. Even without Patrick Vieira, who had joined Juventus, Arsenal easily overcame a depleted United side. Alan Smith announced his arrival with a well-taken strike, but there was little else to smile about. Ronaldo did not play at the Millennium Stadium and he missed the first few games of the season due to his involvement with the Portuguese squad for the Olympics. His absence just added to Ferguson's headache, considering United had major injury worries. Rooney's injury at Euro 2004 had not yet healed, van Nistelrooy was on the treatment table and Rio Ferdinand was still serving his ban for the missed drugs test. It all led to a disastrous start to the season for United, and it allowed the other title contenders to grab an early lead.

A 17-year-old Cristiano in action for Sporting Lisbon against rivals
Benfica in the Portuguese Premier Division in December 2002.

In action for Portugal against Argentina as an Under-21 in June 2003.

Above: Ronaldo looks cool in the winter sun as he arrives for training at Manchester United's Carrington complex in December 2003.

Left: New Manchester United signing Cristiano signs autographs as he leaves Old Trafford after a press conference in August 2003.

Above: Euro 2004, and on home turf Cristiano celebrates after scoring during the semi-final match between Portugal and the Netherlands in Lisbon, June 2004.

Right: His joy in the semis turned to disappointment in the final, where despite some energetic tussles his team lost out to Greece for the championship.

Above: Cristiano looks on during a first team training session at Carrington training ground, Manchester, January 2005.

Left: Two of the deadliest young players in the Premiership – Cristiano and team mate Wayne Rooney.

Cristiano can take on any defence in the world; here he controls a ball in front of veteran Paolo Maldini of AC Milan during a Champions League second leg football match, 8 March 2005.

Above: Laughing with Manchester United manager Sir Alex Ferguson during a Champions League press conference ahead of the match between Benfica and Manchester United in December 2005 in Lisbon.

Below: Holding his head in his hands after a refereeing decision goes against him during the match.

Cristiano was chosen to present the Portuguese football team's new strip, worn at the 2006 World Cup, at the Discovery monument in Lisbon.

A 1-0 defeat to Chelsea at Stamford Bridge on the opening day was a disappointment and an ominous sign for the rest of the campaign. Jose Mourinho, the new manager of the Blues, certainly enjoyed his first taste of Premiership action. United's selection problems forced Roy Keane to play in the centre of defence while midfielder Quinton Fortune lined up at left back. It was a far from ideal start, and the injury problems showed no signs of improving. The fact that Mourinho's Porto had eliminated United from Europe the previous year made the result even more frustrating. Ronaldo, away on international duty at the Olympics, could have made the difference for the Reds, a fact that no doubt occurred to Ferguson in the wake of the defeat.

A narrow win over Norwich at Old Trafford secured the team's first three points of the season, and Ronaldo made his unexpectedly early return to action, coming off the bench for the final five minutes. United were far from their best, and selection problems forced Ferguson to put Liam Miller, David Bellion and Eric Djemba-Djemba in the starting line-up. Ronaldo's introduction eased the pressure in the closing moments, but Old Trafford had expected a far more emphatic win against Premiership newcomers. The United manager had vowed to give Cristiano a two-month break to make up for the player's lack of a summer rest, but the injury situation at the club made that impossible. Instead, Ronaldo was quickly back out in the red shirt as the side needed all the available first team stars they had in the early moments of the season.

Three consecutive Premiership draws led to plenty of questions from the critics. First, Alan Smith's late goal against Blackburn on 28 August earned a 1-1 scoreline in a match where United created an abundance of chances but were not sufficiently clinical. Brad Friedel was excellent in the Rovers goal, but Ronaldo knew that he was guilty of wasting a couple of good opportunities. He played the full 90 minutes and, despite a non-stop summer, felt in good shape. Things got worse when United drew 0-0 at home against Everton. The visitors set up with a very defensive formation and United were unable to make the breakthrough, although they did hit the woodwork on three occasions. One of those attempts came from the boot of Ronaldo, who jinked away from a couple of Everton shirts only to be denied by the frame of the goal. The players had tried their hardest, but it was two more precious points dropped.

International duty occupied Cristiano's attention at the beginning of September. The Portugal squad was ready to put the disappointment of the Euro 2004 final behind them and concentrate on the 2006 World Cup qualifying stage. The team were favourites to top a group that included Russia, Latvia, Luxembourg, Estonia, Liechtenstein and Slovakia. The players were determined not to be complacent, but most neutrals felt that minnows like Luxembourg and Liechtenstein were dream opponents and would offer plenty of chances for Portugal's attackers to find their form. The qualifying campaign began away to Latvia on 4 September. The Latvians would present a tricky challenge, having reached Euro 2004 and put in creditable displays.

After a goalless first half, it was Ronaldo's creative talent that finally broke the deadlock. His goal in the 58th minute brought a sigh of relief all over Portugal, and Pauleta then made it 2-0 a minute later to leave Latvia a mountain to climb. It was never going to slip from Portugal's grasp.

Scolari had called for a winning start and Cristiano had provided the perfect response. He and Pauleta would dominate the scoring in Portugal's qualifying campaign. Four days later, on 8 September, Ronaldo was once more the man to unlock an opposition defence. Estonia had stubbornly held out for 75 minutes, but the floodgates opened after Ronaldo had made the breakthrough. Three more goals flew in to give Portugal a 4-0 victory. The final 15 minutes showcased the danger presented by the Portuguese attack and indicated the important role that Cristiano had adopted in the national setup.

When Ronaldo rejoined his United colleagues, injury problems continued to haunt the side, and another last-gasp equaliser was required to salvage a 2-2 draw against Bolton at the Reebok Stadium. Cristiano came off the bench as Ferguson sought to up the tempo and the winger almost had an early impact when his shot rattled back off the crossbar. The players were relieved to pick up a point but knew that they were slipping behind the leaders. Sir Alex spoke proudly about his team's character, 'I don't think either team deserved to win or lose that game. To come back like that shows our determination. We'll get better, of that there's no doubt.'

On the plus side for United, van Nistelrooy was now back from injury along with Wes Brown, while Heinze and Smith were looking shrewd signings. It was the backup players that were falling short of the desired level of performance. Liam Miller was struggling to live up to his billing as 'the new Roy Keane', and Djemba-Djemba and Kleberson still did not seem suited to the English game. The situation with Kleberson was the most baffling because he had looked such a classy

91

midfielder at the 2002 World Cup, but he had not found that level of performance in his time at Old Trafford. Of the signings made by the club in the summer of 2003, only Cristiano had lived up to his billing.

Having won their Champions League qualifier against Dinamo Bucharest 5-1 on aggregate, United were drawn in Group D with Lyon, Fenerbahce and Sparta Prague. Fenerbahce and Sparta Prague represented rather straightforward opposition, but French champions Lyon would be a dangerous threat. The heart-breaking experience against Porto had reminded the players not to underestimate any opposition, but few in the United dressing room could have hoped for a better draw for the group stage. Ultimately, the European stage is where great teams earn their reputation, and Cristiano was well aware of this. It explains why the likes of AC Milan and Real Madrid will always remain bigger clubs than Arsenal until the Gunners succeed in the Champions League. Ronaldo and his team-mates were desperate to win back the Premiership trophy, but a Champions League triumph would be the highlight of any season.

The campaign began away to Lyon on 15 September where United picked up another draw, on this occasion recovering from two goals down thanks to a van Nistelrooy brace. Lyon put in an impressive display and forced the Reds to dig deep. The French champions had been untouchable domestically in recent seasons and appeared ready to transfer that form into European competition. Ronaldo played a major role in pulling United back into the contest, setting up van Nistelrooy's first with a good cross and then creating the second when his shot fell into van Nistelrooy's path. The comeback was a boost to the team, who were increasingly making life hard for themselves. In these first few weeks of the season, Ronaldo and his team-mates seemed to be forever falling behind and chasing the game. It spoke volumes for their character and desire that in a number of these matches they successfully fought back to take a share of the spoils.

The team finally returned to winning ways on Rio Ferdinand's return from suspension against Liverpool, now managed by Spaniard Rafael Benitez. Mikael Silvestre was the unlikely scorer of both United goals in a 2-1 win. Ronaldo carried his form from the Lyon match into the game, and his skills bewitched the Liverpool defenders, providing the team's biggest threat, even if his delivery was a little erratic. While his awareness and vision needed refinement, his raw skills and dribbling ability made him a real handful. Nobody could get near to him, just as Jerzy Dudek in the Liverpool goal could not reach Ronaldo's 30-yard strike that cannoned off the post.

Ronaldo took his menace to White Hart Lane next, as United began to gather some impetus at long last. A van Nistelrooy penalty secured a 1-0 victory, but it was the Portuguese winger who was behind most of the team's best moves, skipping past his marker and delivering dangerous crosses – one of which was converted by van Nistelrooy, only for the assistant referee to rule it offside. Things were improving for United, and suddenly the squad was starting to look back to full strength. Cristiano's recent form did not go unnoticed and several pundits praised the way that he was playing. Having Ferdinand back appeared to be helping to tighten up the defence, and the team appreciated the much-needed clean sheet.

The next Champions League game was all about Wayne Rooney, who struck a hat-trick on his debut. United supporters had been desperate to see their new signing in action and hoped his return from injury would kick-start the team's floundering start to the campaign. Ronaldo was given a well-earned rest for a game United were never in danger of losing, running out impressive 6-2 winners. Ferguson was sticking to his promise to nurture Ronaldo carefully – he was, after all, still just 20. Old Trafford was believing again and, if the team kept up their current form, silverware would follow. Having struggled for goals in the early stages of the season, Rooney's return was seen as the start of a potential purple patch. He had certainly made a strong start. Ryan Giggs went as far as to proclaim Rooney and Ronaldo as the top two youngsters in Europe.

United drew at home to Middlesbrough on October 3, again needing a goal in the last 10 minutes to rescue themselves. It was frustrating for Ronaldo and his team-mates – for all their efforts, they could not find that knockout blow. Arsenal and Chelsea had made stronger starts and United supporters were beginning to worry about the gap at the top. Only first place would be acceptable, and they would need to step up a gear if they wanted to catch the leaders. Ferguson had spent a lot of money during the summer and expected more from his players. Although Ronaldo and Rooney were still youngsters and had been signed with a view to the future, there was a huge expectation on them to deliver results immediately.

On 9 October, Ronaldo headed to Liechtenstein for the latest World Cup qualifier. To everyone's surprise, Portugal's good start came to a halt with a shock 2-2 draw. It was hard to tell whether the players had underestimated their opponents or whether they had simply endured an off night. Scolari was left to rue his decision to withdraw Ronaldo with almost half an hour to go, when Portugal were still 2-1 ahead. The squad left feeling rather embarrassed, but two dropped points were not worth fretting about. The players would be back with a bang just a few days later.

Russia bore the brunt of Portugal's frustrations four days later in a 7-1 demolition, as Ronaldo ensured that the team got back on track. There was evidence of a more clinical Portugal as they converted chance after chance to leave their opponents thoroughly demoralised. Cristiano was amongst the scorers, grabbing a brace – one in each half. The other goals were shared around as the Portuguese fans enjoyed a feast of football. It was pleasing for Ferguson to see his winger scoring so often for his country, and Sir Alex just hoped that Ronaldo could carry those predatory instincts into his club performances. The Reds desperately required goals from their winger.

When United failed to win again in their next match, away to Birmingham, the players found themselves under intense pressure. The players were unaccustomed to having problems scoring, and it was an anxious time as they drew another blank in a 0-0 draw away to Sparta Prague in the Champions League. With Arsenal visiting Old Trafford in their next league game, it seemed a make-or-break game, even as early as October. The Gunners had extended their marathon unbeaten run in the Premiership to a whopping 49 games, and it was fitting that avoiding defeat against rivals United would take them to the half-century mark. Roy Keane missed out with flu but the team fielded plenty of other stars, among them Ronaldo, Rooney, van Nistelrooy and Giggs.

CRISTIANO RONALDO

In a tense and tetchy contest, the game remained goalless until the 73rd minute, when Sol Campbell was adjudged to have fouled Rooney in the area. After mass complaints from the Arsenal players, van Nistelrooy scored the penalty, in the process erasing the memories of his miss in 2003. Rooney added a second for good measure in the closing moments to seal the win. Ronaldo and his team-mates could celebrate ending Arsenal's unbeaten run, but ultimately they still had much to do to claw themselves back into the title race.

What happened after the match, though, will probably be remembered as much as the game itself. A skirmish in the tunnel at full-time between the two sets of players and both managers saw an Arsenal player throw a slice of pizza that hit Sir Alex in the face. The media tagged the match 'The Battle of the Buffet', and it dominated the headlines all week as everyone awaited news of which player had dared to hurl the pizza at the United boss. The rivalry was as fierce as ever and was showing no signs of calming down, but the mayhem of this contest definitely affected the Gunners, who took a long time to recover from it.

It seemed as though the win over Arsenal would re-ignite United's title challenge. Despite their slow start, the team certainly had the talent to surge back into title contention, and they had recovered from rocky starts in the past – just ask Kevin Keegan. For United, there are few better catalysts for a run of form than a victory over the Gunners and, with this in mind, supporters hoped that Ronaldo and company would return to their best.

But United's inconsistent form continued domestically. They collected one point from their next two league games and failed to score – beaten by Portsmouth and held 0-0 at home to Manchester City. Supporters questioned why a team with the likes of Ronaldo, van Nistelrooy and Rooney were struggling to find the back of the net. It was all the more frustrating for Ferguson as the title slipped further and further away. Ronaldo was certainly guilty of wasting opportunities at Fratton Park as United squandered chance after chance against Portsmouth.

Ferguson fumed afterwards when he spoke to the media, 'It's a kick in the teeth. It absolutely destroys what happened last week [victory over Arsenal]. We missed an incredible number of chances and I couldn't tell you why. For the quality we've got we should be doing better in these games.'

With the crowd so close to the pitch and the intensity of the home fans, Fratton Park was a tough place to visit. United's struggles must have reminded many supporters of the fruitless trips to play Southampton at The Dell in the mid to late 1990s. It was the type of match that championship-winning teams could battle through for victory, but that spirit was sadly lacking in the United performance.

Gradually, United's form improved. Seven consecutive wins in all competitions showed the capabilities of the squad. In the last of those seven victories, Ronaldo finally scored his first goal of the season with a volley from a Gary Neville cross. Whilst the winger was delighted, he knew that he had to contribute more goals to the team. Ferguson hoped Cristiano would get close to the 15-goals mark, but it was an aspect of his game that the Portuguese youngster needed to improve. Currently, the goalscoring burden was weighing too heavily on the shoulders of Rooney and van Nistelrooy, and United were accustomed to their midfielders chipping in with plenty of goals.

The run began with a victory over Crystal Palace in the Carling Cup on 10 November and a 3-1 win away to Newcastle four days later. Ronaldo was rested for the game against Palace but returned to face the St. James Park crowd, who needed no invitation to boo him after a few theatrical tumbles. Cristiano's movement and dribbling tormented a Newcastle team not renowned for its defending as he helped to earn his side the three points.

Fresh from running riot against the Magpies, Ronaldo headed to Luxembourg with the Portuguese squad on 17 November. The result was never in doubt as Portugal racked up a 5-0 win. Cristiano struck one of the goals and enjoyed a very easy evening, pulling the strings and laying on chances for his team-mates. The bid for qualification was back on track. It was undoubtedly a happier journey home than the return after the draw in Liechtenstein. The qualifying group was proving easy work for Portugal's talented squad. They had collected 13 points from a possible 15.

United continued to claw themselves back towards the top with a 2-0 win over Charlton, but Ferguson opted to keep Ronaldo on the bench as the three points were wrapped up. The Champions League group stage was also being safely negotiated, and Cristiano looked ahead with excitement to the second round. Victory over Lyon at home showed that the team had not lost their goalscoring touch, and it clinched qualification and eased some of the pressure on the team. United had blown the French club away on the night and that was no easy feat. With one match remaining, it was just left to see whether Lyon or United would go through as group winners. Domestically, wins over West Brom and Arsenal kept up the team's momentum and ensured that they were still challenging on all four fronts.

The last of those seven consecutive wins came against Southampton, who had a terrible record at Old Trafford in the Premiership. Ronaldo put in a good display and grabbed the last goal in a 3-0 victory. Ferguson was pleased with his young winger, telling the press, 'He's learned about the English game and he's learned from his own players about the way we are. Now without question he is an influential player. He turns games – he changes games and changes the pattern of games.' Now, Ronaldo needed to be a match-winner on a more regular basis.

Having already qualified for the Champions League second round, United fielded a weakened, youthful team away to Fenerbahce in the final group game. It was not an enjoyable night for Cristiano as the team lost 3-0 and surrendered top spot in the group to Lyon, increasing the possibility that United would face tough opposition when the draw was made. It was a result that would come back to haunt United as they were paired with Italian giants AC Milan, as experienced a team as there is in European competition. Ferguson cursed his bad luck but Ronaldo knew that if United performed at their best, they could beat anyone in Europe.

Back in the Premiership, United won three of their remaining four games in December, beating Crystal Palace, Bolton and Aston Villa. Ferguson tried not to overuse Ronaldo during the busy Christmas period, but the winger was happy to see the team heading in the right direction. Including the wins over Bolton and Villa, United strung together eight consecutive clean sheets in all competitions and were back to their miserly best. The team travelled to

Middlesbrough on New Year's Day and won 2-0, with Ronaldo turning in a man of the match performance.

Away from the pitch, the disaster caused by the Indian Ocean tsunami in December 2004 was not lost on Ronaldo. An earthquake in the ocean was responsible for the tragedy and around 300,000 people were killed. The tsunami had far reaching consequences, decimating nearby Indonesia, Thailand and Malaysia, as well as hitting countries further away including Sri Lanka and India. The lives of hundreds of thousands of people were changed forever. Cristiano was aware of the trauma experienced in the wake of the disaster and he knew how highly he valued his own family. To see people lose their loved ones affected him deeply, and he did not hesitate to get involved when he heard a particular story regarding a young boy named Martunis. The seven-year-old, whose mother and sister had been killed by the tsunami, was found after surviving on his own without food for nineteen days.

This discovery especially caught Ronaldo's attention because the boy was found wearing a Portugal shirt and was a Manchester United supporter. Cristiano immediately made plans to invite the youngster to a match at Old Trafford and the Portuguese national team paid for a new home for Martunis and his remaining relatives. *The News of the World* ran a story later, in 2007, regarding Martunis. In the article, Cristiano explained, 'I can't even imagine the suffering he went through during those nineteen days. Football is nothing, winning the title is nothing compared to this. Martunis is a real hero and he continues to be so.'

To be an orphan at such a young age was incomprehensible for Cristiano and he wanted to do whatever he could to help

Martunis. Ronaldo went to meet the youngster in Banda Aceh, Indonesia, and the pair spent the day together. It gave Cristiano a chance to witness Martunis's courage up close, and they managed to communicate by gestures and the help of a translator. The seven-year-old would never forget the experience of meeting the United winger but, even more so, Ronaldo would never forget Martunis' inspirational qualities.

Back at United, Tottenham were the next visitors to Old Trafford – a game that ended 0-0 but will be remembered for Pedro Mendes' 'goal' that Roy Carroll scooped out from well behind the goal-line. The team fired two more blanks in the following two games, embarrassingly drawing 0-0 with Exeter City at home in the FA Cup third round, and more impressively holding Chelsea to the same scoreline in the Carling Cup semi-final first leg at Stamford Bridge. The Blues had taken a firm grip over the Premiership table and United were determined to stop their domestic domination.

As it became increasingly clear that United would not win the Premiership, rumours began to circulate that Cristiano had fallen out with his United team-mates, who were frustrated by his unpredictable service from the wing. One particular source claimed that Ronaldo and Alan Smith had rowed after the disappointing 1-1 draw against Fulham at Craven Cottage. Cristiano found it hurtful to read such stories and he denied them when asked by the media. 'I have never had any problems with any of my team-mates, and I want people to understand that. Nothing happened after Fulham. I admit I was angry at the end because we allowed them to level the game when we had been in control, but so was every player because we had lost two points', he said.

A good win at Anfield on 15 January brought smiles back

to the faces of United fans worldwide, at least temporarily. Rooney grabbed the winner in a 1-0 victory, and Ronaldo provided plenty of threatening counter-attacks, overcoming the predictable boos and chants from the Anfield crowd. The players relished the win but knew it was meaningless unless it led to a long run of victories. With their Champions League tie coming soon as well as the Carling Cup semi-final second leg, it was crunch time. Even if the title was slipping away, there was plenty of silverware left to play for.

Ronaldo led the way with the opening goal in the 2-0 replay win over Exeter City, and he followed it with the opener in a 3-1 win against Aston Villa on 22 January. It was proving a very good patch for him and his team-mates were looking to him more and more to provide the cutting edge. But a 2-1 defeat against Chelsea in the Carling Cup semi-final second leg left a bitter taste in the mouths of United fans and meant that it was one trophy the club would definitely not be winning. Mourinho was having the last laugh.

Middlesbrough were beaten 3-0 in the FA Cup Fourth Round and then Arsenal and United clashed in a titanic battle at Highbury on 1 February. Both teams knew that only a victory would realistically keep them in the hunt for the title. The loser would have no chance of catching Chelsea. It was as simple as that. It was no secret that the two teams respected each other but did not like each other. However, nobody expected the fireworks to begin in the tunnel.

Sky Sports' cameras caught the end of the scuffle which involved an altercation between the two captains, Roy Keane and Patrick Vieira. Keane took exception to Vieira taunting Gary Neville and a row broke out. Arsenal had been unhappy with Neville's physical marking of Jose Antonio Reyes in the league match in October, and it is thought that Vieira was warning the full-back that it would not happen again. Ryan Giggs's autobiography sheds more light on the incident. According to the Welshman, Vieira had apparently pushed Neville in the tunnel after the warm up and word soon spread back to the dressing room. Giggs recalls the reaction, 'When Keaney heard we could see he was angry and going to do something about it.'

Keane's response was to look Vieira in the eye in the tunnel and deliver a message along the lines of: If you want to pick on a United player, try me. As if the contest needed any extra spice!

After the game, referring to the incident in the tunnel, Keane explained, 'If people want to intimidate some of our team-mates, let's have a go at some of their players.' The way that the Irishman had spoken up for his team-mates was an incredible inspiration for Ronaldo as he stepped out onto the Highbury turf. The row had certainly got everyone going.

The match itself was a classic – in all probability, the match of the season – and Cristiano played a major role. Now was the time for the big stars to stand up and be counted, and the Portuguese winger grabbed two priceless goals in a dramatic 4-2 victory – an absolutely thrilling contest. United trailed twice, but Ronaldo scored the second equaliser with a left-footed strike and then put his side ahead with a tap-in after brilliant work from Keane and Giggs. A cute chip from John O'Shea put the icing on the cake and United strolled out of London with a massive three points to keep themselves in the title race. Any win over Arsenal was sweet, but this victory was the stuff of dreams.

Cristiano could reflect on an excellent individual and team

performance, proving that he loved the big occasion. His goal celebration, putting his finger to his lips to tell the Arsenal fans to be quiet, spoke volumes about his confidence and had United fans worldwide jumping for joy. Obviously, it did nothing to improve his popularity with the Gunners' supporters. As well as showing the club's future was in safe hands, the match also served as a reminder to everyone that while Roy Keane was in the latter stages of his career, he was still a phenomenal player and an even better captain. United had stood tall in the face of everything Arsenal could throw at them.

This left United as the only team capable of catching Chelsea at the top and also put the Reds ahead of Arsenal in the race for second place. A betting man would have put his money on United finishing strongly and pushing the Blues all the way, but they had left themselves plenty to do. The good form continued at home to Birmingham in a 2-0 win, marked by Roy Keane's 50th goal for the club as he burst onto Ronaldo's pass. The key was to keep winning, just in case Chelsea slipped up at any point. But Mourinho's side seemed to have the nerve required to get over the finishing line.

Ronaldo and his Portugal team-mates lined up against the Republic of Ireland on 9 February. While it was only a friendly, both sides wanted to put in a good performance. Cristiano played for 70 minutes, but it was not a memorable clash for the Portuguese as they fell to a 1-0 defeat. Ronaldo returned to Old Trafford frustrated by the result and, though it was only a friendly, he still had that boyhood trait of hating to lose in any contest.

A Manchester derby is never an easy contest and City did well to hold the match goalless until Rooney snapped into life to snatch a 2-0 victory on 13 February. Strangely,

Ronaldo had been left on the bench as Ferguson chose a very defensive line-up, but the winger was brought into the action earlier than he could have expected when John O'Shea came off just after the half hour mark. He instantly earned himself plenty of boos from the City crowd but blocked them out and used the chanting as extra motivation. The United players had to work hard for the win and Ferguson must have hoped it would have been a more routine contest.

A trip to Goodison Park awaited United next with a chance to clinch their place in the FA Cup quarter-finals. Rooney received a typically hostile reaction on his return to his former club, but it was Ronaldo who stole the show with an excellent performance. His pinpoint cross found the head of Quinton Fortune in the first half to give United the lead, and then the winger scored the second himself when Everton goalkeeper Nigel Martyn spilled Scholes' free-kick. He received some very physical marking but rose above it to help his side through to the next round.

Ferguson singled out Cristiano for special praise when he spoke to the media after the match, 'The boy Ronaldo is a fantastic player. He's persistent and never gives in. I don't know how many fouls he had. He gets up and wants the ball again, he's truly a fabulous player.'

The draw for the quarter-finals handed United a tie away to Southampton. Having enjoyed some good wins at the Saints' new stadium, most pundits expected United to cruise into the semi-finals. Southampton were in the midst of a relegation dogfight and, while the cup match would be a welcome distraction, morale was pretty low on the South Coast. The last thing that Southampton needed was to face Cristiano and his team-mates in full flow.

AC Milan arrived in Manchester – the scene of their European final success in 2003 – for the crunch Champions League Second Round first leg on 23 February, and most anticipated a cagey contest. United were not able to field a full strength side, yet they had the better of the chances with Fortune going close, having burst forward from midfield. Milan controlled possession in patches with the finesse of Andrea Pirlo, Manuel Rui Costa and Kaka, but the United back four kept a tight rein on Hernan Crespo, the lone striker. Cafu, the Brazilian full-back, caught Ronaldo napping a few times early on, but the winger worked hard to recover and led several promising counter-attacks.

As the game appeared to be heading for a 0-0 stalemate, disaster struck for Ronaldo and United. Clarence Seedorf was afforded too much room on the edge of the area and his stinging shot was fumbled by Roy Carroll in the United goal, leaving Crespo the relatively easy task of tucking home the rebound. The away supporters went crazy; the home fans were stunned into silence. A night that had promised so much had ended in the worst possible way.

The curse of the United goalkeeper in Europe had struck again – Tim Howard's fumble had allowed Porto to progress the previous year – and this may have been the night that convinced Ferguson to remedy the situation by buying a proven stopper. Nevertheless, Sir Alex did not blame Carroll, instead focusing on the lack of composure the team had shown in the final third. Looking ahead to the second leg, Ferguson explained, 'We have got to make sure we don't make any mistakes – and if we score the game changes.' It would take a performance similar to the one in Turin in 1999 for United to save themselves.

United's Premiership form continued to put pressure on Chelsea, and that pressure was cranked up a little more with a narrow, nervy 2-1 victory at home to Portsmouth. The team had Rooney to thank as his double lifted a weary looking performance to gain the three points that they just about deserved. The hangover from the gut-wrenching defeat in midweek was understandable, but now was not the time to falter. There were still some vital matches ahead for Cristiano and his team-mates.

Following on from that below-par display, United headed to Selhurst Park to take on Crystal Palace, who were struggling at the other end of the table. With one eye on the crucial return leg in Milan, Ferguson opted to leave Ronaldo, Rooney and Scholes on the bench, expecting the side to overcome Palace without too many difficulties. Iain Dowie's side possessed the threat of Andy Johnson up front, so Sir Alex did not tinker with his back-line. It was a selection gamble but to have his attacking stars fully fit might just make the difference in midweek.

The Londoners fought hard, but when they were reduced to ten men United scented the three points. Ferguson threw on Ronaldo, Scholes and lastly Rooney to try to salvage the win, but they could not find the net, and van Nistelrooy missed their best chance late on. Resting the big names had backfired and the United manager was utterly frustrated at the dropped points, 'We've given ourselves a real mountain to climb. It's a bad result when you are going for the title.' As Chelsea stretched their lead at the top, United supporters despaired. Everyone at Stamford Bridge breathed a sigh of relief.

However, there was no time for the players to dwell on the title race setback. The biggest game of their season so far arrived on 8 March, as they tried to repair the damage from the Champions League second round first leg against AC Milan. At last, Ferguson was able to choose a full strength attack and there was plenty of hope in the United dressing room. It would only take a moment of Ronaldo magic or Rooney power to put the Reds back on level terms. Curiously, it was only the second time all season that Ferguson had been able to select Ronaldo, Rooney, Giggs, Scholes and van Nistelrooy in the same line-up. This showed how badly the club had been hit by injuries.

Sadly, though, this was to be another heartbreaking European night. United crafted several decent openings – with Ryan Giggs hitting the post – but Milan were always dangerous at the other end. Ronaldo and his team-mates kept themselves in contention for around an hour of the game but when Hernan Crespo, the scorer in the first leg, headed home Cafu's cross, the tie was over. Cristiano kept trying but it was a fruitless task as the Italians closed ranks as only they can.

United could be proud of their efforts, but Milan had the edge in experience and that is so crucial for grinding out results in the knockout rounds. The Italian side had the knack of finding the killer blow at precisely the right time, and this had stung United badly in both games. The fact that a player discarded by Chelsea (Crespo) had scored the goals was an additional annoyance. The two teams were destined to meet again, and when that happened United would be hungry for revenge. For the time being, Ronaldo and his team-mates looked to learn their lessons and move on.

Ferguson was devastated but remained gracious in defeat, 'The margins at this level are very fine and that is what has decided the tie overall. I'm disappointed to go out, but we've gone out to a very good team. Losing the goal at Old Trafford was the killer for us.' Sir Alex marvelled at the energy and desire of Milan veterans Cafu and Paolo Maldini, claiming that he would quit if Maldini was still playing in four or five years. Milan boss Carlo Ancelotti was relieved to see Crespo's goal clinch the tie, explaining that while it was 0-0, he feared United might claw their way back into the game.

For Ronaldo, it was a second consecutive second round exit, and it pained him to miss out on the latter stages of the tournament. He was well aware that it is in the semi-finals and finals that players truly earn their star status and he yearned to join the pantheon of European greats. At least he had time on his side. But, like his manager, he acknowledged that AC Milan simply had too much class and know-how across the two matches, whereas some of United's players were relatively new to that level of competition. Maldini had not allowed Cristiano to influence the tie, but the experience of facing such tight marking would benefit the winger in the long run. Now it was time to concentrate on the Premiership and cup competitions.

There was bound to be a backlash. United's elimination was going to hurt someone, and Southampton were the unlucky victims in a very one-sided FA Cup quarter-final on 12 March. Taking out their frustrations, Ronaldo *et al* racked up a 4-0 win with a very impressive demolition of the Saints, who were left to focus on their fight to avoid relegation to the Championship. Roy Keane opened the scoring early on, and Ronaldo doubled the advantage just before the break with a clinical finish, after an unselfish pass from van Nistelrooy, in a great team move. Seeing the winger strike the ball so cleanly, many wondered why he did not score more goals.

Ferguson took the chance to rest Ronaldo with almost 20 minutes remaining and he left the field content with his evening's work. It had been far too easy for United. He had been a thorn in Southampton's side from the first minute and, as usual, had received his fair share of boos for his trickery. The draw for the last four of the competition revealed that Newcastle would be United's semi-final opponents, and Cristiano was confident of a second consecutive FA Cup final appearance. Arsenal and Blackburn would contest the other semi-final.

A rather meaningless international friendly against Canada was the next challenge for Cristiano. Portugal ran out easy winners and Scolari withdrew his winger at half-time, content with the 2-0 lead. Ronaldo watched from the comfort of the bench as his team-mates sealed a comfortable 4-1 victory to keep morale sky high. The more he played alongside his international colleagues, the more fluent the displays seemed to become. The Canadian players stood no chance of stopping an attacker with the array of tricks that Cristiano possessed. Though the match was very one-sided, he enjoyed the change of scenery and the chance to meet up with his friends in the international squad.

Back in Premiership action, Ronaldo was on the scoresheet again as he starred in United's 1-0 victory at home to Fulham. He grabbed the winning goal after 21 minutes when he turned inside a Fulham defender and rocketed a shot into the top corner. Typically, it would have been easier to pass, with Rooney and van Nistelrooy waiting, but the winger only had eyes for goal. On this occasion, his decision was vindicated by the quality of the strike, but there had been other times during the season when his team-mates had grown increasingly frustrated at his lack of awareness. However, this was his day and he brought out a full range of tricks to entertain the Old Trafford crowd. Sloppiness almost let Fulham steal a point, but it would have been harsh on Ronaldo if his efforts had not produced three points.

The Fulham game had certainly been memorable for Ronaldo, but the draw at home to Blackburn in the next league game was instantly forgettable. The 0-0 result signalled the end as far as United's title hopes were concerned; now the FA Cup was the sole focus. The visitors had worked hard to stop United's flowing style, but it was worrying that the Reds had not managed a goal – especially for van Nistelrooy who had not scored in seven games since his return from injury. Questions were asked of the Dutchman amongst others. A 2-0 loss to Norwich pleased the critics and suddenly put pressure on United to deliver the goods in their FA Cup semi-final. That match was now all or nothing for Cristiano and his colleagues.

Ronaldo was in no doubt, United had to win the semi-final to keep their season alive – just as in 2004, when victory over Arsenal was critical. The players came out and performed as if their pride depended on the result. They were first to every ball and, most importantly, van Nistelrooy re-discovered his scoring touch. Ronaldo showed the less praiseworthy side of his game early on, when he was rightly booked for diving, but thereafter he was excellent. His pace enabled United to start some exhilarating counter-attacks which Newcastle simply could not handle, and the winger deservedly got on the scoresheet with the fourth goal in an emphatic 4-1 victory. Arsenal's semi-final triumph over Blackburn meant that another classic United – Arsenal clash was set up for the

Millennium Stadium – the first meeting between the two clubs since the tunnel scuffle.

In their next league game, the performance summed up their erratic season. Everton, enjoying an excellent campaign despite selling Rooney and still holding onto fourth spot, outfought a lacklustre United. It was such a different display from the cup heroics and even Sir Alex was bemused. Gary Neville and then Paul Scholes were sent off as frustration kicked in. Ronaldo had a poor game, seemingly unwilling to participate in a physical contest and falling in the box under minimal contact when he might have scored. It was the type of performance that he would have to eradicate if he wanted to go on to the next level at the club, and the theatrical tumbling would have to stop. He was earning himself a bad reputation in that regard. All in all, it was a miserable afternoon.

The players continued to try their best in the Premiership, but the incentive of winning the title had gone and, for some, there was a sense that the motivation had disappeared with it. Having become so accustomed to being in the title race all the way until the end of the season, Ferguson had to face the reality that first Arsenal and now Chelsea had overtaken United in terms of consistency. Cristiano had produced some magical displays during the season but had faded out of too many games and wasted too many chances. He knew he was better than that. But when he was on song he was as watchable as anyone in the league. More of those performances would be needed from Ronaldo if the trophy was to be grappled back from Stamford Bridge next season.

Whether it was due to his disappointing display against Everton or simply his need for a break, Ferguson opted to leave Ronaldo on the bench for the next two games. An injury to Gabriel Heinze, who had been a major success in his first season at the club, brought the winger on in the first half against Newcastle in a game that United made hard work of, before securing a 2-1 victory. The match was memorable for a superb volley from Wayne Rooney that brought the Reds back into the game. Ronaldo was an unused substitute away to Charlton, but was apparently not missed as the Addicks were thrashed 4-0 at The Valley, thanks to four different United scorers.

Cristiano was back in the starting line-up at home to West Brom and, in a weakened team, he shone the brightest. As has been the case several times before in his short career, Ronaldo thrived on the pressure of lifting the team, and his creative spark was too much for West Brom to cope with. Bryan Robson, the West Brom manager, might have thought Ferguson had done him a favour when he heard about the changes in the United side but then he saw Ronaldo in full flight! The only criticism of the winger's display was that again he got into scoring positions but did not convert the chances. It proved costly as the visitors sneaked a 1-1 draw at Old Trafford. Ronaldo's efforts could not be faulted, but he rued the missed opportunities and knew that, with the chances he had had over the course of the season, he could have scored as many as 20 goals.

A 3-1 defeat against Chelsea at Old Trafford on 10 May was another sickening disappointment and did nothing to ease the anger and frustration surrounding the club. The Blues had now beaten United three times during the season, twice in the Premiership and once in the Carling Cup. Mourinho had certainly enjoyed the better of his early tussles with Ferguson, and he appeared to have found the secret to beating the Reds. Van Nistelrooy gave United the lead, but it proved a false dawn as the champions proved their quality. This night, as much as any, showed that there really was a gap in class between Chelsea and United. There was much to do for United if they were going to compete for the title next season. Ronaldo had hoped for better in his second season in England.

The final league game of the season saw United travel to Southampton, the scene of many embarrassing afternoons in the late 1990s. The Saints were desperately clinging to their Premiership status, but a defeat against United would seal their relegation and give Sir Alex a measure of revenge for some painful afternoons on the South Coast. In an incredible last day of the season, all of the bottom four clubs could still avoid the drop. United had been involved in some tense end-of-season games in the past, but it was strange for them not to be directly feeling the pressure.

Norwich began the day just above the drop zone, but it was destined to be a tense afternoon. It began well for Southampton as they took the lead, but when United completed the comeback to win 2-1 Southampton were relegated to the Championship. Unbelievably, West Brom, who began the day at the bottom of the table, survived after a 2-0 home win. Ronaldo cast an eye over proceedings but was not involved at St. Mary's, as Ferguson sought to rest a handful of players ahead of the FA Cup final against Arsenal. That match was the last challenge for Ronaldo and a chance to recreate the magic of the 2004 FA Cup final win over Millwall, when he had taken the game by storm.

Quietly, the Gunners had picked themselves up after

losing to United in February and had won the race for second place. While United's form had been erratic, Arsenal had stormed along with a string of victories. Ferguson and the players had to accept that they had finished third and would need to play qualifiers for the right to enter the Champions League. The embarrassment was acute for everyone associated with the club, and there would be major problems if the following campaign did not provide indications of improvement.

All that was left for United was the FA Cup final and a last chance to salvage some silverware from a below-par campaign. The FA Cup was the one competition in which they been consistently excellent, and Ronaldo wanted to emulate his heroics from the previous year's final. He had happy memories of the Millennium Stadium. He felt refreshed after having a break against Southampton and was raring to go. Both United and Arsenal saw the FA Cup as a silver lining for the season, just as it had been for Arsenal in 2003 and United in 2004. But only one team could lift the trophy.

Those who hoped for a repeat of the 4-2 classic at Highbury were to be disappointed, as the game finished goalless, even after extra-time. Although there were no goals, it was still an entertaining contest with United enjoying the better chances. Ronaldo spent the majority of the game on the left flank, terrorising Lauren, the Cameroon defender, with a combination of trickery and pace, prompting Roy Collins of the *Daily Telegraph* to write, 'Cristiano Ronaldo gave Lauren one of his most uncomfortable afternoons of the season.'

On the right wing, Rooney overpowered Ashley Cole on

several occasions, but the breakthrough just would not come. Cristiano's mature and expressive display convinced many sceptics that the best was yet to come from the winger. With further development under Sir Alex's watchful eye, Ronaldo could become one of Europe's finest players. The next few years would be pivotal.

Arsenal had shown limited threat, content to try to smother United's star attackers, and had clearly targeted a penalty shootout long before the whistle blew at the end of extra-time. Jose Antonio Reyes was sent off in the closing seconds for a second bookable offence after a foul on Ronaldo. The game would be decided on penalties for the first time in the history of the FA Cup. In the past, teams had fought out replays to decide drawn finals, but since 1993 that had been abolished. In the lottery of the shootout it was Jens Lehmann, the controversial Arsenal goalkeeper, who was the hero, and Paul Scholes was the unlucky player whose miss proved decisive.

Ronaldo stepped up to take United's third penalty and with typical confidence he found the net, sending Lehmann the wrong way. But Arsenal captain Patrick Vieira scored the winning penalty and lifted a trophy that their performance had barely deserved. The United players lay on the Cardiff turf in shock and dismay. Ronaldo was distraught. He and several others struggled to hold back the tears. After the agony of the Euro 2004 final, he could not believe that he had come so close again, only to be denied. All the United players looked at their runners up medals with disdain.

Sir Alex expressed his disappointment that Vieira had escaped a red card – and that Reyes had not been dismissed earlier – but reflected on the positives for United. 'You could toss a coin for man of the match out of Wayne Rooney and Cristiano Ronaldo because they were great, the pair of them. The season's over now and we can reflect on what might have been as long as we like but we have to look forward to next season now,' he said. Roy Keane, like all his team-mates, found the shootout defeat hard to take, 'It's small consolation to say that we had all the chances.'

It was a bitter note on which to end the campaign. Despite playing some incredible football in patches, United had to endure the unfamiliar feeling of a trophyless season. The club's supporters were not happy. Having spent so heavily in the summer of 2004, Ferguson and the United board would have anticipated a more productive season but, in his defence, the team was still very inexperienced in places and injuries had ruined the beginning of the campaign. By the time United had a full-strength squad to choose from, Chelsea and Arsenal had quickly established substantial leads at the top. However, no one at Old Trafford was looking for excuses. They had not been good enough and that was the bottom line. Ronaldo took stock of his season's experiences, learned his lessons, put it all behind him and prepared to move on with his career.

For Ronaldo's compatriot, Jose Mourinho, it was a dream first season in English football as the Blues captured the Premiership title and the Carling Cup, as well as reaching the last four of the Champions League. Liverpool's heroics in Istanbul had won them the Champions League, with Steven Gerrard inspiring a second half comeback from 3-0 down against United's conquerors, AC Milan. It was a tremendous start to Benitez's tenure as Liverpool boss. All the other big guns had picked up silverware which just made matters worse for Ronaldo and his United team-mates.

Despite the lack of silverware, the feeling remained that United had the players to win trophies. The defence looked solid with Gary Neville, Rio Ferdinand, Wes Brown and Gabriel Heinze. The midfield boasted Ronaldo, Paul Scholes and the admittedly ageing Ryan Giggs and Roy Keane, while Wayne Rooney and Ruud van Nistelrooy represented one of the most potent strikeforces in Europe. There was perhaps a lack of squad depth that needed attention, but the first choice line-up looked remarkably strong.

Many, though, still sensed that there would be several big name arrivals at Old Trafford over the course of the summer. With Chelsea setting the bar higher, all eyes were on United and Arsenal to see how they would respond. Roman Abramovich would no doubt be opening his chequebook again during the close season, putting more pressure on the other title challengers. A massive season awaited Cristiano as his team would increasingly look to him to unlock defences. The club had invested a lot in Ronaldo's development and, with two seasons under his belt in English football, wanted him to become a more consistent and influential player.

As there was no major international tournament to prepare for, Ronaldo ought to have been able to take a proper break away from football during the close season. But international commitments put paid to that idea. Wearing the Portugal shirt for the first time in 2005, Ronaldo helped his team to a 2-0 victory at home to Slovakia on 4 June – the same team who had held Portugal to a 1-1 draw back at the end of March. He was always proud to represent his country and, after a lengthy break from international football, he was raring to go. Cristiano grabbed his sixth goal of the qualifying campaign in the 42nd minute, as Portugal stamped their authority on the group once more.

Remarkably, Ronaldo struck again four days later against Estonia in the next World Cup qualifier. It proved to be the only goal of the game. Cristiano was in fantastic goalscoring form, and he was propelling his team towards Germany 2006. The prospect of playing in the World Cup was enough to motivate any footballer, and Ronaldo was now well on his way towards achieving that aim.

By the time his international commitments had finished, there was little time for Cristiano to take a break from football. With the Champions League qualifiers looming, the start of pre-season would be earlier than usual. He needed to get plenty of rest because a long campaign awaited United.

2005/06:
THIRD TIME LUCKY?

RONALDO'S THIRD SEASON in England saw him continue to improve. United had been powerless to stop Chelsea's emphatic march to the 2004/2005 Premiership title, but a new season meant a fresh opportunity to bring the trophy back to Old Trafford. The club had ended the previous campaign empty-handed, as Chelsea and Arsenal collected the domestic honours, and everyone in the squad was desperate to succeed, no one more so than Ronaldo.

The key aims for him were to improve the number of goals and assists he contributed. His performances had been strong in patches, but he was still suffering from inconsistency, and the team needed him to step up with more stylish displays. Sir Alex Ferguson only made two significant signings in the summer transfer market, bringing in experienced goalkeeper Edwin van der Sar, in whom he had long been interested, from Fulham for £2 million, and hard-working South Korean midfielder Ji-sung Park, from PSV Eindhoven for £4 million.

Van der Sar was the latest goalkeeper to attempt to fill

Peter Schmeichel's shoes. Ferguson had tried a number of candidates, including Mark Bosnich, Massimo Taibi and Fabien Barthez, but no one had inspired total confidence. The Dutchman's experience was a key factor for Sir Alex, who felt certain that he had got the right man for the job.

Park also appeared to be a promising signing. He had impressed both at the 2002 World Cup and during the 2004/05 Champions League, where PSV were unlucky to lose out to AC Milan in the semi-finals. His best position seemed to be as a wide man and so he might be vying with Ronaldo for a place on the right flank. United's summer spending was a tiny outlay in comparison to their rivals, however.

As expected, Chelsea were busy in the close season. Mourinho strengthened his title-winning side with several new additions as he aimed to take that crucial step and bring the Champions League trophy to Stamford Bridge. Michael Essien, the midfielder nicknamed 'The Bison' for his powerful style of play, was signed from Lyon for £24.4 million after a very lengthy pursuit. Shaun Wright-Phillips arrived from Manchester City in a £21 million deal, to offer another dimension on the right flank, and Asier Del Horno completed an £8 million switch from Athletic Bilbao. Chelsea seemed to have covered any weak points from the previous campaign, which was bad news for Ronaldo and his team-mates.

Further news came in the form of Malcolm Glazer's takeover of Manchester United. While Ronaldo was more interested in getting on with his football, it was still a significant development for the players. Glazer had enjoyed success in the NFL American Football league with his Tampa Bay Buccaneers and now wanted to turn his attention to owning a 'soccer' team – since Abramovich, plenty of powerful businessmen seemed keen to buy a football club. In general, the United fans were furious and felt that the club had betrayed them. Some even flocked to a new team called FC United of Manchester, founded in 2005 by angry fans who wished to take their money elsewhere. It all became very bitter as talk of a boycott spread. It had been hoped that the high value of the club would prevent anyone from buying it but Mr. Glazer had other ideas. It added an intriguing subplot to the campaign and created plenty of extra, unwanted media attention at the start of the season.

Having finished third in the league the previous season, United were faced with the unfamiliar prospect of qualifying for the Champions League in a two-legged tie against Debreceni VSC, champions of Hungary. For Ronaldo and his team-mates, it was a reflection of how far the team had slipped during the past few seasons. Cristiano was determined to turn things around and, having shown his quality in two FA Cup finals, all eyes would be on him to see if he could take United to the next level. Arsenal and now Chelsea had raised the bar in the Premiership and, whereas in the past United could afford to lose as many as five games on the way to the title, the margin for error was now minimal.

United put in a good team display in the first leg in Hungary to win 3-0, giving themselves a comfortable cushion ahead of the return leg. Ronaldo relished the chance to thrill the home crowd, and he added United's third goal himself for good measure. The combination of Ronaldo, Rooney and van Nistelrooy blew Debreceni away. Ferguson expressed his delight to the media, 'We acquitted ourselves very well – and the game will help us for the start of the league.' The team would have no excuses for being rusty when their domestic campaign kicked off.

United began the Premiership season away to Everton, for whom Phil Neville was making his debut. It was ironic that his first match in the blue shirt should be against his former club, and it was a strange sight for the Red Devil fans, so accustomed to seeing him in the red of United. Ronaldo missed the game, suffering with an ankle injury, but van Nistelrooy and Rooney ensured that his absence was not felt. Rooney, receiving a predictably hostile reaction from the fans at Goodison Park, was the star of the show. He and Cristiano would be the key to United's title chances. Ronaldo returned to action as a substitute against Aston Villa and instantly sparked the team to victory. His energy caused all sorts of problems and his cross in the 66th minute created van Nistelrooy's winner. Ronaldo also went close to scoring himself late on. As the season wore on, his creativity would be a very important asset for the side.

The second leg of the Champions League qualifier in the Ferenc Puskas Stadium on 24 August was as much of a formality as the first game and United successfully avoided an embarrassing, early exit. Gabriel Heinze popped up with two goals and Kieran Richardson completed the scoring. Ronaldo and team-mates were able to celebrate a job well done and look forward to another season of Champions League football – the financial consequences of failing to qualify would have been drastic for United.

The only low point on the night was a groin injury to Gary Neville, which would keep him sidelined for several months. United's excitement was heightened when they saw the Champions League draw. The team ended up in Group D alongside Villarreal of Spain, Benfica of Portugal and Lille of France. Considering that they had avoided a number of stronger sides, Ferguson and the players were satisfied with the draw.

The team continued their 100 per cent Premiership start with a solid 2-0 win over Newcastle. Ferguson's 4-3-3 formation allowed Ronaldo the freedom to express himself out wide and it was bringing the best out of Rooney and van Nistelrooy too. As the away side, United dominated possession and it was van Nistelrooy and Rooney again on the scoresheet. The signs were promising; United looked as though they would put together a consistent campaign.

The players certainly seemed focused on the task and the attack was in scintillating form. There had been fears that van Nistelrooy would be too isolated up front on his own – as had been the case during Euro 2004 for Holland – but Ronaldo and Rooney had the youthful energy to offer support to the Dutchman. By all accounts, it was a formation suggested by Ferguson's assistant Carlos Queiroz, whose knowledge of European football is highly respected.

Ferguson explained the thinking behind the formation to the media, 'What we're trying to do is get Rooney and Ronaldo into forward positions more often because they can win games for you. So we're utilising the intelligence and experience of Keane and Scholes, while benefiting from the great energy that the young players – Rooney, Ronaldo and Fletcher – provide.' The chance to spend more of the game in the final third, taking on defenders, naturally appealed to Cristiano.

Portugal were also getting the best from Ronaldo. After several months away from the international scene, Ronaldo's twinkling feet were back on 3 September and Luxembourg were the latest team to suffer. It was a comfortable game for the Portuguese players as they overwhelmed their opponents in a 6-0 win. Considering that they had been criticised after Euro 2004 for being goal-shy, Portugal were hitting back at the sceptics and Pauleta, in particular, was showing impressive striking instincts. Scolari decided to take Ronaldo off after 62 minutes, replacing him with Simao, as the match was already sealed by that point.

With a fixture against Russia just four days later, Ronaldo stayed with his international team-mates as they focused on the qualifier ahead. But news from Madeira brought his world crashing down around him. His father, Dinis, who had shared in so many of his son's early football memories, had died in hospital in Funchal from a chronic liver condition. The years of drinking had finally taken their toll on him. He was only 51. It was a very traumatic period for Cristiano as he sought to comfort his family and grieve for his father. Everything else in his life just faded away into the background as he took in the shocking news. The illness had been drawn out, making it all the more painful for Dinis' family – Ronaldo had known the severity of the situation but nothing could have prepared him for the confirmation of his father's death.

Looking back, Ronaldo recalls it as an extremely tough time in his life, 'It's not normal to lose your father at 20 years of age and you learn a great many things about yourself at such times. I have certainly changed a lot in the past two years. I don't have any fear when I go out to play now. My father was No.1 in my life. He is always in my heart.'

Ronaldo now has a picture of his father in his home so that he is always there with him, through good times and bad times. The picture reminds Ronaldo of his father's role in helping him fulfil his potential and become a professional footballer. Cristiano knew that if he could overcome his father's death, he could overcome anything, and he took this attitude into his football. It inspired his performances in the seasons to come. Yet he rarely speaks about this stage of his life, finding it too distressing, and it is only more recently that he has revealed the depth of his feelings at the loss of his father.

To many people's surprise, Ronaldo announced that he would be available for selection ahead of the match with Russia. When asked by the Portuguese management if he wanted to go home to be with his family, Ronaldo had immediately said no. His father would have wanted him to focus on his football and that is what he was going to do. Scolari, as his national team manager, handled the situation very well and gave Cristiano every opportunity to deal with his grief in whichever way he desired. In the end, the Portugal manager had no doubts about putting Ronaldo in the starting line-up.

On that Wednesday night, Portugal added to their points tally as they played out a goalless draw with the Russians. With a place in the World Cup now assured thanks to the team's unbeaten record, everyone in the Portugal camp was more relaxed. However, their inability to unlock the Russian defence made it a frustrating night nonetheless. With just two more qualifying games ahead – both at home – there was a good chance that the side would end with an unbeaten campaign.

All this mattered little to Cristiano at the time. In the circumstances, Ronaldo played fairly well, but it was clear that he was not quite himself out there on the pitch. Though he tried to focus on the qualifier, his personal loss still weighed heavily on his mind. It has always been evident that family is a huge part of Ronaldo's life and he has always remained close to his roots. Dinis had been particularly proud of his son's journey to the top, and the way Ronaldo performed in the next few years would have made his father very happy.

Back at United, there was little to cheer Ronaldo's mood. September was a miserable month for United, full of the kind of inconsistency that had blighted them over the previous few years. Ferguson gave Cristiano leave to be with his family at this difficult time, telling the press, 'We have just told Cristiano to be with his mother until everything is sorted. He will pick his own time when to come back.' His trip back to Madeira meant that he missed the disappointing 1-1 draw with rivals Manchester City at Old Trafford. It was a bad way to begin the month. City were the type of opposition that United needed to be beating comfortably if they wanted to match Chelsea at the top. Some were already questioning United's title chances.

This was followed by a tricky fixture away to Villarreal in Europe on 14 September. Pre-match, Gary Neville had called for bigger contributions from the team's young guns, 'They are sensational players and now is the time that you have to become a man. They have had the years' experience and you have got to be more polished.' United were boosted by Ronaldo's early return from compassionate leave. Certainly, many had expected Ronaldo to take a longer period away from football while his family coped with their loss, but he insisted that he was ready to return to the fray.

The game saw United facing former Red Diego Forlan, who had been a huge success since moving to Spain. Forlan had a message for those back home who had ridiculed him, telling the media, 'I still have respect for Manchester United and their fans. But I am not the joker that many people think I am.' The game ended 0-0 and it was a frustrating night. Wayne Rooney was sent off and his team-mates had to cling on for almost half an hour. Cristiano put in a decent display but did not appear to be entirely focused on the match. It was not the ideal start, but a point away to Villarreal was a solid platform for the rest of the group stage – the Spanish side were regarded as United's toughest opposition in Group D.

Ferguson resisted the temptation to defend Rooney, whose second yellow card was for sarcastically applauding the referee. He told the media that Rooney had left the official with no choice but to punish his actions. The United boss clearly would not tolerate any such behaviour from his players. It was a further reminder to Cristiano that he must not lose his temper. As usual, the team would be playing in lots of testing atmospheres and he could not afford to lash out under pressure.

In one of those hostile atmospheres, Anfield, United only managed another goalless stalemate against Liverpool in mid-September. It was proving a worrying few weeks, especially when Roy Keane limped off the field with a broken metatarsal injury. One goal in three games hinted at problems with the formation. Ferguson was determined to protect Keane's aching legs and so a three-man midfield left the inspirational captain with less defensive work, but perhaps it was holding the team back from showing their true attacking strengths.

To make matters worse, the team dropped more points at home in a 2-1 defeat to Mark Hughes's Blackburn Rovers. Suddenly United's level of performance was being questioned. The team left the field to boos at Old Trafford and Sir Alex faced mockery in the media. Carlos Queiroz did not help matters by commenting to a Portuguese newspaper that 'stupidity has no limits', in reference to all the United fans who had chanted '4-4-2' during the defeat. Clearly, it would take time for the supporters to accept the change from the 4-4-2 formation that had brought the club so many trophies over the preceding 15 years. Ronaldo's form was proving erratic and he was still struggling to produce quality displays on a consistent basis.

On a more positive note, Cristiano picked up an award at the FIFPro dinner and gala in London. Ronaldinho was the big winner on the night, but Ronaldo received the Fans' Young Player of the Year gong for his exciting displays for United. He certainly had a large following, especially amongst young supporters. His club colleague Rooney scooped the Young Player of the Year award, as voted for by his fellow players. It further emphasised the bright future that awaited Manchester United.

Next up for United was a home Champions League fixture against Benfica, and Ronaldo was determined to return to winning ways. A 2-1 victory was achieved but Benfica made life hard for United, who needed an 85th minute winner from Ruud van Nistelrooy to seal the win. Cristiano went close to scoring and his energy pushed the team forward in search of the winner that they knew they needed. With four points from two games, United sat happily at the top of Group D with two matches against unfancied Lille ahead.

Everything looked rosy. The boos at the Blackburn game had changed to cheers as Ferguson was applauded as he headed towards the tunnel at full-time.

The United manager told the media of his delight, 'We were always positive and with persistence you can gain success. We deserved it. There's no point feeling sorry for yourself, you just have to get on with it.' All the players appreciated the way that the crowd at Old Trafford got behind the team and acted as a 12th man in driving the side towards victory. United had left it late but the three points had been secured. The electric atmospheres of European nights always lifted Cristiano, giving him extra energy and stimulating his desire to be a match-winner. It did not get much better than playing in Europe in front of a packed house at Old Trafford.

October was certainly a mixed month. It started excellently with two gritty away wins and United scored three goals in both games. Ronaldo was only a substitute away to Fulham, but he was back in the starting line-up against Sunderland to help the side to a 3-1 win. Yet United were still failing to finish teams off at home. Sandwiched between these two wins, Ronaldo joined up with his international colleagues for the last two qualifiers as they attempted to complete an unbeaten campaign.

On 8 October, Portugal exacted revenge on Liechtenstein for the 2-2 draw back in late 2004. The team were determined to put things right but once more found it very hard against their plucky opponents. Ronaldo came off with the score still 1-1, and Portugal required a very late winner from Nuno Gomes to secure the three points. Somehow, Liechtenstein had caused Portugal a lot of problems in the two qualifying matches. It left many supporters baffled. By this stage, though, nobody minded too much about the scoreline, the main objective was to develop the winning momentum.

In midweek, Ronaldo and Portugal rounded off their campaign with an emphatic 3-0 win over Latvia. From their 12 games, the team had won nine and drawn three with no defeats. It was a very impressive effort. Many across the world now considered Portugal to be dark horses to win the 2006 World Cup because, on their day, they could beat any side. Pauleta grabbed two goals in the victory over Latvia and broke Portuguese legend Eusebio's international goalscoring record in the process. It was a proud moment for the striker. As for Ronaldo, he was substituted at half-time with the team already leading 2-0 and was able to watch on comfortably as his team-mates sealed the result. His seven goals in the qualifying stage represented an excellent contribution and, alongside Pauleta's 11 goals, it inspired Portugal's unbeaten run. Many tipped the 2006 World Cup to be the stage on which Cristiano would truly show his class.

Back with United, Ronaldo's thoughts turned to Europe. Lille arrived at the Theatre of Dreams on 18 October for a Champions League match that United were expected to win with ease, but it proved to be another frustrating game. Paul Scholes was sent off for a second bookable offence with half an hour to go, and the attack just could not break down Lille's dogged rearguard. Ryan Giggs' 100th European appearance was marred by a fractured cheekbone that saw him leave the field with seven minutes remaining to join an ever increasing list of United injuries. A point was disappointing but was enough to keep the Reds at the top of Group D.

Off the field in mid-October, Ronaldo suffered a further setback when he had to answer police questions over rape allegations. A woman claimed that she had been sexually assaulted in the penthouse suite of a London hotel, and Ronaldo voluntarily agreed to speak to police about the claims. His agent, Jorge Mendes, spoke to the media to set things straight on the matter, 'The accusation of rape that has been made against Cristiano Ronaldo is totally and categorically repudiated. As the investigations will demonstrate, these charges are not based on any credible facts.' Ronaldo allegedly told friends at the time that he felt that the whole incident was a 'stitch-up', designed to take advantage of his celebrity status.

Carlos Queiroz also supported Ronaldo, 'He went to make a statement as was planned. Based on those statements, the authorities are going to reach fair and correct conclusions.' The player was released whilst the police made further inquiries and was later cleared of any involvement. It was a distressing time for Cristiano and he could scarcely believe that he had been caught up in the investigation. He was simply relieved that the storm had blown over and that he could now concentrate fully on his football again. It was the type of scenario that Ronaldo had always worked hard to avoid as attention seekers often try to use celebrities to get themselves in the newspapers. It was Cristiano's first major experience of the dangers brought on by fame.

Later on, in November, news spread that Cristiano had been completely cleared of all charges. Ronaldo issued the following statement, 'I have been notified that the police investigation has been closed and no action will be taken against me in relation to the allegations made previously. I have always strongly maintained my innocence of any wrong-doing and I am glad that this matter is at an end so that I can concentrate on playing for Manchester United.' United released a statement of their own, expressing the club's satisfaction that the case was now closed.

In due course, an investigation by the *News of the World* unearthed more information about the woman who had originally made the rape claims against Cristiano. According to one source, she was a prostitute who particularly preyed on rich men. If it had been a trap, Ronaldo had been an unlucky victim. The source suggested that the rape allegation might well have been the kind of tactic that the woman would use to try to discredit a person of Cristiano's wealth and status.

In fairness, a bad situation had been eased a little by the fantastic support offered to Cristiano by club and country. As well as United's backing, Ronaldo received kind messages from the Portuguese Football Federation (PFF). The PFF commented on the rape claims, offering 'solidarity' to Cristiano during such a difficult time. Ronaldo was at least cheered by his selection on the 30-man shortlist for the 2005 FIFA World Player of the Year award, ultimately won by Barcelona talisman Ronaldinho. To be considered worthy of the company of stars like Ronaldinho, Thierry Henry and Zinedine Zidane was a great honour. He was delighted to finish 20th after the voting process, ahead of more established players, including Raul, Pavel Nedved and United team-mate Ruud van Nistelrooy.

Back on the pitch, things got no better at home as, despite leading through an early Mikael Silvestre goal, the players had to settle for a 1-1 draw against Tottenham on 22 October.

Worse was to follow. In the final Premiership match in October, Ronaldo had to watch from the bench as United fell to a humiliating 4-1 defeat at the Riverside Stadium against Middlesbrough. The Portuguese winger came on after an hour, with United already trailing 3-0, and, though he found the net with a 90th minute header, it was too little, too late. Cristiano's aerial ability is an under-rated attribute and he regularly surprises opponents with his terrific spring and bravery. At his height – 6' 2" – he is often taller than his markers and at times United seek to use this to their advantage. Despite his reputation for being a 'pretty boy', Ronaldo is never afraid to compete for long balls and usually attacks set pieces with gusto.

Ferguson fumed after the match, 'It was a shocking performance.' He was not wrong. The players had been humiliated at the Riverside Stadium and their confidence seemed to have disappeared. Usually so solid on their travels, United had been out-fought by Middlesbrough in all areas of the pitch. It was concerning and frustrating for Cristiano, who was a mere spectator for 60 minutes when he felt he could have contributed to the match. The defeat left United in seventh place in the Premiership table and already 13 points behind the leaders, Chelsea, who had made an excellent start. Having pledged to match their rivals' consistency, United were failing to live up to their promise.

Just as significantly, the defeat prompted another outburst from injured captain Keane, who singled out seven of his team-mates for criticism in a slot that would have been shown on MUTV. Ferguson felt he had to act and on 18 November one of the club's greatest players left Old Trafford. He paid Keane a fitting tribute, calling him 'the best midfield player in the world of his generation' and saying, 'He is one of the great figures in our club's illustrious history. Roy has been central to the successes of the club in the last 12 years.' Keane's departure was announced as an amicable agreement but many suspected that a blazing row had followed Keane's explosive comments. It left a huge hole to fill in the midfield and a massive influence and inspiration to replace in the dressing room. The team never fully recovered from the Irishman's exit during the 2005/06 season.

The mood around the club was not improved by a disastrous 1-0 defeat away to Lille in the Champions League, leaving their qualification in jeopardy. The travelling United supporters booed the players off the field at full-time, and Ferguson agreed that it was a poor display. Keane's criticisms prior to his departure seemed all the more justifiable after this result and some players desperately needed to raise their game. Keane's outburst ought to have provided all the motivation necessary, but it had been a very flat performance.

Admittedly, the group contained no weak teams but nor were there any European powerhouses, and there would be no excuses for failure. Ronaldo went closest for United as his header came back off the underside of the bar, but once more the team had struggled to score in Europe, and nobody could dispute the fact that two goals in four games was cause for concern. Van Nistelrooy spoke out about the recent lack of supply – a topic that seemed to create a rift between the Dutchman and Cristiano. Maximum points from their last two games would still put the team through and Ronaldo hoped that there was time to remedy the situation; early elimination was unthinkable.

Chelsea were United's next Premiership opponents and the

game represented a chance to close the gap at the top, though it did not come at the best time for the Reds. The intensity of United's play, epitomised by the tireless Alan Smith, ensured that it was a tight contest, and Darren Fletcher's 31st minute looping header was enough to snatch the three points in a 1-0 win. The goal was conjured by the excellence of Ronaldo, as he tricked Paulo Ferreira and found Fletcher at the back post. It showed the winger's natural ability and it was the kind of creativity that the team was craving from him.

International duty saw Cristiano and Portugal face Croatia and Northern Ireland in friendly matches. Firstly, Portugal took on Croatia, who would be joining them in Germany and could unsettle many teams on their day. The Croatians had a solid track record in major competitions, dating back to their third place finish in the 1998 World Cup in France. After a few quiet matches towards the end of the qualifying campaign, this was seen as Ronaldo's return to top form – the kind of form he had shown early in the qualifying campaign. He was directly involved in the second goal, setting up Pauleta to clinch the 2-0 victory, and his trickery left Croatian defenders utterly bamboozled.

Against Northern Ireland on 16 November the Portuguese players again looked to prove their worth to Scolari. Ronaldo's place in the squad was assured but he was still determined to shine. Northern Ireland had proved capable of surprising big teams and Lawrie Sanchez, their manager, was having a significant impact. They would not be heading to the 2006 World Cup but they would provide a stern test of Portugal's ability to break down plucky defences.

Sanchez knew plenty about Cristiano's quality and admitted his chief concern in the *Belfast Telegraph*, 'He

[Ronaldo] is a brilliant player who can cause havoc for any team in the world. I know a lot of people in Northern Ireland are looking forward to seeing him but we must make sure that the match does not turn into the Cristiano Ronaldo show.' The story showed that Ronaldo was now viewed as a danger man on the international scene as well as domestically. His profile had risen rapidly since his move to United and his form at Euro 2004. With the majority of the Northern Ireland squad playing outside the Premiership, Cristiano was probably a hero for some of them.

Ronaldo only played 68 minutes but proved a thorn in Northern Ireland's side. While some of Portugal's other stars were subdued, Ronaldo oozed class and he crafted the team's goal in the 1-1 draw. His dangerous cross left Stephen Craigan in all kinds of problems and he could only turn the ball into his own net. It was a reminder of how quickly a quality player can change a game. Sanchez could be pleased with his team's performance, but Cristiano had influenced the match just as the Northern Ireland manager had feared.

In the Premiership, back-to-back victories over Charlton and West Ham suggested that the team were back on track, and Rooney put in two brilliant displays, profiting from the return to form of his team-mates. United usually seemed to be at their best when Ronaldo and Rooney were involved in the build-up and the win over West Ham put United second in the table, ten points behind Chelsea, but with a game in hand over the Blues.

Sandwiched between the two Premiership wins, United once again came up short in Europe, drawing 0-0 with Villarreal at home and failing to score for the fourth time in five European matches. Despite controlling possession, the team had only two shots on target. Ronaldo despaired at missing two good headed chances, while Rooney and Scholes also wasted opportunities. United's fate was still in their own hands but only just – a victory away to Benfica was required to put the Reds through to the next round. United fans everywhere were looking worried. It should never have been left so late to seal qualification.

Cristiano was especially pleased in November when he agreed a two-year extension to his contract at the club. His new deal would keep him at Old Trafford until 2010. Plans for the contract had begun during the summer and both parties were delighted with the outcome. Ferguson said, 'It represents our faith in young players at the club and Ronaldo will develop into a fantastic player.' Ronaldo was equally thrilled, telling the media, 'I am very happy and proud to finally put a deal on paper. It is important for the development of my career and I want to be an integral part of the team that achieves trophies for the club.' He now needed to focus on winning those trophies.

On 25 November, United supporters was saddened by the news that the club legend George Best had died; the attacking play in the victory over West Ham was a fitting tribute to one of the finest players to grace the game. Ronaldo had only been at the club for a few years, but it was long enough to understand how highly Best was regarded at Old Trafford, and to hear about the magic he had brought to the number 7 shirt that Cristiano had now inherited. It was a big loss for everyone associated with Manchester United to say a final farewell to a player who had scored 178 goals in 466 games for the club and had inspired the 1968 European Cup triumph, earning himself the European Footballer of the Year award for that season.

United won 3-0 against West Brom in their first home game since George Best's death. It was the perfect way to pay tribute to Best and United produced an attacking display that the great man would have been proud of. Ronaldo came off the bench to open the scoring and, as Ferguson observed, it was very apt, 'It was fitting that we played some great football and that our first goal should come from Cristiano Ronaldo, wearing the No.7 shirt.' Emotions were running high and it was a special feeling to be inside Old Trafford as the club remembered one of its greatest ever players.

But December began in agonising fashion. Despite a good display in a 3-0 win over Portsmouth – with Ronaldo's arrival as a substitute spurring the team on as he crafted the third goal for van Nistelrooy – everyone at United was focused on the crunch contest in the Champions League on 7 December. Needing to beat Benfica – or draw, if Villarreal beat Lille – Ronaldo went into the fixture confident of victory and of being greeted fondly by the supporters of Benfica, his boyhood team. He told the media, 'It will be great to go back and I think I'll get a really warm reception. But our focus must be on the result.' Heading to face Benfica so soon after Best's death, it was impossible not to think of the Northern Ireland international's stunning display in the 1968 European Cup final against the same opposition.

The massive night in Portugal started well for United but ended miserably as the team threw away a good start to lose 2-1. The European dream was over for 2005/06. Everyone had been optimistic when Paul Scholes opened the scoring after six minutes, but two Benfica goals before half-time were massive body blows and left Ronaldo and his team-mates with an uphill task. United enjoyed an incredible 61 per cent of the possession but managed only three shots on target. The equaliser proved elusive.

Ronaldo never stopped trying, dragging a shot wide and searching for that vital equaliser, but it was not one of his better nights. Substituted with just over 20 minutes remaining, he was devastated and had to endure the closing moments powerless to make a telling contribution. His one-finger salute to the Benfica supporters as he left the pitch was inexcusable, but it revealed the true extent of his emotions – he had been desperate to make it to the next stage of the competition. The embarrassment for United was increased by the fact that the defeat put them bottom of the group which meant that they did not even receive the consolation of entering the UEFA Cup – an opportunity that went to third-placed Lille. There were doubtless smirks on the faces of the supporters of United's Premiership rivals.

The aftermath of United's exit was extreme as the media attacked the team's deficiencies. For Ronaldo specifically, there was one main source of grievance. Benfica sent a formal complaint to UEFA regarding Cristiano's gestures and a club spokesman said that Ronaldo 'showed a lack of respect towards Benfica fans.' The winger's behaviour was immediately scrutinised by millions in front of TV sets, and then later by those reading the national newspapers. Ronaldo knew that his response was rash but he defended himself, claiming that the abuse from the Benfica fans had warranted such a reaction. Having spoken before the match about getting a warm reception from the home supporters, it came as a shock to Cristiano that he was treated to so much angry chanting.

A 1-1 draw with Phil Neville's Everton at Old Trafford

made it a miserable week for the club. The major trophies all seemed to be slipping away from Ronaldo's clutches and, hard as he tried when he came off the bench, Everton clung on for a well-earned point. Once again United failed to turn an overwhelming majority of possession (61 per cent) into chances and goals. Liverpool's 2-0 win over Middlesbrough saw them leapfrog United and move into second place in the table. At that moment, it was 'Rafa' Benitez's side who were looking more likely challengers to Chelsea at the top of the league.

Historically, United tend to hit their best form around the Christmas period, and this year seemed no different as the team finally began to produce consistent displays. Victories over Wigan, Aston Villa and West Brom represented a good points return. Ronaldo was making useful contributions but found himself coming off the bench during United's strong run. It was a difficult period as he wanted to help his teammates, but Ferguson seemed to prefer him as an impact substitute, ensuring that he did not burn out. Cristiano's season, though, was about to take a turn for the better as he gave glimpses of his undoubted quality.

He was restored to the starting line-up on 28 December for a 2-2 draw with Birmingham at St. Andrews – a game in which United fell further behind Chelsea. Ferguson was very unhappy with the result and was critical of referee Howard Webb for being swayed by the home fans in his decision-making. Several times the United manager felt that Cristiano had been denied clear free-kicks. Sir Alex told the press, 'It is unfair to the boy because he is such a great player. If the refs watched the game instead of listening to the crowd then that's fine.' He was especially angry about a particular incident when former United midfielder Nicky Butt had fouled Cristiano, only for Webb to wave away claims for a free-kick. Perhaps Ronaldo's reputation had been a factor in Webb's thinking.

At the halfway point in the season, Chelsea had stretched their lead to a massive 11 points. It was going to take a very special recovery from Ronaldo and his team-mates, and a collapse of sorts from the Blues, for the Reds to salvage the title. An excellent 4-1 win over Bolton saw Cristiano stand out as the star man and his return to top form was a welcome sight for all United fans. He scored two second half goals to clinch the match as well as striking the woodwork with a couple of efforts in a contest that United dominated. It was one of those days when all his trickery came off, and he left Bolton defenders and spectators mesmerised.

Ferguson was very pleased and saw this as a major moment in Cristiano's development. He told the press, 'Maybe today will prove to be the best thing to happen to him this season. He missed a lot of chances at Birmingham last week, but he hit the target today and that is really important for a young player.' Nobody needed to remind Ronaldo that he had to hit the back of the net more often to ease the pressure on the strikers. His lack of goals, though, was not for the want of trying.

Cristiano followed this on 4 January with an exciting performance in a 0-0 draw against Arsenal, causing plenty of problems for the Gunners but failing to find the net when well placed. Considering it was a goalless draw, there were plenty of opportunities at both ends and it was a surprise to see it end 0-0. But the absence of Keane and Vieira meant that the match lacked the spark or combustibility of previous meetings. In fairness to the two sides, it was their fourth match in eight days in a ridiculously congested Christmas period. The players could be excused for showing some fatigue, especially as their European counterparts were putting their feet up and enjoying their winter break. The scoreline ensured that Mourinho continued smiling at Stamford Bridge.

The games kept coming. United kicked off their FA Cup campaign away to Burton Albion of the Nationwide Conference, managed by Nigel Clough. Ferguson took the opportunity to rest a number of first-team players but, rather like an insurance policy, he named Ronaldo and Wayne Rooney amongst the substitutes. However, he certainly hoped that he would not need to use them. But it was a day to forget for the Reds as Clough's Conference battlers held out for a 0-0 draw, despite facing the trickery of Ronaldo for more than half an hour. The replay, for which Cristiano was rested, was a different story as United romped to a 5-0 win with two-goal Giuseppe Rossi the star of the show. It was, no doubt, at least a good day out for the Burton players and a story to tell the grandchildren.

Rumours spread in January of behind-the-scenes problems at United. It was reported that a confrontation had taken place in training involving Ronaldo and Ruud van Nistelrooy, and some sources suggested that the disagreement had led to fisticuffs. Ferguson moved quickly to dismiss the rumours but the tension caused by United's struggles had seemingly had an effect. The reasons for the spat were unclear, but there was a feeling that van Nistelrooy was one of those who was particularly vocal about Ronaldo's occasional lack of awareness in crucial moments.

Though he said nothing openly, the United manager appeared to take Ronaldo's side in the argument, and van Nistelrooy's season would not be the same from this point onwards. The incident was well managed behind the scenes, but it was the kind of problem that does not occur in winning teams, and Sir Alex had been spared such difficulties in the past with his all-conquering sides. However, the current slump had changed all that.

United's focus switched to their Carling Cup campaign as they faced Blackburn at Ewood Park in the first leg of their semi-final. Ferguson picked a strong team, including Ronaldo, aware that it might be United's last chance of silverware for the season. Ryan Giggs, who is often rested for Carling Cup games, crafted a goal for Louis Saha in the 30th minute. The Frenchman finished expertly to give the Reds the lead. But Mark Hughes' players possessed the same steely resolve that he epitomised himself in his playing career, and Blackburn equalised six minutes later through Morten Gamst Pedersen. That was the end of the scoring, but it was a very entertaining battle and round two would come two weeks later to decide who made it through to the final in Cardiff. Cristiano had faced some physical marking but had stood up to the challenge commendably well.

However, a 3-1 defeat away to rivals Manchester City on 14 January put United's title hopes on the brink of disappearing. It was a poor display and put the Reds a daunting 16 points behind Chelsea. This was one derby game that Ronaldo will not look back on favourably. Despite early menace and a beautiful through-ball for Wayne Rooney, the winger became increasingly frustrated at the team's shortcomings and the decision-making of the referee. When referee Steve Bennett denied the winger a free-kick, Ronaldo snapped and his nasty challenge on former United player Andy Cole earned him a straight red card. From this point onwards, Cristiano would play a leading role in Manchester derby action and he was regularly singled out for abuse by the City supporters.

The loss forced United to focus their sights on holding onto second place rather than challenging for the title. The fans were not happy. As for Ronaldo, he would have to serve a three-match suspension after an FA disciplinary commission rejected United's appeal against the red card. In fairness, Cristiano could have no complaints about the ban because the lunge was very reckless and perhaps the suspension would give him time to reflect and iron out some of his flaws. During his impetuous days – like the Manchester derby defeat – the young, boyish side of Ronaldo's character became very visible.

Ronaldo's enforced absence saw him miss one of the team's most exhilarating final flourishes. A tense affair with Liverpool at Old Trafford, which the visitors had edged on chances, ended with Rio Ferdinand's late winner that gave United bragging rights over their rivals. The stadium erupted, and Ronaldo was left to curse the fact that he was not soaking up the applause with his team-mates. Any victory over Liverpool was a proud occasion, as shown by Gary Neville's frenzied celebration after Ferdinand's goal.

The winger also sat out United's semi-final second leg with Blackburn at Old Trafford on 25 January. The Reds got off to the best possible start when van Nistelrooy beat Brad Friedel in the Rovers goal after good work by Rooney. But, just as they had in the first leg, Blackburn fought back and United carelessly threw away the lead, as Steven Reid equalised after the Reds had failed to clear. The crowd grew restless, especially when van Nistelrooy then had a penalty saved by Friedel. In the second half, United improved and Louis Saha popped up with yet another Carling Cup goal, which proved enough to win the tie and clinch a place in the final. Ronaldo, a nervous spectator, could look forward to another trip to the Millennium Stadium, though he was disappointed not to have played a part in the victory. Ferguson was happy but critical of the sloppy start, telling the media, 'I thought we were a bit casual in the first half. The players realised that if they didn't match them for effort, we were going to suffer, and they raised the tempo of the game.'

Cristiano's troubled season took another turn for the worst when UEFA decided to charge him with misconduct, for his one-finger gesture at the Benfica fans in December. The matter would be discussed at an appeal, with the possibility of a Champions League suspension that would be carried over to next season. Ronaldo's frustrations seemed to be getting the better of him too often and he knew he had to work on his temperament. In his defence, it had been a testing year for him. His father's death, combined with the rape allegations, had knocked his confidence and shaken him badly. He was the first to admit that he had not been his usual self, and his performances suffered as a result.

On Cristiano's return from suspension, United lost 4-3 in a thriller at Ewood Park against Blackburn, who exacted revenge for their Carling Cup semi-final defeat. Having hauled themselves back from 4-1 down, even Ronaldo's trickery was not enough to find an equaliser as they sought to break down a stubborn Rovers rearguard. Blackburn were fast becoming a bogey team for United as ex-Red Mark

Hughes added to his managerial credentials. Some feel that he may one day take over from Sir Alex at Old Trafford and be Cristiano's next boss.

In a strange way, the defeat away to Blackburn was a turning point in a season that was quickly becoming embarrassing as Chelsea savoured their 15 point advantage. Ronaldo's form over the next few months gave early indications that 2006/07 would be a defining campaign for him. He managed better end product and his link-up play with Gary Neville, who had been appointed the new Manchester United captain in early December, got better and better. Ronaldo appreciated the fact that with few homegrown players left at Old Trafford, it was important that the team's leader on the pitch was both vastly experienced and a product of the club. Neville fitted both categories. Chelsea and Liverpool had taken the same approach with skippers John Terry and Steven Gerrard.

The winger struck twice against Fulham on 4 February as an early celebration of his 21st birthday, which was the next day. His two goals helped United towards a 4-2 victory in what was, strangely, his first home appearance of 2006. Ferguson was desperate for more goals from his midfield, and Ronaldo's display showed that he was improving game by game. But he knew that ultimately the title was Chelsea's to lose and that United might fall short even if they won all of their remaining games. Fulham boss Chris Coleman praised United's 'exciting, attacking football' and admitted that although the Blues were sitting comfortably at the top of the table, they could not match Ronaldo and company for entertainment.

Yet, as Cristiano admitted to reporters, all of United's best efforts came in vain as the players struggled to make major inroads into Chelsea's lead. The Blues were playing some superb football and Ronaldo had to grudgingly admit their excellence. He told the press, 'Chelsea are doing well. They're a very stable team and they lose very few points.' All United could do was keep winning and hope that Mourinho's players let their standards slip. It was critical that Chelsea found themselves under some pressure going into the closing stages of the campaign.

Cristiano simply focused on his own performances, and he hit another double away to Portsmouth as United's attack destroyed the hosts in the first half. Ronaldo's first goal was particularly special, as he hammered a 25-yard left-footed strike past a helpless Dean Kiely in the Portsmouth goal. Pompey boss Harry Redknapp was left spellbound by Cristiano's footwork. Yet again it was clear that the winger could score as many as 20 goals a season if he was on song and Ferguson admitted as much when he spoke to the press, 'I think Cristiano Ronaldo is capable of scoring between 15 and 20 goals a season. Hopefully that will give him more confidence to go on and score more.' Ronaldo took his manager's words on board and sought to contribute more goals to the side.

Gary Neville was also pleased for Ronaldo. Playing behind Cristiano on the right flank, Neville had the best view in the ground of the winger's improvements. He saw Ronaldo strutting his stuff at close quarters and was full of respect for him. 'Ronaldo is capable of doing anything he wants to do. He's got absolutely everything – incredible physique, 6'2", strong, quick, two great feet, good shot, good in the air,' the right-back enthused. It was just a case of bringing all these assets together more consistently in the same performance. The management at the club knew that Cristiano could do it. They saw his potential every day in training.

Having beaten Wolves in comprehensive fashion in the previous round, United travelled to Anfield for their FA Cup Fifth Round clash with Liverpool on 18 February. Ronaldo and his team-mates had only managed a 0-0 draw in the league game on Merseyside and were ready to go one better this time. Cristiano promised that the players were heading into the match concentrating on victory and aware of the game's importance for the fans.

He had been in tremendous form and represented one of United's biggest threats, but this was not one of his better displays as Liverpool outmuscled United to win 1-0. The horrific injury to Alan Smith – a broken leg and dislocated ankle – made it an even more painful day for the visitors. Ronaldo reacted in shock at seeing the condition of Smith's leg, and it was a sight that badly affected him. After such a solid run of results, United had come down to earth with a bump against Rafa Benitez's well-organised outfit and the defeat ended their hopes of FA Cup glory. The Carling Cup was the only realistic trophy for United to target now.

The biggest game of United's season arrived on 26 February, as they travelled to the Millennium Stadium for the Carling Cup final against Wigan. Going into the game as big favourites, United knew that only a comprehensive victory would be good enough, and the players found themselves in a tough situation as the critics sharpened their knives. Having suffered the misery of a penalty shootout defeat in Cardiff the previous season, Ronaldo was desperate to enjoy success at the Millennium Stadium this time.

Just as the FA Cup final of 2004 had represented a lifeline for United as Arsenal stormed away with the Premiership title, the Carling Cup now offered partial redemption for 2006. It would not erase the season's scars, but it would spare Cristiano and his team-mates' blushes. To play in front of a packed Millennium Stadium was always a wonderful treat – the kind of arena in which Cristiano was born to play.

Speaking pre-match, Ronaldo admitted that a defeat would be a disaster yet added, 'I don't believe it is going to end up that way.' He assured United fans that the players were fully focused on doing their job in Cardiff, and revealed that he would dedicate the win to his father's memory as well as to the fans. Cristiano felt that his father would be looking down and smiling at seeing his son playing in another major final. He was determined to put in a brilliant performance.

Wigan had shocked everyone by eliminating Arsenal in the semi-finals and could not be underestimated. Manager Paul Jewell had led his team to a very respectable league position against all expectations, and in the early weeks had been closer challengers to Chelsea than United had. With Jason Roberts and Henri Camara up front, fleet-footed counter-attacks would be a threat, but most felt that Wigan would be entrenched in their own half and thus unable to play to their strengths. Jewell knew that if they let United dictate, they would have no chance of an upset.

Ronaldo took his usual place on the right flank and looked forward to a duel with Wigan's highly rated Leighton Baines. The biggest news pre-match was that Sir Alex Ferguson had dropped van Nistelrooy to the bench in favour of Louis Saha, who had scored five goals in the last four games in the competition. Saha had been excellent and deserved to play in the final as a reward for his good form. But Ruud did not look happy as he watched on from the touchline. After a cagey opening, United took the lead through Rooney, who capitalised on defensive confusion to find the back of the net.

But it was in the second half that Ronaldo and United took the game away from Wigan. Inspired by Ryan Giggs in the centre of midfield, the Reds struck three times in six minutes to settle the match. First, Saha bundled the ball in at the second attempt after a slick move involving Giggs, Ronaldo and Neville. Then Ronaldo capped off a fine display with the third goal. Supplied by Saha, he wasted no time in extending the lead as he beat John Filan and wheeled away in celebration. It was his tenth goal of the season.

Rooney completed the scoring two minutes later from close range. It was hard on Wigan, who had given their all. Ronaldo was substituted after 73 minutes to give Kieran Richardson a taste of the glory, and the Portuguese star watched his team-mates see out the closing moments to clinch the 4-0 win. It had been a very special day for him and he was extremely proud of the performance.

As the squad went up to collect the trophy and their winners' medals, the whole squad wore 'For you Smudge' t-shirts in sympathy for Alan Smith's injury. Ronaldo's beaming smile told the whole story of how much the triumph meant to the United players, and to him in particular. It was important that winning competitions became a habit so that next season the club could focus on the main prizes. It was Cristiano's second taste of silverware at United, and the players had benefited from Ferguson's decision to take the competition seriously.

Many dismissed the Carling Cup win as a meaningless

achievement, but Ferguson was pleased. He told the media, 'Any trophy you win is important and we're delighted. We've never devalued this cup. Credit goes to Wigan because they had a go.' The feeling remained, though, that the Carling Cup was a good achievement but it could never replicate the sensation of lifting the Premiership or Champions League trophy.

On 2 March, Cristiano took a momentary break from United action to play in a home friendly for Portugal against Saudi Arabia, designed to gear the players up for the huge summer of football to come. Saudi Arabia had experience of playing at major tournaments but were not expected to cause the Portuguese too many difficulties. Ronaldo followed up his recent good international form with a superb display, scoring twice and playing a big role in the other goal. His first goal was a header from a Luis Figo corner and his second, in the 84th minute, was a neat, left-footed finish. Maniche's goal, sandwiched between Ronaldo's efforts, came from a rebound after Ronaldo's volley was blocked. With a few more months of Premiership action before the World Cup, the signs were ominous for Ronaldo's opponents.

Back in Premiership action, Ronaldo made it five goals in three league games with United's first in a scrappy 2-1 victory away to Wigan, in a repeat of the Carling Cup final eight days earlier. The Reds were somewhat fortunate to leave the JJB Stadium with the three points, but it had been a gutsy display. Chelsea, seemingly unstoppable, were continuing their relentless march to the Premiership crown, but it was reassuring to see positive signs coming from Ferguson's players. Even if the title had slipped away again, there would be chances to send out messages of intent for next season, when youngsters like Ronaldo and Rooney ought to be hitting their peak.

Speaking to an overseas television network on a preview show, Cristiano spoke about why he loved to play the game with grace, 'It isn't always possible to play beautifully but I think some players in the Premier League basically always do that. I think I'm one of them.' While Ronaldo sought out stylish performances, it was consistency that Ferguson really wanted from his wide man – this was the key improvement that Ronaldo needed to concentrate on. He had all the qualities but needed to put them all together more frequently.

With Ryan Giggs operating in the centre of midfield – while Paul Scholes was still absent – it offered the team extra creativity and the chances kept coming. Newcastle were beaten 2-0 at Old Trafford in a game where they could have reached double figures from their 26 shots on goal. In a 2-1 victory against West Brom, Ronaldo laid on Saha's second goal with a neat pass, and United had won their fifth consecutive Premiership match. That run increased to six with a 3-0 win over Birmingham in Gary Neville's 500th game for the club – an exceptional achievement.

Suddenly, a few people were asking whether it was too late for United to steal the title. Ronaldo and his team-mates were producing some stunning performances, and further wins over West Ham and Bolton cut Chelsea's lead at the top to seven points with six games remaining. With Saha and van Nistelrooy amongst the goals, a few nerves must have been jangling at Stamford Bridge. After all, the Chelsea players had not experienced a tight run-in before. A 2-0 win against Arsenal ensured that United stayed in the title race, even though the odds were still heavily stacked in Chelsea's favour.

Unfortunately for Ronaldo, a 0-0 draw at home to Sunderland on 14 April put the final nail in the coffin for United's title bid and his hopes of a title winners' medal. Despite 66 per cent of the possession, the team could not beat Kelvin Davis in the Sunderland goal. Ronaldo was one of many who were guilty of missing good chances, and a game that seemed like a guarantee of three points finished with rueful looks on all United faces. Ferguson expressed his disappointment in front of the media, 'We got a bit anxious. We were trying to hammer a square peg into a round hole.'

The players hit back in the best possible way, beating Tottenham 2-1 at White Hart Lane. Rooney scored both goals with Ronaldo providing an inch-perfect cross for the opener. The result at least partially eased the pain of the stalemate against Sunderland.

The title was finally surrendered to Chelsea in rather feeble circumstances. United travelled to Stamford Bridge and played poorly, losing 3-0 and suffering the heartache of watching the Chelsea players celebrate their success. An injury to Rooney, with the World Cup on the horizon, added to the sadness in the United changing room. For Ronaldo, it was a disappointing experience, but it made him stronger as a person and increased his determination to make amends the following season. After a 0-0 draw with Middlesbrough, there was time for one more Ronaldo goal before the season ended, as he scored from close range in a 4-0 rout of Charlton – Alan Curbishley's final fixture as the Addicks' boss.

Van Nistelrooy's omission from the team for the Charlton match resulted in more speculation on the fall-out between the Dutchman and Cristiano. European Soccer Correspondent

Graham Hunter explained to Setanta.com, 'In January, Ruud van Nistelrooy and Cristiano Ronaldo, who literally cannot stand the sight of each other, traded punches in training.' This story had circulated at the time but then in May (prior to the Charlton game) there was another, more serious incident. Apparently, a frustrated van Nistelrooy had once more questioned why Ronaldo kept hold of the ball for too long during a training session and the row had escalated. Hunter continued, 'Ronaldo gives van Nistelrooy some lip, it ends up in a fight, and van Nistelrooy needles Ronaldo, and says, "Yeah, go running to your Dad." Ronaldo burst into tears and shouts "I don't have a Dad, he's dead."'

The comment about Cristiano's 'Dad' referred to United assistant manager and fellow Portuguese Carlos Queiroz. But Ronaldo allegedly took the words at face value and thought that van Nistelrooy was insulting his dead father. In truth, though, the tension had been growing between the two players for a while. It left Ferguson with problems to sort out as it threatened to create a bad atmosphere in the dressing room. It dated back to when van Nistelrooy was quoted as saying that Ronaldo's improvements meant that 'at least we now get a cross in after six step-overs.' There was, admittedly, plenty of speculation involved in these reports, but it was a sour note on which to finish the season.

United ended the campaign eight points behind the champions, Chelsea, and just one point above third-placed Liverpool. There was no hiding the disappointment at Old Trafford as the Premiership trophy resided elsewhere for another season. They had finally won the Carling Cup, but Ferguson, Ronaldo and the rest of the squad all knew that the club expected to be challenging for the bigger prizes, namely the Premiership and the Champions League. Cristiano had not taken long to appreciate the fact that the club is never happy with second place in any competition.

The European campaign had been a particular disappointment for United, and Ronaldo had endured a torrid night away to Benfica. With so many talented attackers, it was mystifying that the team had struggled so much to find the back of the net, scoring only three goals in six group games, despite fielding stars such as van Nistelrooy, Rooney and Ronaldo. It certainly baffled Ferguson and the coaching staff, and it would need to be addressed ready for the next assault on the Champions League. Perhaps a different formation would be required.

The biggest problem for United had come in the centre of midfield, where they were unfortunate to lose Roy Keane and Paul Scholes during the season; subsequently, the team failed to take games by the scruff of the neck as they had in previous years. United supporters could legitimately point to several key injuries that hindered their pursuit of silverware. Giggs and John O'Shea did an effective job as a makeshift central midfield, but Alan Smith, Darren Fletcher and Kieran Richardson struggled to convince the fans that they could solve the midfield conundrum. The trio struggled to hold down places in the side, despite their best efforts.

Ferguson stressed the need to be patient as the younger players gained experience. The lack of silverware was certainly frustrating, but it was also easy to overlook the fact that Ronaldo only turned 21 during the campaign, while Rooney was still only 20. They were improving every season and few doubted that they were the future of the club. But the pressure to win trophies is so intense amongst Europe's elite that the highest quality is expected immediately. During the season, Ronaldo and his team-mates had played some excellent football, only to let themselves down by failing to maintain that level in the next few games.

The United manager gave an accurate summary of the season in *The Official Manchester United Yearbook 2006*, 'It's true to say we have had our ups and downs this season but, give or take a couple of matches near the end of the campaign, the important thing is that I feel we are making progress. We have the Carling Cup and I congratulate the players who captured a trophy that I see as a stepping stone to bigger and better things.'

There was little doubt, though, as the players headed off to Germany for the 2006 World Cup, that Ronaldo and company would push Chelsea harder next season. They had stomached more than they could take of watching other teams celebrating with the top trophies. Nobody was happy to settle for second place, and Cristiano vowed to lead the team to the title next time. If the players failed again, they knew their jobs would be on the line and that was something that Cristiano did not even want to consider.

His performances during the season had certainly raised his profile and he was now one of football's most recognisable faces. This has led to hoards of off-field sponsorship opportunities. In 2005, he had agreed a deal with Suzuki to market the Suzuki Swift car. In the advertisement, a group of boys are playing football when the ball spins away and falls at the feet of Ronaldo, who has just got out of his Suzuki Swift. The advert was shown in Europe, Japan, Australia and New Zealand, further raising Ronaldo's profile in the process. Suzuki explained that they enlisted Ronaldo because he emphasised the young, dynamic feel of the car.

In addition, 2005 also saw him agree a sponsorship package with Extra Joss, an Indonesian energy drink. The idea came about as a result of United's Far East Asia tour. In the brand's television advert Ronaldo can be seen looking on in awe at the strength of those who drink Extra Joss. The club's overseas tours made their players huge stars in every corner of the world, particularly in Asia, and a massive group of fans attended any training session or match. As David Beckham found, on-field success is quickly followed by off-field celebrity status.

With his Premiership efforts over for another season and only a Carling Cup triumph to show for it, Ronaldo could have been forgiven for simply wanting to get away from football and have a relaxing break before the World Cup. But Portugal, like most nations, were working very hard to ensure that the players were fully prepared for the strain of a major tournament. This process involved strenuous training sessions and a one-sided 4-1 victory against Cape Verde Islands on 28 May. Pauleta maintained his scoring streak with a fine hat-trick, and Ronaldo played for just over an hour, keeping his fitness levels high, as well as collecting a yellow card. Even though their opponents were vastly inferior, it was a decent workout.

Audiences all over the world were now preparing for the huge month of football ahead. Ronaldo was equally excited as he and his team-mates headed to Germany. It was going to be four weeks of football that he would never forget.

WORLD CUP 2006 AND THE ROAD TO REDEMPTION

EURO 2004 HAD seen Portugal excel in front of their home supporters, reaching the final but losing 1-0 to Greece. The success of the team had roused the whole nation, and the Portuguese people hoped the players could go one better in Germany. The 2006 World Cup would be the last major tournament for stars such as Luis Figo, and many neutrals hoped that Figo would leave the world stage on a high.

Portugal again arrived at a big tournament with a talented squad. The experienced heads were still involved and some of the younger players, including Ronaldo, had matured and improved over the past two years. Goalkeeper Ricardo had earned himself a reputation as a brilliant shot-stopper and penalty-saver, as England had found out to their cost at Euro 2004. The defence boasted Chelsea's Ricardo Carvalho and Valencia's attacking full-back Miguel, while the attack was crammed with the flair of Ronaldo, Figo, Deco and Pauleta. If the defence could keep things tight, there were plenty of options in attack. The key would be converting chances.

Historically, Portugal had created a hatful of chances but struggled to find a striker who could score consistently.

In the media, Cristiano spoke out confidently about his country's chances of success, 'I think Portugal has an excellent team. We have great players and a great coach.' He also added that he had set himself a tough individual goal for the competition, 'Personally, I hope to be better in the World Cup than I was in the European Championships.' Considering that he was one of the stars of Euro 2004, it would take some special displays in Germany to eclipse those performances in Portugal two years earlier.

But while Scolari left Ronaldo on the bench for the early matches at Euro 2004, he made Cristiano a certain starter in Germany. His creativity on the wing was a crucial part of Portugal's game plan, and he would be expected to weigh in with goals to support Pauleta, the team's lone striker. It was a big burden for a 21-year-old.

The 2006 World Cup really marked Ronaldo out as a talented – and controversial – young player. Scolari had continued his successful run, and the team had cantered through the qualifying round, winning nine and drawing three of their 12 matches. Scolari had unleashed Ronaldo at Euro 2004 and he was now a central figure, capable of dominating any game with his pace and trickery. He had developed his vision and consistency playing for United and seemed ready to enjoy the best form of his career. With the whole world watching, Cristiano sensed that it was time to grasp the opportunity with both hands.

Scolari's main concern over Ronaldo was the winger's temperament. The World Cup would be full of emotion and he could not afford to see Cristiano get sent off for lashing out. Scolari told the press, 'Cristiano Ronaldo worries me because the majority of our opponents provoke Cristiano and he does not know how to deal with it. He must keep his head not to react in this way. I want him to bear this in mind. We're trying to make him understand referees do not always penalise fouls.'

This comment was prompted by Ronaldo's angry reaction in a warm-up friendly against Luxembourg, when he had responded to a bad challenge by grabbing an opponent by the throat. Cristiano knew he was in the wrong and vowed not to let his temper get the better of him in the World Cup. He did not want a moment of madness to jeopardise the team's chances. Seemingly, the bookmakers did not believe that Ronaldo could keep his emotions in check because they offered odds of 12-1 on the winger receiving a red card during the tournament. There would be testing moments ahead, but Cristiano was confident that he had the temperament to overcome any provocation.

Portugal received an enviable group for the opening stage of the World Cup as the team was drawn alongside Mexico, Angola and Iran in Group D. They could not have wished for a much better start. Whilst Ronaldo and his team-mates were not complacent, everyone knew that nothing short of top spot would be acceptable. Finishing in first place was especially critical as it would probably pair Portugal with Holland in the next round, rather than the slighter superior Argentina. Some of the other groups had two major threats – Italy and Czech Republic; England and Sweden – but the Mexicans were not expected to carry quite the same danger for Portugal.

The tournament began well for Portugal, who gradually

found their form without comfortably beating any of their opponents. They were made to work hard in their first match to secure a 1-0 win in Cologne over former Portuguese colony, Angola, who could take great pride from their stubborn display. Pauleta scored early on, but the team failed to add to their lead despite controlling possession for long periods. Ronaldo savoured the electric atmosphere in his first ever World Cup appearance.

It was not a result that sent a message of intent to their rivals, but Portugal had collected the three points and, at this stage, wins were much more critical than quality performances. Tournament winners rarely hit the ground running but instead go through the gears as the competition progresses. After all, Portugal had lost their opening match of Euro 2004 and still found themselves playing in the final. Scolari seemed happy enough with his players' winning start, telling the media, 'We got the three points. We'll build on that. A victory, even by the narrowest margin, is excellent. That's what we wanted – three points in the bag.'

Figo was less enthusiastic about the performance, 'We came in here well prepared and played well at times but there were periods when we went off and lost our rhythm.' Pauleta echoed these comments, saying, 'We have to step it up if we want to go much further in this tournament. We really need to do better.' But there was plenty of time to do so and, with Iran as their next opponent, there would soon be a chance for Ronaldo and his team-mates to improve their goal difference.

Former German international midfielder Dietmar Hamann, amongst many others, predicted a comfortable victory for Portugal in their second group game against

Iran in Frankfurt. Hamann claimed, 'This could be the game in which Cristiano Ronaldo shows the world what he is all about. I'm a massive fan of the kid. I remember playing United a couple of years ago on a wet night at their place. Ronaldo did more with the ball on a messy pitch than most good players can do on a dry one. He now provides end product.'

Portugal did indeed beat Iran, and the 2-0 win was a very special night for Cristiano, even if the team only played well in patches. The winger scored the team's second goal from the penalty spot – his first ever World Cup goal – after Deco, restored to the starting line-up, had given Portugal the lead with a fine long-range strike. Ronaldo's display was one of the highlights as he showed his full repertoire of tricks and he thought he had bagged a second goal, only to be denied by the offside flag. A team with more clinical forwards might well have scored four or five against Iran's defence.

The victory secured Portugal's place in the next round, giving them maximum points in Group D. Scolari was thrilled with the achievement – the team had not reached the second round for 40 years, 'This is an historic moment for Portugal. We're elated. We still want to beat Mexico to ensure first place in the group.' The players looked thrilled but this squad had ambitions of going much further than the second round.

Portugal's match with Mexico would decide the leadership of the group. The Mexicans had beaten Iran but surprisingly drawn with plucky Angola, so only a win over Portugal could snatch top spot. Most expected that Holland would await the winners; Argentina the losers. Portugal had kept two successive clean sheets and, with the defence holding firm, there was a solid base for Ronaldo and his fellow attackers. By drawing 0-0 with Angola, Mexico had shown that they did not have the ruthless streak in front of goal. The Portuguese nation looked on expectantly.

Maximum points were secured on 21 June with a 2-1 win over Mexico in Gelsenkirchen. Portugal were able to rest a few players, including Ronaldo, ahead of the second round, and the replacements certainly did not let the side down. Maniche continued his excellent form, scoring the first goal, and Simao made it 2-0 from the penalty spot after a ludicrous handball by Mexico captain Rafael Marquez. Mexico pulled a goal back but when they were reduced to ten men, the game petered out. Ronaldo understood the decision to rest his body for the challenges ahead, but he was itching to be part of the action. Scolari spoke happily about his team's progress and looked forward to facing the Dutch – Portugal's semi-final opponents at Euro 2004 – who had finished second in Group C. He told the press, 'It wasn't a game where everything was at its best. There are three games to go until the final, and they're the hardest.'

The Portugal manager, who had turned down the England manager's position at the end of April 2006, boasted a magnificent tournament CV. He had guided Brazil to their 2002 World Cup success and taken Portugal to the final of Euro 2004. The Portuguese team was in safe hands and hopes were high. Many had expected Scolari to take over in charge of England, and it seemed as though the Brazilian was about to accept the offer, only for him to change his mind.

Portugal faced Holland in the next round in Nuremberg, and the two teams were very evenly matched, with plenty of talented attackers on both sides. Sadly, the game will live long in the memory for all the wrong reasons. Portugal were eventual winners, triumphing 1-0 thanks to a Maniche strike, but the game was marred by overly strict refereeing. Referee Valentin Ivanov gave out 20 cards (16 yellow, 4 red) yet the game contained just 25 fouls. A rough challenge on Ronaldo forced him to reluctantly limp out of the match with a thigh injury after just 34 minutes. He had to watch the chaos from the touchline – it was not the way he had imagined the night turning out. The whole episode left both teams very bitter, and Portugal were forced to prepare for their quarter-final with England knowing that Deco and Costinha, who had been sent off, would be suspended.

Scolari spoke proudly of his players, calling it a 'heroic victory'. He added, 'FIFA always talks about fair play but tonight we saw several gestures that were anything but. There were excesses on both sides – but the sending off of Deco was provocation.' Deco had been given his first yellow card for a lunge on Johnny Heitinga, who had refused to return the ball after Portugal had put it out of play. The Dutch should have shown better sportsmanship by giving possession back to their opponents, but it still did not excuse Deco's nasty challenge.

The overall performance said much about the spirit in the Portugal camp as everyone pulled together to achieve the win. Figo told the media, 'From the start of the tournament our great strength has resided in our unity and the great support of the whole country. The team should be congratulated for demonstrating such character.'

Scolari later revealed that he would appeal against the dismissal of Deco, 'The Federation could send a letter to

FIFA because of the first yellow card. The ball was ours, we had possession, but the Dutch player was told by his coach to continue playing. There should be fair play guidelines from FIFA; the time has come for FIFA to think about this.' The nature of the game gave Ronaldo and his team-mates an unfair reputation for being physical and dirty.

In addition to the suspensions, Figo and Ronaldo were struggling with injuries that they had picked up in the physical clash. Cristiano now faced a race against time to be fit to line up against England in the quarter-final. He was determined to take on a number of his club colleagues, including Gary Neville, who he would face down the Portugal left flank. Already Ronaldo's performances were earning rave reviews. In a Portuguese side that was more functional than free-flowing, he stood out as the player who could unlock opposition defences and provide the speed and trickery on counter attacks.

The fact that Scolari had rejected the England job, and had such a good track record against England, provided an intriguing subplot to the game. Some fans saw Scolari's rejection of the manager's post as a snub and were still bitter over the eliminations at the past two major tournaments. Ronaldo knew that it would be extra motivation for the England camp and the team's supporters. It was going to be an incredibly tense match.

A more pressing issue, though, was Cristiano's fitness. An update on the thigh injury from the Portugal team doctor, Henrique Jones, provided reason for optimism ahead of the clash with England, 'Ronaldo has just had a scan; he's got muscular swelling in his thigh and we hope that it will ease. He's having medication and he will have two daily treatments. We are hopeful that he will recover.' The whole nation had its fingers firmly crossed, especially with Deco and Costinha already unavailable. Scolari explained that he would wait until just a few hours prior to kick-off before deciding on whether or not Cristiano was fit enough to play.

Ronaldo did pass his fitness test to play against England in Gelsenkirchen, where he enjoyed a duel with United colleague Gary Neville, who had also brushed off injury to play. Usually employed on the right wing, Scolari opted to use Cristiano on the left and he caused problems for the England defence. He enjoyed dancing past Neville on a couple of occasions early on. While the Holland game was eventful throughout, the England–Portugal match burst into life in the second half when Ronaldo and Wayne Rooney became involved in an incident which would dominate the headlines for months.

Rooney had been starved of supply in his curious role as a lone striker and, as he became tangled with Ricardo Carvalho and Armando Petit, he seemed to stamp on the grounded Chelsea defender. Referee Horacio Elizondo, who had a perfect view of the incident, was immediately surrounded by Portuguese players urging him to produce a red card. Among them was Ronaldo, Rooney's United team-mate. Elizondo appeared to hesitate but then did indeed produce a red card. To many it seemed to be the correct decision, though Rooney protests his innocence to this day. The whole drama was over in a blink of an eye yet it had changed the game completely.

The reaction of Ronaldo and the rest of the Portuguese side left England furious, however. Cristiano did not help matters by winking at the Portuguese bench moments after Rooney's dismissal, and it became all the more foolish when the wink was captured by television cameras, leaving English fans across the country baying for Ronaldo's blood. In a few minutes of controversy, Cristiano's behaviour had ensured that he would face a major backlash from English supporters throughout the following Premiership season. But according to Rio Ferdinand, Ronaldo later explained that the wink was just acknowledgement to the Portugal bench that he understood Scolari's message to fully exploit their numerical advantage.

It begged the question of whether Portugal had deliberately targeted Rooney's suspect temperament as a way to gain an advantage in the match. As the players lined up for kick-off in the first half, Cristiano had pretended to head-butt Rooney and the Portuguese defence gave the striker plenty of physical treatment. If it had been a ploy, it had worked because Rooney was off and Portugal were now in the ascendancy.

For the remainder of the night, Ronaldo continued to carry the biggest threat to ten-man England, but the glaring lack of quality strikers was letting Portugal down – Pauleta simply did not have the skill, height or pace to trouble England. Neville, John Terry and the rest of the back line gave heroic displays, while the best of all came from the tireless Owen Hargreaves who covered every blade of grass. Portugal threw everything at England but created very few chances, most of which were crafted by Ronaldo. 120 minutes of gripping action could not separate the two teams, and the match went to penalties; an all-too-familiar feeling for England at major tournaments.

Sadly for England, the shootout followed the usual pattern. Simao gave Portugal a 1-0 lead, Ricardo saved from Steven

Gerrard, Hugo Viana missed, Owen Hargreaves scored. 1-1. Armando Petit missed. Ricardo saved from Frank Lampard. Helder Postiga scored. 2-1. Ricardo saved from Jamie Carragher. Then Ronaldo himself stepped up and fired the winning spot-kick past Paul Robinson before a joyous celebration. It was somehow appropriate that Ronaldo, both hero and villain, was the man who scored the winning penalty. Ricardo took the plaudits, becoming the first goalkeeper in World Cup history to save three penalties in a shootout. But it was cruel on England, who had shown great spirit to force the shootout.

Cristiano now had his sights fixed on the semi-finals. He told the media, 'I'm full of confidence and I shoot strong. I was tired in the second half but I haven't played for a week so it was okay. We have four days to recover now so I think everyone's going to be ready.'

Scolari was dignified in victory, having eliminated England from a major tournament for the third time in succession, once with Brazil in 2002 and now twice with Portugal. England fans were sick of the sight of him. The Portugal manager said to the press, 'Congratulations to England – with ten players they were incredible – it was an electrifying match. We didn't take advantage, we shot too much from outside the area. England closed the way to goal very well and it was like playing against 11.'

England manager Sven-Goran Eriksson was devastated by his team's elimination but was proud of the players. He insisted that the players had practised penalties regularly and so found the outcome heart-breaking, 'I really don't know what more we could do about it.' The fact that Eriksson had arranged to stand down from his post after the tournament saved the Swede from some of the flak in the wake of the quarter-final exit. His fate had long been sealed in the eyes of the English public. It did little to help Ronaldo from avoiding criticism.

As Portugal advanced to face France in the semi-final, the English media went all out in their bid to make Ronaldo the villain of England's World Cup exit, ignoring the fact that it was Rooney's temper that had really cost the team. Much was made of the fact that Ronaldo had contrived to get his own club team-mate sent off, and Manchester United were urged to take action. Ronaldo, whose reputation as a diver had already angered opposition supporters, would now face the most hostile atmospheres of his career.

Numerous experts spoke out against Ronaldo's actions, including Martin Jol, the Tottenham manager, who said, 'The biggest disgrace of all was Cristiano Ronaldo because he tried to influence the referee. What about sporting values?' Many agreed that Ronaldo was in the wrong and that his behaviour showed no signs of sportsmanship. It was all anyone could talk about as fans all over England reflected on the team's elimination.

Ricardo, the Portugal goalkeeper, was one person who defended Cristiano in the aftermath of the game. He explained to the media, 'There always has to be a scapegoat when someone loses. I don't think [Ronaldo] influenced the referee. The referee was right on top of it.' The Portuguese goalkeeper was not far wrong regarding England. Whether it is the penalty takers who miss or players who are sent off, somebody must be blamed. England's exit from major tournaments must be someone else's fault – it could never be as a result of the team playing poorly.

Cristiano moved quickly, though, to quash the idea of a rift between himself and Rooney, telling the press, 'There is no problem at all between me and Rooney. At the end of the game, we exchanged a series of text messages. This reinforces that I have a fine relationship with Rooney. Between the two of us, everything is clear. I complained to the referee about the foul but I didn't ask for a red card.' He revealed that Rooney had told him to ignore the English media, who simply wanted 'to stir things up'. To some, this story seemed far-fetched, but both players maintained that their relationship was unaffected.

While from Rooney's perspective it was disappointing that Cristiano had got involved, the suggestions that Ronaldo had betrayed Rooney were over the top. As the winger himself explained in *Four Four Two*, it was not personal, 'Everyone does what he has to do for his country and I did what I had to do. Every player plays for his national team with great love and I was giving great love for Portugal. You don't expect a thing like that to be used as an excuse for their defeat.' He was not the first, and will not be the last, to run to the referee in order to try to influence a decision. Rooney himself, along with so many others, has been seen to do exactly the same. It is not the best advertisement for the game, but it happens.

The way that Rooney discusses the incident in his autobiography, *My Story: The Way It Is*, reveals more about the matter. How much truth there is behind Rooney's version of events after the match is open to debate, but the distribution of blame is not. The striker writes, 'I sent a text to Ronny. I told him to forget about what happened. I wasn't blaming him for interfering. Then I wished him good luck in the semis.' Though it was through no fault of Rooney's, the

United striker managed to escape most of the criticism for the incident, which he insists was a result of him landing off balance on Carvalho rather than anything vicious. It was impossible to tell whether there was any malice involved, and only Rooney himself truly knew the answer.

Steven Gerrard's autobiography suggests that Rooney was actually angrier with Ronaldo than he let on and had quizzed the Liverpool captain on the coach after the match about the wink. Gerrard was furious about the swarm of Portugal players who had surrounded the referee. In his autobiography, he writes, 'F**king Ronaldo was at the front. Portugal's deviousness got one of my best mates sent off in the World Cup.' He did not help the situation by calling Ronaldo 'a disgrace' for his role in Rooney's dismissal. Gerrard also claimed that if his Liverpool team-mates Xabi Alonso or Luis Garcia had done the same in a match against Spain, he would never have spoken to them again. In his autobiography, he adds, 'Sadly a dark side stains Cristiano Ronaldo's game.'

The fact remained, though, that on that day, on that pitch, in a World Cup quarter-final, Ronaldo and Rooney were on opposite teams. Regardless of their mutual club allegiance to United, Ronaldo was representing Portugal, Rooney was representing England. Regularly in football, the notion of friendships being put to one side for 90 minutes is mentioned without anyone questioning the truth behind it. When Cristiano rushed to the referee and, as he maintains, pleaded for a free-kick, he was not trying to seal his club colleague's fate but seal Portugal's progression to the semi-final. This match was about much more than Ronaldo and Rooney, and it would be wrong to think that Ronaldo had time in the heat of the moment to stop and think that, because it was a friend of his, he must not appeal too strongly about the foul.

Rio Ferdinand echoes these sentiments in his auto-biography, *Rio: My Story*. The defender says, 'In the heat of the moment, isn't the other player just the opposition, not a club mate?' Ferdinand is adamant that he did not blame Ronaldo and had believed Cristiano when his club colleague told him that he didn't try to get Rooney sent off. It put the likes of Ferdinand and Gary Neville in an awkward position, as they tried to take the sting out of the controversy surrounding their two United team-mates.

Certainly, regardless of who was to blame, the long term result of the red card was that Ronaldo was vilified, not Rooney. Looking at the similarities with Beckham's dismissal against Argentina, there are striking resemblances. England had made solid starts in both matches, the game was level at the time, the red card resulted from lashing out, England battled bravely to force penalties and lost. Beckham became a figure of hate, Rooney largely managed to quietly prepare for pre-season. Had Diego Simeone been playing in the Premiership, things might have been very different for Beckham when he returned for the 1998/99 campaign.

Meanwhile, Cristiano ignored the comments of others and prepared for the French, who had surprised many by beating first Spain and then the favourites Brazil to reach the World Cup semi-finals. Zinedine Zidane had been their hero, rolling back the years with some vintage displays as France's playmaker. Ronaldo knew Zidane would represent the biggest danger, along with Arsenal's Thierry Henry, but he was confident that Portugal's attackers would also cause problems if they were on top of their game.

In the build-up to the semi-final, there was much controversy over comments made by French coach Raymond Domenech about the Portuguese side. Firstly, when he had been manager of the France Under 21s, he criticised a Portuguese Under 21 side including Cristiano. Domenech called the Portuguese players 'savages, who believed they were still living in the time of the conquistadors.' The media reminded the world of this, and Ronaldo was quick to defend his team's behaviour.

Prior to the game, Domenech said, 'Portugal are a team with talent, are well organised, know how to defend – and how to provoke their opponents.' This latest statement added extra spice to the contest, as did the words of French defender William Gallas. Gallas told the media, 'In this sort of match we must be careful of the Portuguese – they like diving, you can see that.' It was a claim that seemed all the more ridiculous considering Thierry Henry's theatrical fall that created France's crucial second goal in the second round against Spain. But few in the Portugal camp saw the funny side of it.

Sadly, though, the semi-final in Munich proved to be a bridge too far for Ronaldo and Portugal. Just after the half hour mark, Ricardo Carvalho fouled Henry in the penalty area, and Zidane slotted home the spot-kick. The goal was enough to clinch a 1-0 victory and a place in the World Cup final for the French. Ronaldo was booed throughout the 90 minutes – particularly after one very theatrical fall – presumably by a combination of neutrals and hopeful England fans who had booked semi-final tickets. In a prelude to how he would respond back in England, the winger seemed to relish the hostility, and it inspired some excellent runs at the heart of the

French back line. He was the main threat for Portugal and defenders twice had to make important blocks.

Otherwise, though, the Portuguese looked fairly ordinary, lacking any other attacking ideas and unable to put France under enough pressure. The urgency expected in a World Cup semi-final was sadly missing. Cristiano and Scolari both blamed the referee, with the Portugal manager unleashing a tirade at the official after the final whistle. Scolari admitted that France's penalty was fair but was adamant that there should have been a penalty awarded to his team for a foul on Ronaldo. Cristiano told the media, 'Anyone who understands football saw that the referee wasn't fair.'

The 1-0 semi-final defeat was a disappointing end to the competition for Ronaldo, whose performances in the tournament had further developed his reputation as a fantastic young player. While it was the end of the road for the likes of Figo, Cristiano would certainly be back again on the world stage – in less controversial circumstances, he hoped.

It was doubtless little consolation for Ronaldo when he earned himself another award in 2006 to go with his Carling Cup success. It emerged that he had been named Top World Cup Gay Icon by a Dutch gay magazine, winning the poll for the second year in a row. According to the magazine, readers voted for Ronaldo as 'the most beautiful, the most attractive and the sexiest player at the showpiece event'. He reportedly finished ahead of a number of other top players, including David Beckham, Michael Owen, Ruud van Nistelrooy, Fredrik Ljungberg and Kaka. No doubt news of his achievement reached the Manchester United dressing-room.

Nothing could improve Cristiano's mood, as it would be

France who advanced to the final to face Italy, a repeat of the Euro 2000 final and certainly not a final that many experts had predicted. Generally, it had proved a defenders' tournament as big name stars such as Ronaldinho, Adriano and van Nistelrooy had failed to make an impact, while the likes of Fabio Cannavaro and Lilian Thuram had been immense. No one anticipated a high scoring final!

Scolari's frustration at his team's lack of goals was evident in the post-match press conference, 'We did everything possible but if you don't score you don't win the game. We did everything we could, we did our best. We have to accept this. We had a few chances but, unfortunately, didn't do it and lost.' Scolari's furious reaction at the end of the game was presumably regarding the penalty decision, but he refused to discuss the matter. Eusebio, the Portuguese great, was a little more upbeat and admitted on Portuguese television that it was just not Portugal's day, 'The luck factor was not on Portugal's side today. The players deserve to be congratulated.'

It was not all over yet, though, for the Portuguese as they faced Germany in the third place play-off on 8 July in Stuttgart. It was a difficult game to get motivated for as everyone involved was still hurting from losing the semi-final, but both sets of players tried to put the pain to one side to end on a high note. In front of their home fans, Germany had enjoyed a super tournament, and Italy had left it very late to win their semi-final, scoring twice in the closing moments of extra-time. Willed on by the crowd, Germany swept Portugal aside in a forgettable match for Ronaldo and his team-mates. It seemed a harsh way for Cristiano's tournament to finish. Figo came off the bench to make his final appearance for the national team and set up Nuno Gomes for Portugal's consolation goal.

Figo and Pauleta both announced their retirement from international football after the match. Figo told the media, 'It is hard for me to end my international career in this way. I did everything I could and the team gave their all.' Pauleta called it 'the saddest day of my career'. It was an emotional time for all those associated with Portuguese football, and for Cristiano it felt like the end of an era.

Ronaldo and his Portugal team-mates could only watch as Italy went on to lift the trophy in Berlin, winning a penalty shoot-out 5-3, after a 1-1 draw. It was a tense match between two sides that had been written off in comparison with the praise heaped on Argentina and Brazil. Like Portugal, Italy and France had arrived in the latter stages of the tournament thanks to superb defensive work and just enough moments of attacking flair. It was an all-European World Cup final for the first time since Italy and West Germany contested the 1982 showpiece. Cristiano was just disappointed that Portugal were not involved.

The final will forever be remembered for Zidane's shameful headbutt on Marco Materazzi, ending the Frenchman's magnificent career in disgrace. Having been so calm and composed throughout the competition, it was a bizarre moment. However, this did not prevent Zidane – controversially FIFA's Golden Ball winner at the World Cup – from being named in most pundits' team of the tournament. Similarly, Ronaldo's misdemeanours were overlooked as he was selected in many of the same line-ups. While he had infuriated many England fans, his profile had certainly been boosted by the quality of his displays during the tournament.

Meanwhile, Ronaldo seemed to be busy making his own plans. Perhaps still affected by his team's failure to reach the final, Ronaldo spoke out about leaving Manchester United, with the prospect of angry England fans awaiting his return. The winger put himself in the shop window, announcing to the press, 'I should get out of Manchester as the circumstances are not right. Will it be Real or Barcelona? It will be one of them. For some time I haven't had any support from my chief executive or my coach. They should have come out in my defence but no one did.' It was a very bold statement and it certainly sent waves of panic around Old Trafford.

Sir Alex Ferguson had already assured United supporters that Ronaldo would be going nowhere and immediately took steps to defuse the situation. It turned out that Ferguson had tried to contact Ronaldo after the England game but had his old phone number – this had triggered Cristiano's concerns. Ferguson, assistant manager Carlos Queiroz, and David Gill, the chief executive, flew out to discuss the issue with Ronaldo after the World Cup, and pulled out all the stops to convince the youngster to return to Manchester.

The United manager revealed in *Planeta Ronaldo*, 'Cristiano had fears about the reaction back in England. I explained that we had gone through the same thing with David Beckham when they were burning effigies of him after the 1998 World Cup. I told him that English people talk more than they actually do anything. They might make a lot of noise but they wouldn't harm him physically.'

Ferguson also suggested that Ronaldo might feel safer if he moved house into the countryside and gave the winger all the advice possible to help him prepare for the reaction of the English crowds. The first few months would be critical. If Cristiano could silence the boos with his performances, the atmospheres at away games would become increasingly easier to handle. It was not going to be easy, but Sir Alex felt sure that his winger could deal with the pressure.

United moved quickly to back Ronaldo, explaining in a statement, 'The club can confirm there is no possibility of Cristiano being sold. The club will not listen to any offers for Cristiano.' Nevertheless, rumours still circulated that the winger wanted to leave United, with Spain his likeliest destination. At this stage, his future at Old Trafford looked very much in the balance. But gradually it became clear that Ferguson's efforts to reassure Ronaldo were starting to have some effect. Speaking to the press in his hometown of Funchal, Ronaldo explained, 'I have no reason to leave the club which has always supported me and has always helped me to evolve as a player. Things will be worked out next week.' It was still not the definite statement of commitment that United wanted, but it was an improvement. Ferguson remained confident that Cristiano would commit himself to the team's bid to reclaim the title.

Predictably, as the affair rumbled on, Ronaldo was linked with other clubs. Real Madrid were rumoured to be offering him a bolthole away from the English fans, but manager Fabio Capello played down talk of the player arriving in the Spanish capital, whilst admitting his admiration of the winger's talent. Links with Real would persist throughout the campaign, as reports persistently circulated in the press in both countries. Capello was trying to rebuild Madrid's team and, naturally, a talented young winger would be an attractive signing.

As they had in 1998 with Beckham, United handled the controversy with care and eventually Cristiano decided to return and face the boos. Ferguson's reassurances to Ronaldo had proved to be worth their weight in gold and, looking back, the air fare to Madeira had been his best piece of summer spending. Ronaldo was aware that he would receive some less than pleasant abuse on away trips throughout the season. It would be a daunting adventure, but he felt ready for it and he knew he had the support of Manchester United – that counted for a lot in his mind.

This still left the small matter of Wayne Rooney, however. Many questioned whether Ronaldo and Rooney could play in the same side. But for his part, Rooney spoke out in support of his club colleague, 'I bear no ill-feeling to Cristiano but am disappointed that he chose to get involved.' However, rumours persisted suggesting that Rooney had been so furious after the match that he had wanted a confrontation with Ronaldo and that, claiming that he would never play alongside the winger again, he had to be restrained from bursting into the Portuguese changing-room. Some sources quoted Rooney as saying he would 'split Cristiano Ronaldo in two' – a comment that Rooney strongly denied. Alan Shearer, working as a pundit for the BBC during the World Cup, suggested in the heat of the moment that Rooney would want to hit Cristiano next time he saw him.

The media thrived on the story, relishing the chance to portray Ronaldo as the villain and thus unsettle United's pre-season. Numerous stories circulated suggesting that Ronaldo had reason to be apprehensive about returning to the United dressing-room, as his team-mates were still smarting over his behaviour in the World Cup. But remarkably it seemed that Cristiano and Rooney were now ready to put the incident behind them for the sake of United's title hopes. The pair made up in front of the cameras at the team's training ground, and the striker proved that he was on good terms with Ronaldo by shaking his hand and giving a jovial wink. The squad saw the funny side of things, and instantly the focus at pre-season training turned to the challenges that lay ahead. The issue had been put to one side, internally at least.

The public, though, still held Ronaldo responsible for England's World Cup exit and he was vilified nationwide. Some angry supporters took out their frustrations by voting for other candidates in the FIFA World Cup 2006 Best Young Player poll, denying Ronaldo the award that he had seemed destined to win. In the end, Germany's Lukas Podolski won the award. Others invested in 'I hate Ronaldo' t-shirts, available on the Internet. Meanwhile, dartboards were sold with a picture of Cristiano in the middle and the message 'Put a dart in the tart'. Tempers were running high. Plenty of jokes were circulated on the Internet on the topic of the World Cup incident, but they did little to calm the heated atmosphere.

Ronaldo's maturity, though, revealed itself in the face of the criticism and angry chants. He managed to channel the abuse into more inspired displays on the field. Cristiano said, 'I play good matches when people shout at me in the stadiums. It is like a special incentive for me to receive so much booing when I touch the ball.' Clearly, it would take more than a few thousand angry supporters to faze Ronaldo. Maybe the hostility would even bring out the best in him.

As he stepped out to face the fans, baying for blood, there

seemed not a trace of fear, no indication that he was intimidated. He simply got on with his job to the best of his ability. The England supporters were happy to find any scapegoat to blame for the team's premature exit, and Ronaldo's wink had earned him that role. Cristiano kept quiet on this topic but privately he found it deeply frustrating and irritating that he was being used as an excuse for England's failure – how much influence did the English think he possessed? The two teams had fought out a 0-0 draw and Portugal had triumphed on penalties. To Ronaldo, it was as simple as that.

Cristiano is now able to look back on the controversy and laugh at his comments about leaving United. Speaking to *Four Four Two*, he admitted, 'It was just after the World Cup; I was hot-headed. We say things we don't mean to say. But it's in the past. I'm at United, I'm happy and I want to continue.' His immediate reaction to the aftermath of the World Cup incident did not just show him as being hot-headed, it also highlighted the very human feeling of fear. Initially, the situation ahead of him was one that he simply was not ready for.

United's explosive start to the 2006/07 season owed much to Ronaldo's excellent early form. After enjoying a very good World Cup – in which he made many pundits' team of the tournament – he carried the same level of performances into the Premiership campaign. His pace and dribbling mesmerised defenders and, with Rooney and a fit Louis Saha proving a good partnership, United looked menacing.

It had been a relatively quiet summer in the transfer market as Ferguson only purchased Michael Carrick and Tomasz Kuszczak. Carrick cost the club £18.6 million and was

Showing his talents off the
pitch – modelling.

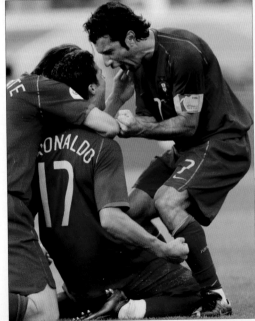

Team mates Luis Figo and Nuno Valente celebrate with Cristiano after he scored Portugal's second goal from the penalty spot during the World Cup game against Iran at the Frankfurt stadium, 17 June 2006.

Above: Rooney gets the red card after the infamous tangle with Ricardo Carvalho during the England vs Portugal quarter-final World Cup match, which saw Ronaldo embroiled in controversy.

Below: Scoring the winning penalty in the shootout against England to break English hearts and put Portugal through to the semi-finals.

Above: Being challenged by French defender William Gallas (*left*) and forward Franck Ribery (*right*) during the semi-final World Cup football match, 5 July 2006. Portugal failed to progress, losing 1-0.

Below: After the World Cup. Putting the sending-off incident behind them, Ronaldo and Rooney get back to the day-job at the Man Utd training ground, August 2006.

Enjoying life off the pitch. Here he attends Christina Aguilera's 'Back to Basics' concert at the MEN Arena, Manchester.

Inset: His younger sister Katia on holiday with him in Madeira in the summer of 2006.

Above: With Sir Alex Ferguson after agreeing a new five-year deal at Manchester United, April 2007.

Below: Cristiano is a globally marketable star. Here he signs autographs for local fans after training in Macao on a tour of the Far East.

After a blistering 2006-07 season, Cristiano was deservedly named as Manchester United's Player of the Season in May 2007. He became the first player in English football ever to be voted PFA Player's Player of the Year, Young Player of the Year and Fans' Player of the Year in one season.

Ronaldo's day of glory, the 2008 Champions League final versus
Chelsea in St Petersburg. Scoring the headed goal which put the Reds
in the lead after 26 minutes; and watching the tense penalty shootout in
which he missed his own spot-kick.

bought to occupy the more defensive, anchor role in midfield. He was not the big name signing that some supporters had hoped for – after links with Argentine Javier Mascherano and Lyon's French midfielder Mahamadou Diarra – but he had a proven track record in English football and an excellent range of passing. He was also familiar with the club's other England internationals and so fitted easily into the dressing-room dynamic. Kuszczak was a goalkeeper with Premiership experience who could provide reliable cover for van der Sar, if and when required.

With Paul Scholes returning to the side after his eye problems, it would be as though United had an extra new signing. In his absence from the side, football fans could be forgiven for forgetting just how talented Scholes was and how much he added to the United team. His presence in the side provided more experience, too, and his knowledge would be vital for Carrick, who would be playing alongside him. With Ronaldo and Giggs occupying the wide roles, the team certainly looked strong.

The biggest news involving United was the departure of Ruud van Nistelrooy, who joined Real Madrid for £10.3 million. Rumours circulated suggesting that the striker had fallen out with Ronaldo and that the bust-up had hastened van Nistelrooy's exit. Ferguson seemed to have taken Cristiano's side in the argument, and the Dutchman decided it was time for a change. He had been a phenomenal player for United, scoring 150 goals in 219 appearances since his arrival in the summer of 2001. However, it was no secret that the Dutchman had never enjoyed Ronaldo's service from the right wing as much as his predecessor David Beckham's pinpoint delivery. Seemingly, Ronaldo's unpredictable nature had not fitted well with van Nistelrooy's strengths. The Dutchman would be re-united with Beckham in Madrid.

In the meantime, Louis Saha had regained full fitness and Ferguson believed that the club could afford to let van Nistelrooy go. He was experimenting with different formations – some of which required only one central striker – and he was encouraged by the returns of Saha, Alan Smith and Ole Gunnar Solskjaer from injuries. United were raring to go and, looking around him, Ronaldo knew this was his best chance yet of winning a championship medal. It was the perfect motivation, and it fuelled the determination that he had displayed ever since his first days in youth football. Van Nistelrooy's departure placed more emphasis on Ronaldo and, with Ferguson having put his faith in the future, it was time for the youngsters to deliver.

Fulham came to Old Trafford on the opening day of the new Premiership campaign with a notoriously bad away record in the league, and they truly lived up to that billing. United went ahead early through Saha and the goals just kept coming. When Ronaldo struck in the 19th minute, Fulham trailed 4-0. It was the perfect way for the United players to declare their intentions of regaining the Premiership trophy. The game finished 5-1, and few could look past the brilliance of Ronaldo who had troubled Fulham all afternoon with his pace and skills, linking up well with Rooney and Saha. The only question marks remained over his ability to produce such performances on a regular basis.

There was absolutely no sign of any hostility from his team-mates, and he got great vocal support from the Old Trafford crowd. Anyone hoping for animosity between

Ronaldo and Rooney would have been sorely disappointed as the two were hugging rather than being at each other's throats, and it was Rooney who supplied the cross for Cristiano's goal. The result certainly served as a message to United's fellow title challengers. So much of the pre-season had been spent emphasising the need for a ruthless start to the season in order to keep pace with Chelsea, and the players appeared fully focused.

In United's first away game of the season, Ronaldo, as expected, was greeted by non-stop abuse from the Charlton fans at The Valley, but his response was to terrorise their defence on the way to a 3-0 win on a wet, August night. In a way, he was at least accustomed to the boos because he usually received that reaction for his perceived tendency to go to ground too easily. So he knew what he would be facing and was able to block it out. He did not find the net this time but came close, seeing his shot cannon back off the crossbar. Goals from Darren Fletcher, Saha and Solskjaer clinched the win, and everyone at United was thrilled to see crowd-favourite Solskjaer back in action.

Another good away win against newly promoted Watford gave the club three wins out of three and, with Chelsea having already lost 2-1 at Middlesbrough, United had made the positive start that they were aiming for – sending out a message of intent to their rivals. But Ronaldo was well aware that the bigger challenges lay ahead and that the Blues would bounce back. There had already been a noticeable change in the way that Cristiano was performing this season, compared to the previous few years. The skills had not changed but his decision making had improved, and he was making the most of all his attributes.

After the disappointment of failing to reach the World Cup final, Ronaldo was soon back on international duty. He was part of a young Portuguese side for a friendly with Denmark on 2 September. Figo and Pauleta had retired, and Scolari took the opportunity to blood some youngsters. Nani, the latest Portuguese prodigy, starred with a goal and a fine all-round display, while Ronaldo's appearance lasted 66 minutes. Denmark were too strong and wily on the night for their inexperienced opponents and scored the last two goals of the game to win 4-2. Sir Alex Ferguson was presumably rather unhappy that his star winger was involved in friendly action just weeks into the new Premiership season, but at least Ronaldo had not completed the whole match.

It was one of a number of occasions when Sir Alex felt that Portugal were not showing enough care over Ronaldo's fitness. Seeing his winger playing when not 100 per cent fit, or when in danger of burning out, angered Ferguson, especially when Scolari selected Cristiano for rather meaningless friendlies. The issue was complicated by the fact that the player loved representing his country and probably made himself available occasionally when many players would have pulled out, citing an injury problem. It tells the whole story of how much it means to Cristiano every time he puts on the Portugal shirt.

Four days after their friendly defeat against Denmark, Portugal began their qualifying campaign for Euro 2008. The draw had put Ronaldo and his team-mates alongside Poland, Finland, Belgium, Armenia, Azerbaijan, Kazakhstan and Serbia. It gave them a very good chance of reaching the competition in Austria and Switzerland. Ronaldo, Scolari and the rest of the squad appeared happy with the outcome and fixed their sights on gaining qualification for a tournament they felt they could win.

Poland looked to be Portugal's most likely challengers in the group, having displayed their quality in reaching the 2006 World Cup. Ronaldo knew that the team could take nothing for granted and would take a professional approach into every match. With minnows Kazakhstan and Azerbaijan in the group, though, the Portugal camp was still confident of securing top spot. The Portuguese were certainly the favourites – this was a tag that they were becoming increasingly accustomed to. Ronaldo's scintillating domestic form was a great benefit to the national side as they plotted their route to Euro 2008.

Portugal's first fixture took them to Finland on 6 September, but the team could only pick up a 1-1 draw. To everyone's surprise, Finland took the lead, but a Nuno Gomes goal just before half-time ensured that the teams went in level at the interval. When Ricardo Costa was sent off before the hour mark, Portugal had to settle for a share of the spoils, despite Cristiano's creative influence. With Poland losing their first game, four days earlier, against Finland, it seemed as though the Finns were breaking into the race for qualification. Suddenly, a point away in Helsinki appeared a decent result for Ronaldo and co.

In the Premiership, the club's high levels of consistency continued as United overcame Tottenham 1-0 at Old Trafford, despite some shaky moments. Ryan Giggs, having an inspired start to the season, grabbed the goal after goalkeeper Paul Robinson could only parry Ronaldo's vicious, swerving free-kick. Cristiano has always worked very hard on his set-pieces and his technique allows the ball to move in the air, often confusing goalkeepers with the change of direction. United had started the Premiership season perfectly, but no one was getting carried away. Ronaldo and Giggs were looking dangerous, and the defence looked more secure than the previous campaign, with Nemanja Vidic proving to be an inspired signing.

The Champions League draw put United in Group F, along with Celtic, FC Copenhagen and Benfica – as favourable as the club could have hoped for. All three teams were very beatable, and it offered the added incentive of facing Benfica again after the Portuguese club eliminated United in Lisbon the year before. Solskjaer, the hero of that legendary Champions League night in Barcelona in 1999, was confident that the club could repeat those heroics, telling the press that the team had great offensive strengths, 'We are good enough at counter-attacking and, obviously, with Wayne Rooney and Cristiano Ronaldo, we have players who can beat men and do things on their own.' It would take plenty of spirit and consistency too.

For Ronaldo, it was another opportunity to return to the club that he supported as a boy, though this time he knew his presence would be met with boos after enduring so much abuse the previous season. These were the same fans to whom Ronaldo had given the one-finger salute that was punished by UEFA. But every trip back to his homeland was a reminder of how far he had progressed in such a short space of time. His Sporting days truly seemed a distant memory now.

The first European game was at home against Gordon Strachan's Celtic, and the media fed on the tense relationship between Strachan and Ferguson. The Scottish side caused

United a lot of problems, but Solskjaer showed his value once more with the winner in a 3-2 victory. Ronaldo missed the game, as Ferguson decided to rest his young winger after the pressures of the first few weeks. His manager wanted to maintain his form, knowing how crucial Cristiano would be throughout the campaign. As the season wore on, Ronaldo would have very few breaks.

Cristiano would, though, be back to face Arsenal at the weekend. But worryingly, Giggs had limped from the field during the game and was doubtful for the big clash with the Gunners. It was a blow for the Reds, as the Welshman had made such an impressive start to the campaign – back to his best form. At least a fresh Ronaldo would still provide plenty of menace out wide.

But the old enemy Arsenal inflicted United's first defeat of the season. In a very poor United display – one of Wayne Rooney's worst in the red shirt – Arsenal grabbed a late winner to take the three points that their performance probably deserved. Ronaldo was United's only real threat going forward but, hard as he tried, he could not unlock the Arsenal defence on this occasion. Unfortunately for Cristiano, it was his mistake which gave away possession in a crucial area in the build-up to the winning goal. Cesc Fabregas's dribble and pass found Emmanuel Adebayor, who calmly beat Tomas Kuszczak, deputising for Edwin van der Sar. It was a reality check for Ronaldo and United. Though they had started well, this game had shown that they could not afford to be short of their best if they hoped to keep pace with Chelsea.

Nerves began to surface amongst the United fans during a 1-1 draw with Reading at the Madjeski Stadium. But trailing to a Kevin Doyle penalty, Ronaldo stepped up just when the team needed him, in what would become a running theme for the season. He had been great all afternoon and, receiving the ball on the left touchline, he dribbled at pace, created room for a shot and drilled a fizzing strike into the bottom corner. Although United did not go on to win the game, the draw had shown their character; Ronaldo in particular seemed to be responding to the criticism over his lack of consistent end-product.

Reading manager Steve Coppell could only look on with admiration, telling the media after the game, 'He is a brilliant dribbler, he can cross, he can shoot and he is a good header of the ball.' On the day, Cristiano was probably the only factor that prevented Coppell's side from taking the three points. United were also still adjusting to the arrival of midfielder Michael Carrick from Tottenham and learning about his style of play. Carrick had not shone in his first few games, but it was early days.

Ronaldo and United erased those negative Benfica memories by winning 1-0 away at the Estadio da Luz in the next Champions League match. It was a real smash-and-grab for United, having been below-par for much of the contest. Ronaldo's pass reached Saha, who found the top corner of the net, and the defence held out for a vital return to winning ways. It was a memorable moment for Ronaldo – his most telling contribution of the night – and provided closure on the intense disappointment of crashing out of Europe the previous season in front of the same mocking fans. Again, United supporters were seeing evidence of the improvements in Cristiano's game: the understanding of when to try his tricks and when to look for an easier ball.

This was the type of game that United had thrown away in previous seasons, but the 2006/07 side appeared to have the fighting spirit to grind out results.

Much was made of Ronaldo's bet with Sir Alex that he would score 15 goals during the season. He had not managed it so far in his United career, but Cristiano knew that more goals from midfield would be absolutely vital for the side's title hopes. His start to the season suggested that he had taken up the challenge eagerly. It was a target that would be monitored continually in the media throughout the season. If he achieved the milestone, United would probably go very close to winning the title.

On 7 October, Portugal collected their first win of the qualifying campaign, beating Azerbaijan 3-0 at home. Ronaldo starred as he bagged two goals – one in each half. He was relishing his role as star man, and the Portuguese media heaped praise on his match-winning display. But a 2-1 defeat away to Poland in midweek, in Portugal's third group match, caused plenty of concern. Ronaldo and his team-mates never recovered from a terrible start in which they fell 2-0 behind inside 20 minutes. A late Nuno Gomes goal was a mere consolation. Four points from three matches was far from the anticipated start to the qualifying campaign, yet it was rather similar to the start made by World Cup winners Italy in Group B.

Back at Old Trafford, three more wins – over Newcastle, Wigan and FC Copenhagen – ensured that United headed into their clash with Liverpool on 22 October in top form. While Ferguson was able to bring Ryan Giggs and Gary Neville back into the side, Ronaldo missed the match after failing to overcome flu. Having missed training in the run-up to the game, he was included as a substitute but would only be used if necessary.

United were relentless, even without their most in-form attacker, and gained a dominant 2-0 victory in Paul Scholes' 500th game for the club. The team ended a superb October with a 4-0 rout of Bolton, in a fixture that has often tripped them up. Rooney, who had suffered a rather lengthy goal drought, hit back at his critics with a hat-trick and Ronaldo grabbed the other, adding to his goal tally. It was a performance that reflected the adjustments that United had made following the disappointment of losing out to Chelsea in 2005 and 2006, and Ferguson deemed it the best football the side had played for a long time. It was a massive bonus for United to have big contributions from the midfield areas – both Cristiano and Ryan Giggs had made good goalscoring starts to the campaign.

November saw continued excellence in the Premiership but a string of failures in the cup competitions. Ronaldo kept up his pursuit of the 15-goal mark with a wonderful free-kick against Portsmouth in a 3-0 win, only to experience a tough winter night in Southend as the Reds were dumped out of the Carling Cup in a 1-0 defeat. While this loss meant that United would not retain the cup, in truth the squad was aiming for bigger prizes. Important away victories against Sheffield United and Blackburn owed much to Rooney and Saha respectively, yet Ronaldo put forward a contender for miss of the season by skying a simple chance in the win at Bramall Lane.

Between the victories over Sheffield United and Blackburn, Cristiano found time to represent Portugal in a Euro 2008 qualifier against Kazakhstan on 15 November. It was important for Portugal to bounce back from the defeat to Poland in October. In a one-sided contest, Ronaldo was once again among the scorers in a 3-0 win. For a midfielder, his goalscoring record was very impressive, and it took a lot of pressure off the other forwards. Simao struck the two other goals, and Scolari was relieved to see the players back in form.

Having coasted along in the Champions League, United suffered 1-0 defeats to FC Copenhagen and Celtic in November, putting themselves under unnecessary pressure in their final game, at home to Benfica. It was a familiar story, but Ronaldo and his team-mates were determined not to suffer the same fate as the previous year. It was a night that still haunted them.

In the midst of his busy season, Ronaldo was forced to elude another opponent – this time a Dutch stalker! The *Sun* newspaper claimed that a woman had followed the star home on a flight and was knocking at his door. The paper quoted Ronaldo as saying: 'According to the girl, she saw in my eyes that she was the love of my life. It was a very strange situation.' It seemed that for one reason or another, Ronaldo would not stay out of the headlines for long during the 2006/07 campaign. Nor would it be the last time that rumours of a Ronaldo romance appeared in the press.

With every passing season, he has become a better judge of when he should stay in and when he can go out. Yet there was nothing that Cristiano could have done to prevent the stalker situation. He claims to enjoy trips to the cinema and to restaurants, but he is always burdened by the need to keep a low profile. Ronaldo could not live a 'normal' life, especially after the summer of 2006. Until the commotion died down, he had a very limited choice of things to do in his spare time.

The biggest match of Ronaldo's season arrived on 26 November as champions Chelsea came to Old Trafford for the clash of the top two Premiership contenders. Chelsea were eager to show they were still a step ahead of United, while the Reds were determined to make it clear that they would challenge Chelsea all the way. As many had predicted, the game was largely a stalemate. United shaded the first half and led at the break, through a neat Saha finish, but Chelsea's energy and relentless drive brought them a deserved equaliser in the second period.

Ronaldo was faced by England left-back Ashley Cole, in a duel that was probably the most exciting of the contest. The winger rates Cole highly, 'He is a wall, very difficult to get past because he anticipates well. He is the defender who gives me the most trouble in the English League.' To his credit, Cole did a superb job despite Ronaldo's constant menace. It would prove a temporary peak for Cole, whose form slumped badly over the rest of the campaign, hampered by injury and a lack of confidence.

Interestingly, when some of his team-mates seemed to have settled for the 1-1 scoreline, Ronaldo was still attempting to create openings. With a lack of support, he was forced to go on solo runs, and time after time he progressed deep into Chelsea territory. He gave the Blues big problems and never looked like running out of energy. Both Ferguson and Mourinho tried to claim an advantage in their post-match interviews, but the draw certainly seemed a fair result.

A solid 3-0 win over Everton on 29 November – with Gary and Phil Neville as the two captains – kept United ahead of Chelsea at the top, as Ronaldo sent United on their way with a well-struck opening goal from the edge of the area.

Ferguson rested a number of first-team players for the game against the Toffees but decided he could not risk leaving Ronaldo on the sidelines. As the team's most creative influence, the winger was the undoubted star in an otherwise rather lacklustre team display. Sir Alex withdrew his winger with just over 20 minutes to go, and Cristiano received a great ovation from the thankful home supporters.

If Ronaldo's inspired performances continued, Mourinho and his players would be hard pressed to keep up with United. Heading into the vital month of December, Cristiano was more hopeful than ever that he and his team-mates would be lifting the Premiership trophy in May.

CHAMPIONS AT LAST

RONALDO'S FORM SO far in the 2006/07 campaign had been very good, and the controversy surrounding the World Cup seemed a distant memory. United's fixtures in December brought even more quality from the Portuguese winger, and the month belonged to Ronaldo. In their six Premiership games, the team collected 15 points and Ronaldo struck seven goals. He had won the Barclays Player of the Month award for November, and there was little doubt that he would be winning it for December too. In doing so, Cristiano became only the third player – after Dennis Bergkamp and Robbie Fowler – to win the award two months in a row. It spoke volumes about the way he was performing.

On 3 December, United travelled to Middlesbrough in the Premiership, looking to maintain their advantage at the top, and Ronaldo was never far from controversy during the afternoon. In the 19th minute, he burst clear in the area, rounded Boro goalkeeper Mark Schwarzer but then tumbled over. Referee Chris Foy pointed to the penalty spot and the

Middlesbrough players reacted furiously, convinced that Ronaldo had dived. Contact appeared minimal, but the winger was running at speed and may have stumbled due to his own momentum. Either way, the spot-kick was converted by Louis Saha and United led 1-0.

There were a few nervy moments when Middlesbrough equalised after half-time, but a Darren Fletcher header clinched the points for the visitors. This, though, was not the end of the matter. Gareth Southgate, the Middlesbrough manager, was evidently fuming about the penalty incident and vented his fury against Cristiano after the match. When asked whether he thought Ronaldo had dived, Southgate replied, 'Yes, it's as simple as that. I cannot see it was a penalty for love nor money. Ronaldo has a history of it. Our keeper has done everything to get out of the way, but the lad has gone down once again. He did it again afterwards with a free-kick against George Boateng.'

Sir Alex Ferguson stood by his player and dismissed Southgate's inexperience as a manager, 'Gareth Southgate's very naïve, of course. He's just a young manager. We'll have to give him a chance to settle in.' Ferguson later targeted the English media for a supposed witch hunt against Ronaldo, 'For me it's a clear penalty. But you [the media] have had it in the papers for the last three days. I hope I'm wrong but I have a feeling it's the revenge of the English press. I think you've been waiting for months to do this.'

The Portuguese star gave his own opinion on the matter, claiming the furore did not bother him, 'The people in England criticise me for anything I do. They love that. Since the World Cup I have just tried to do my best. If I'm criticised by somebody else, I really don't care.' He added that Gareth Southgate should 'understand football much better'.

United then switched their attention to the European scene and their clash with Benfica. Jose Mourinho could not resist stirring up trouble in the build-up to the match, singling out Ronaldo's alleged diving for comment, 'Benfica know Ronaldo well, they know how to deal against his game, so I think it is not easy to get one of his penalties.' The diving argument was rearing its ugly head once again, much to Ronaldo's annoyance.

On a more positive note, Eusebio acknowledged Cristiano as the key figure in the game, saying, 'Today, Cristiano Ronaldo is better than Wayne Rooney for United. If Ronaldo is not on the field – or not playing well – then I think it is immediately a totally different game for the English club.' Spurred on by a man of the match performance from a fired-up Ronaldo, the Reds sealed their qualification from the Champions League group stage with a 3-1 victory against the Portuguese side, fighting back from a goal behind. The result will have disappointed Mourinho, who cheekily admitted that he would be cheering on Benfica.

At times, Ronaldo was keeping his side ahead of Chelsea almost single-handedly, and not since Eric Cantona had a United player produced such an inspired contribution to a title challenge. In a matter of weeks, he scored twice against Aston Villa, Wigan and Reading. Opposition managers were running out of superlatives for him. Wigan boss Paul Jewell had nothing but praise for the winger after he came off the bench to mastermind United's win, 'Cristiano Ronaldo is brilliant. Not only is he quick, he is also a fantastic footballer. He is good in the air and he lifted the crowd.' Ferguson had hoped to rest the winger but with the game goalless at half-time, he could not afford to miss the chance to extend the team's lead at the top. Chelsea had surprisingly dropped two points at home, and Cristiano's two-goal cameo changed the game, putting United four points clear of the Blues.

When the team won 3-2 against Reading on 30 December, Royals manager Steve Coppell, an ex-United player himself, said to the media, 'Ronaldo is probably the player every manager in the league would like to have in his team. It is not just the goals he is scoring but the way he's doing it. He's playing with more responsibility and is winning friends everywhere.' The three points came as a nice early birthday present for Sir Alex, who turned 65 the next day. Cristiano's goals took his tally to 12 for the campaign, and Ferguson knew that he was close to losing their bet. The United boss told the media, 'He is getting better and better with every game and teams are struggling to cope with him. I've had a bet with him that he won't score 15 goals. But he doesn't know it's a Scottish bet. That means I raise the target to 150 once he gets to 15!'

Ronaldo's solo strike at Villa Park was particularly special, and the manner in which the United players celebrated that goal showed just how important and well-liked the winger was. Cristiano has an interesting philosophy on his friends in football. While he gets on very well with Gabriel Heinze, Patrice Evra and Rio Ferdinand amongst others, they are his friends at work and this is a significant distinction. Away from the club, it is his family with whom he spends most of his time. He told *Four Four Two*, 'I've got few friends, but the ones I've got are real friends.'

Ferguson was thrilled with his wide man at Villa Park,

claiming: 'Ronaldo was unbelievable, he was a revelation today and he is as good as anyone in the country.' The team's only defeat of the month came on 17 December at Upton Park, in Alan Curbishley's first game as West Ham manager. Ronaldo, subjected to more loud boos from a packed and hostile crowd, went close several times for United, beating players and creating chances for others. Sadly, it was not United's day and, at the end of a Sunday when Chelsea came back from 2-1 down to win 3-2, the gap at the top was now just two points. But by the end of December, the lead had been extended again.

Injuries in the Chelsea squad to important stars such as John Terry and Petr Cech saw the Blues drop some crucial points and gave added hope to all those connected with United. Jose Mourinho could not believe the bad luck that his team were encountering, and soon became frustrated at the lack of funding he received ahead of the January transfer window. He also lost patience with several players, including summer signing Andriy Shevchenko. Competing on three fronts was always going to be draining for both United and Chelsea, but Ferguson had formed a good blend of young players and those with experience of winning the Treble in 1999.

A sizeable portion of neutrals were now firmly backing United as the ABC ('Anyone But Chelsea') mentality strengthened. For the likes of Neville, Giggs and Scholes, it was a refreshing change from the contempt that most supporters had for United during their glory years in the late 1990s. Meanwhile, Ronaldo was winning over the doubters and, gradually, his antics at the World Cup slipped out of conversation, replaced by the excitement generated by his exhilarating displays. The Christmas period had been profitable for United and the pundits were in awe of Ronaldo's inspirational effect on his team-mates – *Match of the Day* panelists frequently sang his praises. Nevertheless, everyone at the club knew that the job was only half-done.

Ronaldo picked up another award in December, when Portuguese newspaper *A Bola* selected him as the Portuguese sportsman of the year for his 'contribution to the expansion of Portuguese football across the world'. There was satisfaction to be had in the fact that Jose Mourinho only finished third, with Nuno Gomes in second place. The significance of the award came from the obvious rise of his already high profile back in Portugal. United supporters hoped that Mourinho's failure to the win the award was a good omen for the remainder of the season.

The New Year brought Henrik Larsson to Old Trafford in a big coup for United. The veteran Swedish striker, who had won the Champions League with Barcelona the previous year, arrived on loan while the Swedish league had a mid-season break. It meant that Larsson could spend around nine weeks at United before returning to his Swedish club, Helsingborgs. With Saha never truly injury-free, an extra striker of Larsson's quality was a huge boost for United's title quest, and a proven predator could only benefit from Ronaldo's service. The news came very suddenly and took most of the Premiership by surprise. Ferguson could not stop smiling.

A draw at St. James' Park on 1 January was followed by two wins over Aston Villa and then a massively disappointing loss against Arsenal. The Gunners managed to score twice in the final seven minutes to snatch the three points, after Rooney had given United a precious lead with Ronaldo, of course, involved in the build-up. Victory had turned to defeat in a devastating collapse, and questions were asked of United's fitness levels as they seemed to fade in the closing moments. Ferguson was quick to dismiss the notion, but it was a painful blow and left the players determined to prove the critics wrong.

However, Chelsea had lost earlier in the day at Anfield and so United had not lost any of their lead at the Premiership summit. It would be a critical moment in the title race, as Ronaldo and his team-mates were torn between relief that their advantage had been preserved, and frustration that they had not deepened Chelsea's problems by extending their lead at the top. All eyes would be on United's response. The players certainly reacted encouragingly to the defeat at the Emirates Stadium, Arsenal's impressive new home. A 14 game unbeaten run followed and put Ronaldo on course for his first Premiership winners medal.

Ronaldo's team-mates were fully appreciative of his efforts. Paul Scholes told *Football Focus*, 'The amount of goals and assists he's had has been frightening. I haven't seen anybody take players on, score goals and make goals like he has in the first half of the season.' For Scholes, usually so quiet and keen to avoid interviews, to come out with such praise was a big compliment, and everyone associated with United hoped that the form continued. They were not to be disappointed.

Portsmouth were beaten by two Rooney goals, and then Watford and Tottenham were both hit for four as United upped the tempo in the title race. Ronaldo's pace and ball skills terrorised defenders, and he scored his 14th and 15th goals of the season from the penalty spot, one against

Watford and one against Tottenham. He had won the bet! Undoubtedly, Ronaldo had been the star man for United and the main reason that the club had been able to raise their game to the new levels set by Chelsea. If he continued to perform so well, the title was seemingly destined to return to Old Trafford after a three year wait. He was relishing the responsibility of being the team's talisman. Now Cristiano had the 20-goal mark in his sights.

With Saha out injured, Ronaldo had happily taken over the penalty taking duties. Throughout his career, he had shown faultless nerve when striking spot-kicks and had been successful in shootouts against England, at Euro 2004 and the 2006 World Cup. His self-confidence meant that he could handle the pressure and backed himself to beat any goalkeeper in the world from 12 yards. His record during the season reflected the fact that he was the right man for the responsibility. With United's free-flowing attack and his own dazzling trickery, the team earned plenty of penalties, and he won a number of duels with opposition goalkeepers. Considering the problems that English players had endured with penalty-taking, it made sense for a foreign player to do the job.

But as Ronaldo had explained prior to the Tottenham game, it was all about the team effort, 'Something like the Golden Boot doesn't concern me. I want to win the Premier League. We have been the best team in England so far, but that will count for nothing if we let our standards slip. I enjoy scoring goals, but the pleasure comes from what it means to the team.' This perfectly summed up the improvements in his game – the switch of emphasis from his own achievements to the greater team cause. The 4-0 win at

White Hart Lane typified this team spirit, as John O'Shea took over in goal from the injured Edwin van der Sar in the closing stages and did an admirable job.

Off the field during the 2006/07 season, Ronaldo was linked with Hollyoaks actress Gemma Atkinson. The rumour was first spread in the newspapers and then made its way into magazines. Atkinson, who appeared on *Soapstar Superstar*, was the latest woman to claim a relationship with the winger, and she had leaked the news back in January. It came as a surprise to most as the pair had not even been photographed together. So often celebrity relationships are rumbled by the paparazzi, but there had been no warning about Cristiano and Gemma until the first newspaper article appeared.

Ronaldo's mother, however, reacted angrily and quickly sought to put the record straight. Dolores claimed that Atkinson was definitely not Ronaldo's girlfriend and seemed genuinely upset about the story. She explained to the media, 'He doesn't have a girlfriend. I don't know her and I don't care if she's beautiful.' But a friend of Atkinson's offered a different insight into the alleged relationship. She told the *Sun*, 'Ronaldo's mother is probably just being protective. I've seen the texts they send and they're definitely boyfriend and girlfriend. Gemma's a down-to-earth lass and not interested in him as a publicity stunt.'

There was little further comment from either Ronaldo or Atkinson on the matter, and the speculation soon died down, despite the newspapers and magazines trying to claim she was the latest addition to the band of WAGs. But then Cristiano was quizzed on the matter by *Four Four Two* and he gave a surprising response. Asked whether he and Gemma were a couple, he answered, 'No, no, it's just newspaper talk. I've heard her spoken of, but I don't know her.' He was happy to be single and free to enjoy his youth independently. He felt that the prospect of settling down and getting married was something for the future. Whatever the truth of the matter, the pair had been very successful in keeping their business out of the headlines on the whole.

Cristiano took a break from English football as Portugal faced Brazil in a friendly on 7 February. The match was watched with great interest as two of the top sides in the world collided at Arsenal's Emirates Stadium. The five times World Cup winners provided a proper test of Portugal's progress. Fans came flocking to see some of the planet's top players – Ronaldo and Deco for Portugal; Ronaldinho and Kaka for Brazil.

Incredibly, the match remained goalless until late on when Simao and Ricardo Carvalho sealed a proud 2-0 win for Portugal. As seemed to be the usual routine, Ronaldo played just over an hour but could not find a way past Brazil's defence. Former Brazil manager Scolari was thrilled with the result when he spoke to the media after the game, 'The victory will give us more confidence for the upcoming matches in March. We beat a team that is ranked number one and has won the World Cup five times, and this will raise our self-esteem and confidence.'

It may have only been a friendly but to beat Brazil in any game is a fine achievement. The players knew that they were close to putting together the tournament-winning formula, and Euro 2008 was a very serious target – with Ronaldo and several other young stars ready to take the world stage by storm. Ronaldo's early season form at United had shown major improvements in areas of his game, and it was interesting to compare his performances in 2007 with those of 2003/04 to see the new found consistency and scoring touch.

Ronaldo returned to Old Trafford on a high, and as the race for the Premiership title continued, United were showing no signs of faltering. Charlton and Fulham were unable to stop the Reds, though it took a late Ronaldo winner to see off the plucky Cottagers in late February. Cristiano just would not let the team drop points as he ran again and again at the Fulham defenders in search of the goal that would keep up the team's solid form. Eventually, the winner came. Ronaldo received the ball near the halfway line and surged on towards the Fulham area, beating several defenders. He was rewarded when his low shot found the bottom corner via a slight deflection, sparking wild celebrations.

As was so often the case over the course of the season, Ferguson spoke proudly of Ronaldo's efforts against Fulham, telling the media, 'Ronaldo just kept going and deserved to get the man of the match. I must say that was the most difficult game we have had all season.' Reading were beaten via a replay in the FA Cup fifth round, and United headed to Anfield full of confidence for a Premiership fixture which rarely fails to live up to expectations.

United arrived at full strength, ready to face one of their biggest football rivals. But after an even first half, it was the home side that forced the pace and dictated the play. Craig Bellamy caused problems for a United defence that had been imperious all season, and Ronaldo, Rooney and Giggs were kept at bay by a Liverpool defence led by the excellent Jamie Carragher. To make matters worse, Paul Scholes was sent off with four minutes remaining for swinging an arm at Xabi Alonso, leaving his team-mates to see out the closing moments. At this point, even the most optimistic United supporters would have seen a 0-0 draw as a decent result.

But the players had other ideas. In stoppage time, Giggs was fouled by Finnan, and from the resulting free-kick United snatched all three points. Ronaldo, quiet for long patches of the game, fizzed a dangerous free-kick into the area, Pepe Reina in the Liverpool goal could only parry the ball and it fell to substitute John O'Shea who calmly slotted the ball home. Liverpool supporters were furious; the away fans went crazy.

Having looked in danger of taking nothing from the game, Cristiano and his team-mates had stolen the win, and the winger had conjured something out of nothing once again. He just could not stay out of the spotlight, and it was symbolic that it was his delivery – criticised in the past – that had created the winning goal. It was a huge psychological moment in the season and reinforced Ronaldo's belief that this could be his first Premiership title triumph. The joyful celebrations after the final whistle showed just how vital the win was for the club, and this was probably the weekend when United fans really believed that the trophy was coming back to Old Trafford.

Four days later United wrapped up their Champions League second round tie with Lille, with a 1-0 second leg win to go with a 1-0 victory in France. The first leg had seen major controversy as the Lille players and coaching staff reacted furiously to Ryan Giggs' quickly-taken free-kick that gave United a late winner. Lille felt that the referee had let them down by allowing the kick to be taken early, and it looked like the French club's players were going to boycott the game by walking off, only to change their minds.

The debate rumbled on and it added an extra edge to the return match. Ronaldo's display in France was poor, and he was substituted by Ferguson. After the game, the United manager vented his anger over the actions of the Lille players: 'I have never seen that before in all my years in football. That is a disgrace and UEFA have to do something about that because it was pure intimidation of the referee.' Sir Alex told his players not to get involved in the chaos, making the Lille players and management appear all the more foolish.

In truth, though, while United's stars were below par over the two legs, Cristiano and company were still too good for Lille. The team had not always produced their best football in Europe during the season, but now awaited the quarter-final draw with great interest and plenty of confidence. Eliminating Lille further banished the memories of the previous year's early exit, as the French club had been one of the sides against whom the Reds had laboured unsuccessfully.

Cristiano was excited to have progressed beyond the second round for the first time in his career, and United's European campaign was undoubtedly a significant improvement on the last few years. Ronaldo's craving to play on the big stage in the Champions League was about to be satisfied.

United were drawn to face Roma, a talented side but not of the calibre of Chelsea or AC Milan. Francesco Totti would undoubtedly be a threat, and the Italians were not a side lacking in confidence, sitting comfortably in second place in the Serie A table. In fact, Mancini, Roma's Brazilian winger, had drawn comparisons with Ronaldo for his silky footwork, showcased by a special goal in the previous round against Lyon. It would be an exciting contest, and pundits would need to reach for their calculators to count the stepovers.

St. Patrick's Day brought a goal fest at Old Trafford, as Bolton conceded four against United for the second time in the season. A blistering start, with Ronaldo and Rooney as the catalysts, saw a 3-0 lead established after just 25 minutes. It had been a fixture that many regarded as a potential banana skin, but United had battered Bolton into a very early submission, before finishing 4-1 winners. The link-up play between Ronaldo and Rooney was exceptional, and the lightning-fast second goal, scored by Rooney, summed up the team's counter-attacking prowess.

The treble pursuit continued with a 1-0 win over Middlesbrough in the FA Cup quarter-final replay, and Ronaldo simply could not avoid controversy, especially in matches against Gareth Southgate and his players. United made heavy weather of winning the game, requiring a Ronaldo penalty to clinch the victory. Predictably, it was Cristiano who was brought down in the area by a Jonathan Woodgate challenge and, once more, Boro were unhappy with the winger.

Ronaldo, collecting his Man of the Match champagne, assured the media after the game that he had been touched for the penalty and that, while he might have been able to stay on his feet, he had been knocked off balance by the foul. In the past, the winger had called for referees to give flair players like himself more protection, and they certainly seemed to be answering his call this season. Everything was going his way.

Responding to inquiries as to why he was always involved

in these controversies, a playful smirk lit up Cristiano's face as he suggested, 'Maybe I'm too good.' Some may have found this self-confidence a little too much to bear but it was hard not to smile at the swagger that Ronaldo had now adopted. He said, 'The team got to the semi-final. This is the big objective,' and admitted that the whole United dressing-room was buzzing after the result. Some had questioned the top clubs' commitment to the FA Cup and Carling Cup, but anyone who saw the delight in Cristiano's eyes knew that he was genuinely thrilled by the history and excitement of the FA Cup.

Ronaldo transferred his blistering domestic form into the international arena as he was selected for Portugal's home qualifier against Belgium on 24 March. He led the team to a 4-0 victory which re-asserted their undoubted quality. Cristiano oozed class as he struck two goals and kept his team in contention for Euro 2008. All four goals came in the second half as Portugal upped the tempo. His first goal was a header from a Ricardo Quaresma cross and his second, Portugal's fourth, came after he danced inside his marker and placed a low shot past the Belgian goalkeeper.

There was major controversy prior to the game, though, after Belgian goalkeeper Stijn Stijnen issued a statement to the *Gazet van Antwerpen* newspaper about the tactics that would be used against Ronaldo, 'After two minutes we will normally have massacred him so much that he will have to leave the pitch on a stretcher. What else do we need to do? Portugal have greater quality and that's why we have to do things our way.' This incredible comment came just after Middlesbrough's George Boateng had lashed out and predicted that someone would seriously injure Cristiano one day. It appeared to be blatant intimidation, but seemingly it had simply provoked a brilliant performance from Ronaldo. He was above responding to taunts of that nature. Nevertheless, it had all become rather nasty and, although Stijnen tried to make amends by claiming that his words had been misinterpreted, no one was convinced. Ronaldo appeared unfazed as he had done all season. He let UEFA get on with investigating Stijnen's comments and concentrated on his own game.

Belgium might be a fading force in European football, but it was still superb for Ronaldo to have dominated the action so convincingly. The result was a boost because Portugal were trailing Poland and Finland in the group table, and, even though it was early days, it was important to return to the form that had seen the team achieve so spectacularly at Euro 2004 and the 2006 World Cup. Unfortunately, Poland's 5-0 victory against Azerbaijan saw them maintain their lead at the top of Group A. In midweek, Serbia provided the next task for Ronaldo and his colleagues. Portugal had been below par in their two away games thus far in qualification and were keen to replicate their home form on their travels. They began brilliantly, taking the lead through a goal from Tiago, but Serbia's equaliser after 37 minutes was a big blow. Hard as Portugal tried, there was no way through the Serbian defence, and they had to settle for a draw. Cristiano left the field disappointed with the result, but he had played well across the two qualifiers.

Ronaldo returned to England with even more confidence than when he had left and as determined as ever to secure the Premiership title. United's fine run continued with a 4-1 victory against Blackburn, fighting back from a goal down.

Trailing 1-0 at half-time, Old Trafford began to fear the worst, but then Scholes popped up with an equaliser and United pulled away down the stretch, demonstrating a killer instinct when it mattered most. Ronaldo breathed a sigh of relief because for 45 minutes the visitors had threatened to throw the title race wide open. Fortunately for Cristiano, the team had enough spark and spirit to fight back, playing some great football along the way. The gap remained six points, and time was running out for Chelsea to make inroads into that lead. Ronaldo's form was showing no signs of relenting either, and his name was at the top of many people's list for Player of the Year, ahead of Didier Drogba.

The games came thick and fast in April over the busy Easter period, and United began the month with the away leg of their Champions League quarter-final with Roma. In the hostile Stadio Olimpico, United were already handicapped by the absence of captain Gary Neville and Nemanja Vidic, and Roma came out all guns blazing. To make their task even tougher, two reckless challenges by Paul Scholes earned him a red card and left United to play the final hour of the game with ten men. While United looked threatening on the break, the Italians dominated and took the lead just before half-time, via a deflection.

But this United team had the same spirit as the 1999 treble-winning squad. There was the same belief that no situation is irreversible, and in Ronaldo they had a player seemingly capable of taking on an entire defence. At times in the second half he glided past three or four challenges, leaving top class defenders in his wake. He sparked those around him, and it was his run and pass that allowed Solskjaer to cross and Rooney to equalise expertly. Ferguson directed applause in

Cristiano's direction for his part in the move. The Olimpico was momentarily silenced as the ten men of United had drawn level. But it lasted no more than seven minutes, as a Mancini strike stung the palms of Edwin van der Sar who could only knock the ball into the path of Roma striker Mirko Vucinic. 2-1.

Considering that United had players missing and lost Scholes in the first half, a one-goal deficit was not bad at all, and Roma would come to rue missing the opportunity to put the tie to bed. Ferguson was unhappy with the referee but not too disappointed with the result. He told the media, 'Considering we played with 10 men, mostly against 12 men for an hour, it's a good result for us. I don't think we got a decision all night but that's European football.'

Christian Panucci, the Roma full-back, had nothing but praise for Ronaldo's contribution, 'If he takes off with the ball you will never catch him. You could compare him to Valentino Rossi. If I was given the same engine as him then perhaps I could catch him.'

Chelsea's relentless pursuit of United finally gained reward on 7 April. Having beaten Tottenham earlier in the day, Jose Mourinho and his players saw United stumble at Fratton Park against Portsmouth. It has not been a happy ground for Ronaldo and United in recent years, and sloppy errors handed Portsmouth two goals and reduced the lead at the top to just three points – with the titanic clash at Stamford Bridge ahead. Perhaps the drama and intensity of the match in Rome had been too much for some players as performance levels dropped and a bit of complacency kicked in. There was a clear lack of urgency, and it was hard to believe that there was so much at stake for the players in red. Ferguson looked furious; Ronaldo looked downcast. At least United didn't have long to wait to make amends. The mouth-watering return leg against Roma awaited, and Cristiano and his team-mates were determined to silence the doubters.

The Roma game was perhaps the second most incredible night in United's recent European history – only topped by the Champions League final heroics in the Nou Camp in 1999. Ferguson told the press, 'That's absolutely the best night of European football we've had here.' Roma – a team glittering with stars like Francesco Totti, Mancini and Daniele De Rossi – were destroyed in a staggering display of pace and clinical finishing. Without playing too badly, Roma were beaten 7-1. Ronaldo was in his element, running the show and bringing the Old Trafford crowd to their feet. He ran at players, turned defenders inside out with his dribbling and stepovers, and capped the performance with two goals. Only a hat-trick could have made the night more perfect for him. He told the media, 'To win 7-1 against Roma in a quarter-final is just great. Every player is very confident.' The game would live long in the memory.

What should have been a nail-biting night turned out to have the feel of an exhibition game with United leading 4-0 at half-time. Onlookers were stunned; it was a result that left the Italian press humbled and highly critical of Roma's efforts. United had been simply irresistible on the night, and made the rest of Europe stand up and take note. So Ronaldo and United advanced to the semi-finals for the first time in his short career at Old Trafford, where they would face AC Milan, who overcame FC Bayern Munich 4-2 on aggregate. Milan had eliminated United in 2005, and Ronaldo hoped that he and his team-mates had learned their lessons from that tie.

Cristiano made it a great week for United when he ended the speculation over his future and finally put pen to paper on a new deal, keeping him at Old Trafford until 2012. The winger said, 'I am delighted. I am very happy at the club.' His manager, Sir Alex Ferguson, was equally thrilled, 'It is fantastic news. He has a great relationship with the team, staff and the fans and he will go on to be one of Manchester United's great players.' Sir Alex also praised Cristiano further, saying, 'He is one of the best signings I have ever made... the measurement of his improvement this year is astronomical.'

Securing Ronaldo for another five years was a massive boost for everyone connected to the club and ended any chance of a record transfer to Real Madrid. Interest from the Spanish giants, amongst others, had cast doubt over Ronaldo's future. Many Red Devil supporters feared that the lure of the Galacticos would be too strong, and Madrid had made no secret of their desire to capture his signature. Speaking at the Laureus sports awards in Barcelona, United director Sir Bobby Charlton spoke out about the conduct of those clubs chasing Ronaldo, 'I don't think it's correct. Ronaldo is our player, and while he's under contract to us I don't think it's anybody's right to come and start the process of trying to change him into being one of their players. That is not the way to do business.' Ultimately, United had kept their man and, on paper at least, Ronaldo would be a lynchpin of the team for years to come.

By staying at Old Trafford Ronaldo had shown loyalty to the club in return for the treatment he received after the World Cup. Ferguson and United had looked after Ronaldo in the wake of the incident in Germany and had placed great faith in the youngster. He owed his manager and the United fans for supporting him when he was public enemy number one, and insisted that he had never contemplated a move abroad. He was happy in Manchester and saw no reason to leave a club that was still fighting for three major trophies. As the *Mail on Sunday* reported, Ronaldo claimed he spoke regularly with Ferguson during the campaign and a transfer was never a possibility, 'We spoke about a new contract every week. I told the boss all the time I wanted to stay. Now we have concluded the deal.' Cristiano regarded the United fans as the best in the world and saw no reason to leave a club where he was clearly adored.

AC Milan had eliminated United in 2005 en route to the momentous final against Liverpool, and United had failed to score in the 180 minutes in the tie, which did not bode well for the upcoming semi-final. Ronaldo's inexperience had been evident but, two seasons later, he was more mature and certainly United's most likely match-winner. United were just two games away from the final in Athens, but this would be a very testing match-up, as United's youth and pace went head-to-head with the Italians' experience and cunning.

In the meantime, the Premiership required the team's attention in equal measure as they approached the finishing line. The difficulty in competing on three fronts is that every game is critical, and there was no time to dwell on the incredible European performance against Roma as a vital FA Cup semi-final against Watford awaited the team at the weekend. It proved no great obstacle as Ronaldo and Rooney continued to be the tormenters-in-chief, and Ferguson was able to withdraw the Portuguese winger in the latter stages.

Watford had failed to come to terms with Ronaldo all afternoon as he scored one and created one for Rooney in a 4-1 victory. The next day, Chelsea narrowly beat Blackburn – 2-1 in extra-time – to set up the FA Cup final that the neutrals had dreamed of.

There was no time for Ronaldo and his team-mates to take a breather, as they were in action again in midweek, at home to Sheffield United. The tired legs were beginning to show, as well as defensive vulnerability in the absence of Gary Neville, Rio Ferdinand and Nemanja Vidic. The players dug deep for a 2-0 win, but Neil Warnock, the Sheffield United manager, had every reason to be proud of his team. The visitors went close on a number of occasions and were denied a clear penalty. But the football gods were smiling on Ronaldo and his colleagues as United stayed in pole position for the title. Chelsea won 4-1 at Upton Park the next night with an impressive display to keep up the chase, sitting just three points behind United. The Reds, though, had a vastly superior goal difference, and this made the lead four points in theory.

Jose Mourinho spoke out angrily at the end of April about the favourable refereeing decisions that he felt United had been given, claiming that a 'new rule' existed that meant United could never concede a penalty and Chelsea could never win one. This signalled the start of a media war with United as first Ronaldo, and then Ferguson, waded in to have their say on the matter. Ronaldo took offence at Mourinho's comments, saying that the Chelsea manager 'does not know how to admit his own failures.'

Mourinho answered back, telling the press, 'If Ronaldo says it is a lie penalties were not given against United, then he is lying. If he is a liar he will never reach the highest level that he desires in football.' Ferguson was also unhappy that the Chelsea manager's words might put unnecessary pressure on referees, telling the media, 'Mourinho seems to be on some sort of personal crusade. I am surprised no action has been taken. It's calculated. If we get a penalty against us, Mourinho wins that war. That is wrong. It is a rant all the time now. I don't think it is fair to the game.'

Mourinho then went even further, giving suggestions about the reasons for Ronaldo's behaviour, 'Maybe it's about a difficult childhood, no education.' That final comment was the last straw for Ferguson, who fumed, 'It is really below the belt to bring class into it. I don't know why he has done this. Maybe he is trying to unsettle the boy. Just because you come from a poor, working-class background does not mean to say you are not educated. What Ronaldo has are principles – that is why he has not responded to it. Other people are educated but have no principles.' Given Ferguson's own working-class upbringing in Govan, Glasgow, it was a subject that he was very sensitive about. Many agreed that the Chelsea manager had gone too far with this latest outburst.

Sir Alex also pointed to several incidents that showed that Mourinho had had favourable treatment from referees, while at Porto and as Chelsea manager. The feud had become a lot more serious and, with the pressure set to be cranked up another notch in the closing weeks, supporters would not dare to take their eyes off the title run-in. United still held the advantage but their match away to Chelsea – their penultimate game of the season – seemed destined to be crucial in deciding whether the trophy would stay in London once again or head north to Manchester.

But then United faltered at home to Middlesbrough, drawing 1-1, playing poorly and exhibiting worrying signs of wilting at the height of 'squeaky bum' time. Old Trafford despaired at the loss of precious points, and the body language of the United players revealed their concern. Middlesbrough had defended stubbornly and, perhaps, should have received a penalty late in the game as United threw bodies forward. Ronaldo went straight down the tunnel at full-time, such was his disappointment at the result.

Ferguson tried to remain positive in front of the press, 'We're still in the lead and have now just got to get the players' energy back for Tuesday.' The two points dropped by United presented Chelsea with the chance they had been waiting for – perhaps Mourinho's outburst had had the desired effect. But Newcastle were able to hold the Blues to a 0-0 stalemate at St. James Park, and the Reds had been let off the hook. It was a moment that Mourinho would rue, and the United players vowed not to give Chelsea another chance.

It was hardly the ideal preparation for the huge Champions League semi-final first leg at Old Trafford against AC Milan. The team's form had been patchy, and the injuries in defence were still restricting their chances. Milan arrived full of confidence but without their Brazilian striker Ronaldo, who was ineligible. Manager Carlo Ancelotti refused to reveal whether or not there would be any particular defensive plans to contain Cristiano. Rumours suggested that veteran Paolo Maldini might be given the task but Ancelotti denied this, 'The Portuguese player moves from left to right and Paolo plays in the centre.' The Milan manager also diplomatically side-stepped questions about who was the better player – Kaka or Cristiano? Ancelotti explained to the media, 'I agree they are among the top of their profession at the moment, but it's extremely difficult to say who is the best. That will be decided by the player who manages to determine the outcome of the game.'

The lack of confidence within the United back four was threatening to spread throughout the side, and this was the biggest fear for the supporters. It quickly became clear that the Old Trafford crowd had missed these big European occasions because the atmosphere inside the stadium was electric, and the supporters were more vocal than ever. They were all hoping for a night of Cristiano Ronaldo magic – and so was Sir Alex. But Milan's wily veterans were unlikely to be intimidated by a raucous crowd. Nobody dared to take their eyes off Old Trafford.

It was a night that began perfectly for Cristiano and United, as Milan goalkeeper Dida made a mess of a Giggs corner and Ronaldo provided the finishing touch in the ensuing scramble. Old Trafford rejoiced and prayed for a repeat of the Roma demolition. But Milan were not Roma, and United's defensive frailties were exposed twice before the break to give Milan two priceless away goals. Kaka, the majestic Brazilian, struck both sucker punches; the first a neat left-footed finish, the second a fine solo goal after a mix-up between Wes Brown and Gabriel Heinze. Kaka, Ronaldo's main contender as the best player in the world on current form, was upstaging the Portuguese winger and finding far too much space between United's midfield and defence.

A vastly improved second-half performance saw United claw their way back into the tie, aided by injuries to Milan legend Paolo Maldini and ex-Rangers midfield terrier Gennaro Gattuso. Rooney was the hero as he struck twice to give United a lead to defend in Italy, and the United supporters left Old Trafford with hope. Ronaldo had endured a rather quiet night by his exceptionally high standards, but he was regularly confronted by two or three hungry Milan defenders. Too often he sought to wriggle away from his markers and lost possession when an easier pass was available. In the second leg, with Milan chasing goals, he hoped that he would have more space to exploit. Ferguson took plenty of positives from the night, telling the media, 'We've got a magnificent chance now. Some of the football we played was absolute quality. We kept playing our football and dominated the second half. We're in front – and they know that.'

In the meantime, a trip to Goodison Park to face Everton was the main focus, and Toffees manager David Moyes was fearful of Ronaldo's talent, 'Some of the things he does are breathtaking. The other night I just sat back and thought all you can do is applaud. The bit we're all impressed by is his maturity and he seems to have cut out that bit where he seemed to be going over easily. He gains greater respect for that.' With Chelsea and United both playing in lunch-time kick-offs, it was a critical weekend in the title race. There would be plenty of bitten fingernails by three o'clock.

Surprisingly, both went behind to early goals, but Chelsea had soon hit back to lead Bolton 2-1 at half-time. Ronaldo, having picked up an injury in training, was only a substitute – much to Moyes' relief – but with Everton going 2-0 ahead just after the interval, he was soon preparing to come on as Ferguson contemplated the disastrous consequences of a defeat. Bolton's equaliser at Stamford Bridge provided another twist in the title race, and what followed at Goodison

Park was a reminder of just how much courage and character the United squad boasted.

A gift of a goal fell into the path of John O'Shea from a goalkeeping error and then, with Ronaldo introduced in search of an equaliser, a Phil Neville own goal brought the scores level. It was remarkable to see the energy that the winger gave to his colleagues. With both matches at 2-2, a winner from either United or Chelsea would have a major impact on the title race. It was United who got it. Rooney, facing his former club, turned Tony Hibbert and calmly slotted the ball in the far corner. Ronaldo went close to extending the lead before Chris Eagles came off the bench to make it 4-2. Chelsea had been held 2-2, United's lead was up to five points and Cristiano had one hand on the Premiership trophy. His introduction had lifted his team-mates, and his infectious desire had clawed his team back into the game. The celebrations that followed revealed just how crucial the victory was, with Ferguson joining the players on the field to salute the supporters and show off his victory jig. The United manager announced after the game, 'We have a five-point lead and a superior goal difference. I will be giving my old mate Big Sam a hug and a kiss when I see him – maybe two kisses.'

After three tough seasons of enduring the success of others, the United players and management were closing in on a massive achievement. The spirit that the team had displayed against AC Milan and Everton led many to feel that the treble was still possible. Milan stood in United's path, but confidence was at a peak in the dressing-room and English fans hoped that the speed of Ronaldo would be a constant threat on the counter-attack. The key to the treble win in 1999 had been keeping up the winning momentum, and

United knew that going out of the Champions League at this stage could have a knock-on effect domestically.

The trip to Italy, though, turned out to be a night of European heartache for Cristiano and United, as Kaka once more inspired AC Milan, who played as well as they had done all season when it mattered most. United were outclassed in a 3-0 defeat, with Ronaldo's display sadly below-par. It was a frustrating experience for the winger, as he often found himself confronted by both right-back Massimo Oddo and snarling midfielder Gattuso, limiting his trademark dribbles. Cristiano had clearly been singled out as the danger man for United and he was tightly marked throughout.

Ferguson admitted to the press that Ronaldo had under-performed, 'Cristiano had a disappointing night. He knows that but he is a young man and on nights like these he sees the professionalism and experience of AC Milan. It is good to see where he has to go.' Paul McCarthy was harsher with his assessment in the *People*, 'Ronaldo looked tired, leaden-legged and a shadow of the man who has tormented defences for pleasure this season.' But he was not alone in playing poorly as the defence had a night to forget, particularly Gabriel Heinze and Nemanja Vidic, on whose fitness Ferguson had gambled.

It seemed like a step too far for the United players, as though the stress and fatigue of fighting for three trophies was finally taking its toll. It just showed what an incredible effort it had been to come back from 2-0 down in Turin in the 1999 semi-final. Though missing out on the final in Athens was agonising, the feeling amongst many experts was that this group of players was not far from emulating the efforts of the treble-winning squad.

The players were quickly in action again after the elimination from the Champions League as a vital Manchester derby awaited on the Saturday, and Ronaldo would be in the thick of the action. There was no time for the players to feel sorry for themselves. The morale was fairly low on the way home from Milan, but Ferguson spoke to his players and put them back on track. There was so much still at stake. If United won, it would force Chelsea to win away to Arsenal the following day or surrender the title. Manchester City had clearly decided on a game plan to unsettle Ronaldo. In the opening minutes he suffered heavy challenges, including a blatant stamp from left-back Michael Ball. The referee did not see the incident, but Ferguson was fuming. Ronaldo showed his maturity by dusting himself down and getting on with his task – more evidence of the improvements in his game. He refused to let the incident affect him, showed no signs of petulance and let his feet do the talking. He would have the last laugh on Ball.

United struggled to break down a resilient City defence until just before the break. Ronaldo was left one-on-one against Ball – a pitiful mismatch. A couple of stepovers later and Cristiano had tempted the defender into a foolish lunge, resulting in a penalty. Even Mourinho could not have any complaints about this one. Ronaldo had responded to Ball's vicious stamp in the best possible way, by embarrassing him with his skills. He took the spot-kick himself, calmly sending Andreas Isaksson the wrong way, to give United a 1-0 lead. His penalty-taking had been absolutely perfect for the team this season. It was United's goal of the month – the only goal the team scored in May!

The game petered out in the second half as signs began to

show of the exhausting campaign, and City almost punished their local rivals for dangerously coasting along towards victory. Out of the blue, Ball won City a dubious penalty, but Darius Vassell's unconvincing spot-kick was well saved by Edwin van der Sar. United held firm and the celebrations after the game emphasised the fact that the title race was almost over – City had missed the chance to dent their rivals' bid for the trophy. The players threw their shirts to their supporters, hugging each other as if the Premiership was secured. Ferguson was ecstatic, 'What you saw today was human courage. It wasn't a great performance but derby games are like that and in the end we got through it.' Few could deny that Ronaldo was the spark again for the Reds.

The newspapers were full of admiration for United. The *Daily Mirror* announced, 'To win the Premiership you need great ability, luck and bucketloads of character. At Bolton, United showed their class; at Anfield their good fortune; and at Manchester City their strength of character.' *The Times* called Ronaldo 'the matchwinner'. Interestingly, in the fixture the previous season, Cristiano had lost his temper and got sent off. The same could easily have happened again here, but the new and improved Ronaldo stayed composed and delivered the goods when it mattered most.

The trophy would be sealed if Chelsea failed to beat Arsenal the following day. As for Ronaldo, a first Premiership winners medal was within touching distance. When Chelsea could only draw 1-1 at the Emirates Stadium, the race was over, and it was appropriate that it was Ronaldo's goal against Manchester City that had secured the Premiership crown. Ferguson, Ronaldo and everyone associated with United could uncork the champagne and toast a famous title success. For Ferguson and Ryan Giggs it was an incredible ninth Premiership triumph, and they enjoyed it just as much as Ronaldo. It capped a superb season for the winger, proving all the pre-season doubters wrong. He had come a long way since the infamous incident with Rooney at the World Cup, and the whole issue seemed to have been the making of him.

United still had two league matches remaining, against Chelsea and West Ham, but few seemed to care now. Both Ferguson and Mourinho began to look towards the FA Cup final, and the two teams played out a dull 0-0 draw at Stamford Bridge. Chelsea sportingly formed a guard of honour for the United players – just as United had previously done for them – but few of the starting line-up had actually made enough appearances for a championship medal. The contest was not totally without incident, as Alan Smith and several others ensured that the game did not lack a physical edge. The United fans in the away end kept everybody entertained with their chants, including, 'Mourinho, thanks for listening, you kept our trophy glistening, we're back today, to take it away, walking in a Fergie wonderland.' It was a chance to truly revel in baiting Mourinho, who became increasingly unhappy in the Chelsea technical area.

But it was sad that such a massive fixture had been reduced to an end-of-season game with the feel of an exhibition match. Everyone hoped for better at Wembley. Ronaldo later revealed that Mourinho had sought out him out at Stamford Bridge and apologised to him in person for his comments in the media a few weeks earlier. Cristiano told the *Daily Mirror*, 'Mourinho has apologised to me and now I have no problem with him. I am pleased that this has happened. As far as I am concerned, the whole thing is now in the past.' It seemed as though the two managers had decided to 'draw a line' under the issue as Ferguson had promised.

The final Premiership game was another poor spectacle as the players went through the motions, losing 1-0 to West Ham – a result that kept the Hammers in the top flight and relegated Sheffield United, who were beaten 2-1 by Wigan. Ronaldo was introduced as a second- half substitute, but the West Ham back four held firm for the priceless win. The rather feeble display cast a small cloud over the championship party that followed, but it was soon forgotten when the trophy was brought out. Club captain Gary Neville, who had been absent for the latter part of the season with an ankle injury, and Ryan Giggs lifted the trophy; Old Trafford rejoiced. Ronaldo was delighted – jumping around and celebrating with his team-mates. His long wait for a title triumph was over. The team's success was reflected by the fact that eight United players were chosen in the PFA Team of the Year – van der Sar and the whole back four, Giggs, Scholes and Ronaldo. Clearly, their fellow professionals had been mightily impressed with the way that United had turned things around after a few difficult years.

It was the end to the campaign that Cristiano had dreamed about, and it was impossible not to imagine how his father would have enjoyed the moment. One could picture Dinis racing around Funchal on the Monday morning with the newspapers, telling anyone he could find that his son had won the Premiership title. His family back in Madeira were certainly delighted to see that Ronaldo had achieved his goal and played such a pivotal role in the team's success. It was just a shame that his father did not witness the special moment. Speaking to the Express, Ronaldo's mother, Dolores, echoed these sentiments when she admitted, 'Dinis drank himself into an early grave which left Cristiano devastated. He would have loved him to still be around to see the player he is today.'

The final focus for the season was the FA Cup final, the first at the new Wembley. Fittingly, Chelsea would be United's opponents. After enjoying the luxury of a well-earned rest during the meaningless last two games of the campaign, Ronaldo and several other key players were raring to go and determined to end on a high note. For Chelsea, defeat would be disastrous, having only the Carling Cup to show for their efforts in 2006/07. But United were equally desperate to lift the trophy and clinch the Double, putting the finishing touch on their season. In front of a packed crowd at Wembley, it was a mouth-watering prospect.

But it turned out to be a poor final for the new Wembley. A slow, tired game played by tired players – it was simply one game too many for most of the stars on show. United still had the better of the game, shading it in terms of chances thanks to Rooney's determined, physical display. Ronaldo was strangely subdued and struggled to make an impact, as Chelsea, like AC Milan before them, often placed two markers on him. His Portugal team-mate Paulo Ferreira kept him at bay, as Ronaldo found himself spending the majority of the game hugging the left touchline, unable to influence the game as much as he would have liked. For long stretches, Chelsea's defensive mindset stifled United's attacking intent.

Having made such an impact in showpiece finals in 2004, 2005 and 2006 at the Millennium Stadium, Cristiano could not reproduce that form at the new Wembley – he and several others just seemed to have run out of energy at the end of a long season. He loved the big occasion but knew that this time he had not shown his best when it mattered. The trademark dribbling runs were not in evidence, and he faded as the match headed into extra-time. Giggs had a great chance to put United ahead in extra-time, but he scuffed his finish from close range. It would be United's last good opportunity of the game.

In the end, it was Didier Drogba and Chelsea that left their mark on the new stadium as the Ivory Coast international beat van der Sar late in extra-time, after a neat one-two with Frank Lampard, in one of the few moments of real quality in the match. Ronaldo and his team-mates trudged up to collect their runners-up medals from Prince William on what was certainly a forgettable day for the Reds. Despite the Chelsea players' claims, it did not make up for surrendering the title to United, but the Blues were able to end their campaign on a high, and Jose Mourinho completed his set of English winners medals in the incredible span of just three seasons, to seemingly cement his future at Stamford Bridge. There had been rumours of Abramovich trying to recruit a new manager, and reports suggested that Jurgen Klinsmann, who had been in charge of Germany at the 2006 World Cup, and Juande Ramos, Sevilla's impressive boss, had been approached. But now Mourinho seemed the favourite to be in the hot seat for the 2007/08 campaign.

Much of Manchester was at least cheered by Liverpool's 2-1 Champions League final defeat against AC Milan the following Wednesday. Ferguson had predicted the result, claiming, 'I'd bet for sure that Milan will win the Champions League, I'm absolutely certain of it.' Once again, United had been eliminated by the eventual tournament winners. A packed crowd in Athens was certainly a stage that Cristiano would have loved to have experienced, but it was not to be.

The target for the season for Ronaldo and his team-mates had always been to reclaim their position as the top side in the country and to end the four-year wait to reclaim the Premiership trophy. This had been achieved and would rank alongside Ferguson's most spectacular achievements at the club. The challenge now was to return to the days of the dynasty – the late 1990s – when United were able to put together back-to-back title wins. There was immediately talk of potential transfers as Ferguson made it clear that he would spend in order to keep pace with his rivals. Liverpool now had new owners, the duo of George Gillett and Tom Hicks, and hoped to be capable of rivalling Chelsea in the transfer market.

Owen Hargreaves was one name that was frequently linked with United, standing out as a solid candidate for the much-needed anchorman role in midfield. Ferguson had tried to bring him to the club in January, but Bayern Munich had rejected a number of bids. A tireless, tough-tackling holding midfielder would give Ronaldo even greater licence to join in with attacking raids, safe in the knowledge that he was not leaving his back line exposed. Cristiano had experienced Hargreaves' energy first-hand during the 2006 World Cup quarter-final in Gelsenkirchen.

Ronaldo had won over all the pundits over the course of the campaign, and he had the awards to show for it. He collected the PFA Player of Year and PFA Young Player of the Year awards – the first time since Andy Gray (1977) that anyone had won both awards in the same season. While Didier Drogba at Chelsea had enjoyed a brilliant run of form, the fact that Ronaldo had led United to the Premiership title seemed to tip the scales in his favour. At times he had taken on the opposition single-handed, driving United on when it appeared that the three points might be in jeopardy. Games at Villa Park and Craven Cottage stand out as particular examples of Ronaldo's inspirational qualities and of the improvements that he had made.

The awards night in London was a special evening for the Portuguese star as he reaped the rewards of his phenomenal transformation over the course of the season. He was delighted, 'It is amazing and a big honour for me to win trophies like this in the English Premier League. I am very proud. My colleagues have voted for me and that is fantastic because the players know the qualities of players.' He acknowledged that he still had many improvements to make but, at 22, he had plenty of years ahead. Sir Alex Ferguson went further, calling Ronaldo 'the best player in the world.'

He followed this up by winning the Football Writers' Player of the Year award in May. Didier Drogba was once again second, followed by Ronaldo's club colleagues Ryan Giggs and Paul Scholes. Chairman of the Football Writers Association (FWA), Paul Hetherington, said, 'There have been no agendas carried over from last summer. Cristiano has been a runaway winner, and deservedly so. We also know we have a player who is absolutely delighted and honoured to receive this accolade.'

The true extent of Ronaldo's turnaround can be seen from the fact that at the beginning of the season he was an incredible 20-1 with the bookmakers to win this award. Yet here he was, lifting the trophy amidst the applause of the same experts who had written off his chances of resurrecting his career in English football. With United boasting three players in the top four in the vote, it reflected the stylish manner in which the team had won the Premiership trophy back from Chelsea.

The tributes had come flooding in for Ronaldo over the course of the season. Leighton Baines, the Wigan left-back, said, 'He's got so much ability, he can go left or right, is good in the air, and is really strong as well. He is one of the best players around.' Aaron Lennon, of Tottenham and England, added, 'I would have to say Ronaldo is the player I admire most. He is the best player in the world. The way he plays week in, week out is unbelievable. He's improved so much in the last couple of years.' Lennon would do well to learn from Ronaldo's new found consistent end product as this was an area that often let the Tottenham winger down at crucial moments. Cristiano was definitely an example to follow for others wishing to take their play to the next level.

At the end of the campaign, Chelsea and England captain John Terry, ever dignified in defeat, also heaped praise on Ronaldo's play, 'I could watch United just to watch him. He does things no one else in the world is doing at the minute. He's the best in the world. At his best, not many people can stop him. He has done all his talking on the pitch.' Terry's Chelsea team-mate Didier Drogba, who finished runner-up to Ronaldo in the PFA Player of the Year vote, spoke graciously too, 'What Cristiano Ronaldo achieved this year is just extraordinary. He has matured. He will be stronger in the future seasons. Today, without a doubt, he is the best Premier League player.'

PFA chief Gordon Taylor claimed, 'Cristiano is the most exciting player in the country at the moment – the quickness of his feet and the skills he possesses make you think, at times, that he is from another planet.'

Ronaldo had agreed to stay at Old Trafford during the summer of 2006 in a bid to take the title away from Jose Mourinho's Chelsea, and he had repaid Ferguson's faith in him with a staggering total of 23 goals in all competitions, including 17 in the Premiership. The Scot had nothing but compliments for his winger, 'He is one of the best signings I've made and his improvement this year has been amazing. In terms of top-flight football where do you find a winger who has scored 20 goals? It is incredible.'

Ryan Giggs was quick to praise Ronaldo's character, recalling the aftermath of the World Cup incident, 'Sometimes situations like that make you as a player. You have seen that many times at this club. It is all about character and determination. Cristiano has shown that this season.' It had threatened to be the most awkward and unhappy year of Ronaldo's life, but it had turned out to be a dream come true. He had gone from villain to hero in the space of 12 months. It is hard to tell whether his stunning season was a response to the boos or the culmination of his learning process at United, but either way his campaign ranked up there with the best ever in a Premiership-winning team.

As Bobby Charlton said in a BBC documentary about Ronaldo, this title would probably be remembered as Cristiano's achievement, and the fact that he accomplished this mission had proved to be his redemption in England after the World Cup. In Charlton's opinion, a dazzling season was the only way back for Ronaldo in the Premiership after the media storm in the summer. Such was the quality of his displays, few mentioned the incident with Rooney by the end of the campaign. Charlton himself knew plenty about succeeding in English football and he was absolutely correct about Ronaldo's path to forgiveness.

A measure of Cristiano's new found popularity came via one of the more bizarre headlines of the 2006/07 season. A story emerged that a seal sanctuary had chosen to name a seal after Ronaldo. The rescue centre already has seals named Peter Crouch and Hernan Crespo so Cristiano was in good company. Inevitably, the news article invited a whole host of diving related headlines!

So, the Premiership had been sealed, and this time it was the Portuguese face in Manchester, not London, that was smiling at the end of the season. Ronaldo's transformation over the past ten months had been nothing short of incredible and, looking back, he felt immense pride over what he had achieved. While he would have loved to grace the Champions League final, or make a killer contribution in the FA Cup final, it was close to the perfect season for United's number 7. With no World Cup or European Championships tournament during the summer, Ronaldo was able to enjoy a longer rest than usual. It was long overdue, as he had barely had time for a break between the 2006 World Cup and the new Premiership season. His youthful energy had got him through a long, gruelling campaign and he had fully earned a relaxing holiday. But even as he planned a restful spell away from football, his mind was focusing on the new campaign and how he could continue to leave defenders in a spin. He would undoubtedly face even closer marking when the action kicked off again in August. His name was renowned, and opposition teams all over Europe now regarded him as United's biggest threat.

Ronaldo was back on our television screens unexpectedly soon under the worst possible circumstances. When English toddler Madeleine McCann was kidnapped while on holiday in the Algarve in Portugal, Cristiano added his voice to the attempts to find her. He made a statement urging anyone with information to come forward. England captain John Terry and Portugal team-mate Paulo Ferreira did likewise. It was a very sad situation, but he was happy to do anything he could to help the investigation.

The 2006/07 season had marked Ronaldo's emergence as a truly world class player, and he had the sponsorship deals to match. He had agreed the most important deal of his career to date when he signed a contract with giant sports corporation Nike in 2006. Cristiano began by advertising the skin-tight Nike Pro training tops, alongside other big stars such as Italian Fabio Cannavaro and Frenchman Thierry Henry. Nike sponsors so many top sports stars that it was a compliment to Ronaldo's popularity when the company approached him. As his former coach, Sardinha Afonso, explained to the BBC in a documentary, 'Every child wants to be like Cristiano, from Europe, to Asia, America and Africa, the whole world does.' Ferguson was happy to see Ronaldo involved in these projects, so long as his concentration did not waver in training or in matches. There were plenty of other, more harmful distractions for a footballer and Cristiano had chosen well. His deal with Nike meant that he would mix with other top players and in the process he would raise his global profile. Sir Alex knew that this would only benefit United's merchandising sales in the long run.

Ronaldo's ever-increasing status in football resulted in

more and more offers. It led to him accepting three more sponsorship deals as he sought to reap the rewards of his fame. Firstly, he signed with Xerox Fuji to support their latest campaign and featured on TV displaying his ball skills. Then he added his backing to FIFA Street 2, a street football computer game. Ronaldo was happy with the deal as it was a concept that was close to his heart and had been an important part of his childhood, 'The game mirrors the same ideals and philosophies that I use in my approach to everyday football. I played on the street growing up, where I had one-on-one battles, so it's exciting to be a part of the EA SPORTS family and contribute to a style of football I've been playing all my life.'

Next, he signed with Coca Cola in another very lucrative deal. By joining forces with Coca Cola and Nike, Ronaldo had shown his new found popularity in European football and the scramble to sponsor him indicated his marketability. Having starred at the 2006 World Cup and led United to the Premiership title, Ronaldo quickly became one of Nike's most prized players. He was earning a large amount of money from his various sponsorship deals – the only downside was that he was very busy attending to the needs of all his sponsors. Having signed the agreements, he was never shy to fulfil his obligations to the various companies, and his management company, Gestifute, has thus far steered him in the right direction. Time away from football was invariably spent working with his sponsors, meaning that there was really no such thing as a break for Cristiano.

Another Euro 2008 qualifier dominated Ronaldo's thoughts as he lined up for Portugal away to Belgium on 2 June. It proved to be the win away from home in qualification that the team had been craving. A 2-1 victory was achieved thanks to goals from Nani and Helder Postiga. Ronaldo was pleased with the display, but the Portugal camp was well aware that Poland had won their sixth consecutive game, strengthening their grip on top spot. However, with games in hand, Cristiano knew that Portugal had every chance of closing the gap on Poland at the top. When the Poles suffered a surprise 1-0 defeat away to Armenia, Cristiano sensed that his team had to pounce on the slip-up.

The rest of the qualifying campaign would be crucial as Ronaldo and his team-mates sought to fight back and claim top spot. Fixtures against Kazakhstan and Azerbaijan looked like guarantees of maximum points whilst Portugal would be playing at home against Finland, Serbia and Poland and still had two games to come against lowly Armenia. The home match with Poland might well be the one that decided who claimed leadership of the group. Confidence was high in the Portugal squad, and Scolari urged his players to aim to take maximum points from the remaining fixtures. Nobody wanted to endure the embarrassment of failing to live up to expectations.

Nobody was disputing his ability, but what was more uncertain was just how good he might become. He had already been tagged by many as the best player in the world, and Sir Alex Ferguson had made rather premature comparisons with Maradona and Pele. It was all debatable and would be decided over time – Ronaldinho and Kaka would have something to say about it, having masterminded the past two Champions League successes for their respective clubs. Ronaldo still has plenty to prove on the world stage. Pele echoed these sentiments when he discussed the subject with Italian sports newspaper *La Gazzetta dello Sport*, 'Kaka is the best player in the world, without doubt. Cristiano Ronaldo is the best player in England. But from that to being the best player in the world there is still some way.' Despite Pele's preference for Kaka's obvious quality, it was still a great compliment to be called 'the best player in England' by arguably the best footballer to ever play the game. With Kaka three years older than Ronaldo, there was still time for the Portuguese star to overtake his Brazilian counterpart. It was a discussion that dominated the press in Europe after the end of the season.

Those at United certainly understood the quality of their Portuguese star. His monopoly over the end of season awards led to glowing praise from team-mates, and the official Manchester United magazine listed the tributes. Michael Carrick claimed, 'He's world class and he's still so young,' while Darren Fletcher explained, 'Some of the tricks Ronaldo does, you can't even get your head around them.' Defender Rio Ferdinand delivered the most complimentary assessment, 'Cristiano Ronaldo has been unbelievable this season. Not only has he produced goals, he's added so much more to his game. He's certainly been the best player in Europe in my opinion. There is no other player as exciting as him.'

With Wayne Rooney classing Ronaldo as a main threat for the team, and Ryan Giggs recognising Ronaldo's improved awareness of others, the dressing-room had spoken out with spectacular praise. Prior to the Champions League quarter-final second leg with Roma, Rooney was even more complimentary of Cristiano, 'At the minute, Cristiano is by far the best player in the world. He is winning games on his own this season. He has been unbelievable. Hopefully, he can work some of his magic tomorrow and get us into the semi-finals.' Roma captain and playmaker Francesco Totti revealed that Cristiano was the player his team was most concerned about, telling the media, 'Ronaldo can decide a match on his own.' The winger certainly did not disappoint on that night as he tore Roma to shreds.

For Ronaldo, the kind words from his team-mates, his fellow players and the United management were the comments that he treasured most – even more than compliments being thrown his way by the media. The season had been very special but it was over. Now it was time to look ahead to the next season and the bid to retain the Premiership title and conquer Europe. Having re-asserted themselves domestically, the Champions League was the big target for Ronaldo, Sir Alex and United. That would be the way to bring down the curtain on the Ferguson era in style. Having signed his new deal, it seemed likely that Cristiano would outlast his manager at Old Trafford and experience life at United in the post-Ferguson days. It is more than likely that Ronaldo would even be the focal point of the post-Ferguson era at the club.

As David Gill pointed out, the inking of Ronaldo's new deal was vital. Gill told the media in July, 'It was important in the sense of Manchester United being a club that does not sell its best players. For Cristiano to commit to Manchester United until 2012, and hopefully beyond that, is absolutely fantastic. But it shouldn't surprise us. We are the Premiership champions. Why wouldn't he want to stay?'

United were very busy in the transfer market during the early summer months of 2007. All eyes were on Chelsea, expected to spend huge sums in response to surrendering the title, and Liverpool, backed by their new owners. However, it was Sir Alex Ferguson who moved first to strengthen his Premiership-winning side. He knew that he could not rest on his laurels after the title triumph and decided to make the type of big-money signings that he had not made for several seasons.

In the space of a matter of days, United had wrapped up the signings of England international Owen Hargreaves, Brazilian youngster Anderson (pending a work permit) and Portuguese winger Nani. The capture of Hargreaves marked the end of a lengthy pursuit, as Bayern Munich eventually gave up on their struggle to keep him and chose to accept the £17 million bid from United. The player spoke of his delight at sealing the move, 'It has been a long time coming. It was probably the worst-kept secret in football, but it's great to be here. I think it's great to finally reach a positive conclusion, especially after all the time and energy that's been put in from everyone involved! A new era is starting for me now and I hope to achieve even more.' Hargreaves' defensive qualities would allow Ronaldo even greater licence to roam further forward.

It was an important move because the absence of a genuine anchorman had become more and more apparent as the season progressed, especially in the two games against AC Milan when the exceptional Kaka had run riot. Just to stop and watch Kaka's movement was enough to see how much difference a player in Hargreaves' mould would have made in these matches. With so many top clubs in Europe employing a number 10, playing slightly deeper than a central striker, a true holding player was essential to European success, even if it was not so important in the Premiership.

AC Milan had the tireless Gennaro Gattuso and Massimo Ambrosini; Chelsea had Claude Makelele and Michael Essien; and Liverpool had Momo Sissoko and Javier Mascherano. So it was a step in the right direction for United and if Hargreaves bolstered the side defensively, Ferguson's two other transfer coups gave the attack a huge dose of fresh, youthful impetus. Anderson, signed from Porto, had broken into the Brazil squad as a result of his brilliant creative displays at club level, while Nani was expected to have a similar impact to that of Ronaldo. Both players would be treated with care by Ferguson and introduced to English football gradually. The strength of United's current squad meant that, whereas Cristiano was thrown straight into the action in 2003 due to injuries and a lack of other options, Sir Alex could afford to take extra caution with Anderson and Nani.

Having spent more than £50 million, Ferguson had shown the ambition to conquer Europe that would appeal to Ronaldo's desire for silverware. It had, in part, been Sir Alex's vision for the future that had helped Cristiano to decide that he would sign his new deal at the club, and there was excitement all around Old Trafford as the new faces were revealed. In late June, United received the good news that Anderson's application for a work permit had been accepted and the transfer could be finalised. The Brazilian was thrilled, telling the media, 'To join Manchester United at 19 is incredible. Everything will be different in England – I know that – but I am certain I will adjust quickly to life in England. I am proud – and my family is also. For me, everything is new, it's a dream come true.'

Cristiano wasted no time in praising the quality of Nani and Anderson, the club's two new attackers. He told the media, 'I can only say that United will be stronger because they have signed two great players. Anderson and Nani are phenomenons and the side will be improved a lot by their participation.' Ronaldo knew from his own experiences that United were a good club for teaching and nurturing young players, and he promised to help the duo settle in their new surroundings. They would be able to converse in Portuguese if required, and their arrival would force Ronaldo to raise the bar again with his performances.

But there are few wingers of Cristiano's type in the Premiership, making it all the more special for United to have a wide man capable of taking on and beating defenders. Only Shaun Wright-Phillips and Aaron Lennon spring to mind as wingers who consistently seek the by-line with their dribbling. The other rather unique aspect of Ronaldo's game is his ability to use both feet effectively against opponents. Not only does this allow him to attempt more shots on goal, but it makes life tough for defenders because when he is dribbling at them, he has the option to go inside or outside. Full-backs never know which direction he will go, nor which way they should try to force him to go. His mid-dribble Cruyff turn at speed allows him to change direction and cut inside at will. One-footed wide men, such as Stuart Downing of Middlesbrough, are much easier to defend against because it is clear that they always want to cross the ball with one particular foot. It adds to Cristiano's unpredictability.

With the distinct lack of Number 10s – like Zidane, Kaka and Maradona – in the English game, wingers take on a greater role as creators of chances for strikers. Skilful playmakers just behind the forwards are far more common elsewhere in Europe, but in the Premiership it is wide men like Cristiano who dictate the game and are relied upon to provide the assists. Seemingly, this responsibility has brought out the best in him. The different styles in other European leagues go some way to explaining why United have had problems coming to terms with the likes of Kaka and Zidane roaming free in the Champions League.

Just when it seemed as though United's summer spending was over, Ferguson unveiled another big name target. The club had made no secret of its interest in finding a new striker to partner Wayne Rooney, and Sir Alex opted to pursue Argentine Carlos Tevez from West Ham. After a slow start to the season, Tevez had exploded into life in 2007, and his performances played a massive part in the Hammers avoiding relegation. Ferguson liked what he saw and, at 23, Tevez would have the chance to play alongside Ronaldo and Rooney for years to come.

Tevez certainly seemed enthusiastic about the potential move, telling the press, 'For me, Manchester United will be a sensational destination and to be a member of Sir Alex Ferguson's squad will be absolutely spectacular. My dream is to be an idol in English football and I can achieve this now.' The deal appeared to be finalised but, after all the controversy over Tevez's move to West Ham and the influence of businessman Kia Joorabchian, the Premier League was determined to monitor the terms of the contract to ensure that there was no third party influence. United's transfer fee had to be given to the Hammers, not to Joorabchian. This held up proceedings and left everybody wondering whether Tevez would ever be able to wear the red shirt. The player headed off to represent Argentina at the Copa America in Venezuela while the complexities of the deal were ironed out.

Cristiano awaited news on Tevez's arrival eagerly, knowing that the Argentine would add more thrust to the team's attack. David Gill, the club's chief executive, spoke of his frustration over the delay in negotiations as the issue rumbled on for weeks. He said, 'It's become over-complicated. The process is ongoing. We still have to sort out the paperwork.' The obstacles in the transfer were annoying the United fans, too, as they eagerly awaited confirmation that Tevez had become a Red Devil. Manchester United finally got their man on 10 August, bringing to an end one of the summer's most prolonged transfer sagas. After Kia Joorabchian paid West Ham £2 million to release Tevez from his contract, the Premier League approved the Reds' deal for the player – reported to be a two-year loan. Ferguson was delighted to get his man, despite the complications, telling the assembled media, 'I am happy with what the Premier League did because eventually we get a player in the right circumstances, with everything clarified and cleared by the appropriate authorities.'

Ossie Ardiles, the Argentine who made such an impression himself in English football, claimed that United would not be disappointed with Tevez, 'United are a team that will give him the great stage he craves. He will be a success very quickly, there is no doubt about that. He will fit in. He will be the conductor of the orchestra.' For Ronaldo, it was hugely exciting to consider the prospect of an attack including himself, Ryan Giggs, Rooney and Tevez. There would be no excuses for a lack of goals next season as the team would be very much attack-orientated.

There was talk of this United team being the new *Galacticos*, taking over that tag from Real Madrid. But Cristiano knew that Ferguson's interest was in points and trophies, rather than entertaining crowds with attacking football. Sir Alex had bolstered the defence in January 2007 with the signings of Patrice Evra and Nemanja Vidic, and now he was focusing his attention on the front line. Everything about United's summer deals suggested that Ferguson wanted one last assault on the Champions League before he retired from management. The incredible Treble of 1999 was now too distant a memory for him and, like Ronaldo and the rest of the squad, he craved more success in the competition. The previous season, United had been close to reaching the final, and with the additions to the squad there was plenty of optimism.

Elsewhere, it was a very hectic summer in the transfer market. Liverpool were busy trying to complete the signing of striker Fernando Torres from Atletico Madrid. Rafa Benitez had been negotiating with the Spanish club for some time in an attempt to solve the team's goalscoring problems and eventually got his man in a deal worth around £20 million. Liverpool's new owners had answered their manager's plea for big-name arrivals. Benitez then sealed the signing of Ajax youngster Ryan Babel, who had impressed at the Under-21 European Championships. Liverpool were also contemplating an audacious bid for United left back Gabriel Heinze, whose agent made it clear that his client wanted a move away from the club. It was disappointing news for Cristiano, who regarded Heinze as one of his best friends at United. When Ronaldo struck the winner against Fulham in February, he ran straight to Heinze, who was warming up on the touchline, to celebrate. He understood the reasons for his Argentine friend wanting a new challenge, but it still saddened him to see Heinze on his way out of Old Trafford. After yet another prolonged transfer wrangle, Liverpool failed to sign the Argentine, with Ferguson unwilling to sell a player to their oldest rivals, and Heinze eventually signed for Real Madrid.

Arsenal, meanwhile, were smarting from the departure of Thierry Henry, who moved to Barcelona in a £16.2 million deal, and were busy desperately dismissing speculation about the possible departure of Arsene Wenger. The Gunners were at a serious disadvantage as United, Liverpool and Chelsea were able to bring in big names at such high prices. Wenger had to content himself with lesser known players such as the Croatian international Eduardo da Silva, who arrived at the Emirates in a deal thought to be worth around £7.5 million, and defender Bacary Sagna from Auxerre, who cost £6 million. It was not the summer that many Arsenal fans had hoped for, and even some of the players appeared disenchanted. Defender William Gallas spoke out, questioning how the club planned to replace Henry. The Gunners would have an uphill struggle to improve on last season's fourth place finish.

Chelsea had been relatively quiet for the majority of the summer, despite speculation linking them with Valencia's David Villa, but pulled off a coup by snapping up Peruvian forward Claudio Pizarro on a free transfer, along with Steve Sidwell from Reading and Tal Ben Haim from Bolton. Brazilian defender Alex arrived from PSV in a curious deal. Chelsea had signed the player a few years ago, given him to PSV so that he could earn citizenship and then arranged to buy him back for $1. From a neutral's perspective, United seemed to be dominating the close season and had made the strongest additions to their squad.

The Blues were already playing catch up, and some of the signings that they had made appeared to be fringe players rather than first-team stars. Mourinho moved to remedy the situation by securing the signature of Florent Malouda, the Lyon winger, to bolster their squad after a rather desperate pursuit. It was easy to forget, though, that Chelsea had the likes of Michael Ballack and Andriy Shevchenko, who had both underperformed in 2006/07 but would be raring to go again for the new campaign and itching to prove the critics wrong. Everybody knew that they had more talent than they had shown in their first seasons in English football.

Ferguson seemed willing to let a few of his squad seek new clubs during the summer. While Liverpool had made their interest in Heinze known, Alan Smith and Kieran Richardson were also made available by Sir Alex. Everton, Middlesbrough, Sunderland and Newcastle all entered the chase. Richardson appeared keen to gain first team football by moving away from Old Trafford, and he clinched a £5.5 million move to Roy Keane's Sunderland in mid July. But Smith was very reluctant to leave United. He was adored by the club's fans and felt capable of fighting for a place in the team. Certainly, the quality of Ronaldo and Giggs had limited Richardson's opportunities, and the arrival of Tevez would push Smith further down the pecking order, with Rooney, Saha and Solskjaer also competing for a spot up front. Buying young foreign players did make it harder for United's academy players, like Richardson, to break through into the first team, but few minded if Ronaldo was holding back United's youngsters, so long as he kept bringing trophies to the club.

All of this new talent would soon be on show. United's pre-season began before most people had recovered from the thrills of the previous campaign. As usual, the team embarked on their Far East tour, gaining match practice against a host of useful club sides eager to impress their illustrious visitors. Ferguson took a full squad with him, except those who were nursing injuries and those who had been in Copa America action. Cristiano enjoyed the excitement of another new beginning and, as anticipated, he was one of the most sought-after signatures for the autograph hunters who swarmed around the squad at every opportunity.

The opening match saw United face Japanese J-League champions Urawa Red Diamonds in Saitama. As was to be expected, United looked a little rusty and trailed 1-0 at half-time. A strong second half comeback saved their blushes. First, Darren Fletcher grabbed an equaliser, and then Ronaldo put his side ahead with a strike that found the bottom corner. It was his first significant contribution. United should have sealed the match, but Urawa did not give up and levelled the match at 2-2. Both teams seemed relatively pleased with the result, and it had been a good workout for Cristiano as he searched for match fitness before the Premiership season kicked off.

Next, the tour moved to Seoul where United faced FC Seoul. It proved to be a bit of a mismatch, as Ronaldo and his team-mates ran out easy 4-0 winners and found life a lot easier than in the previous match. Cristiano opened the scoring and then masterminded goals for Chris Eagles and Rooney. He only played for 45 minutes, but the Seoul defence were unable to handle him. The short taste of the action helped Ronaldo to prepare himself and his body for the season ahead, though he would certainly experience better marking than the Seoul players could muster. They seemed to be star struck, and Cristiano and United had taken full advantage.

The third match of the tour saw Ronaldo continue his scoring streak as he netted one of the team's six goals against Shenzhen FC in Macau. Though it was only a short cameo, he again impressed and showed signs that he was continuing his 2006/07 form. The 6-0 win was a valuable warm-up for the new campaign, but Ferguson had a few concerns to ponder. Scholes and Neville were set to miss the start of the season through injury, while Hargreaves was still not match fit after an ankle problem. It became all the more important to keep Ronaldo fresh. Alongside Rooney and eventually Tevez, he would carry the goalscoring burden again during this campaign.

Having featured prominently in all three friendlies so far, Ferguson left Cristiano on the bench for the majority of the last match against Guangzhou. Nani stole the show with a lovely chip as United collected a 3-0 win. When Ronaldo was introduced for a late cameo, it brought the biggest cheer of the night. Some had feared that a slight knock might keep him out of the game, but the supporters were not to be disappointed. It marked the end of a solid tour for the club – massive merchandising profits had been made and three matches out of four had been won. Injury worries aside, the trip had been very successful, and the players were now itching to get their league campaign started.

It was always a moving experience for Cristiano to see the

hoards of people who gathered to welcome the players at various stages of the tour. Ronaldo could not help but recall how different things had been on the 2006 tour where he was shadowed by security guards for protection after the World Cup. A year on, everything ran more smoothly. It was particularly special to see the youngsters that had come along in the hope of catching a glimpse of their favourite players, who they could normally only watch on television. The majority were kitted out in the latest team strip and had bought no end of club merchandise. Seeing the frenzied supporters when the United squad arrived, it was easy to understand how the club made so much money from the sale of merchandise in the Far East. There was little doubt that Cristiano had taken over from David Beckham as the most popular player in this part of the world.

Ronaldo gives United incredible income from the Far East. The figures coming out of Old Trafford indicate that the club has over 40 million fans in Asia. Chief executive David Gill commented on the enticing options that the club's popularity offered, thanks to players like Ronaldo, 'Where next? I think Africa is an interesting one. There's clearly a great following for the Premier League.' Cristiano's reputation – along with Rooney's – safeguards the club's future merchandise sales. While those two young stars are still at Old Trafford, shirt sales will continue to boom and United will seek to expand their fan base even further. Experts have predicted that Ronaldo is destined to be the most marketable player of his generation.

When he was first given the number 7 shirt, United could scarcely have imagined the impact that he would have on the world market. Beckham had been such a revelation as a marketable asset that everyone expected a drop in sales after his departure. But Ronaldo had filled that role spectacularly well, particularly after his 2006/07 displays. While Beckham concentrates on conquering the US market after his multi-million pound deal with Los Angeles Galaxy, Cristiano is quickly replacing the former England captain as the leading football icon in the Far East. It has proved a masterstroke for the club to pair the famous number 7 with the marketable Ronaldo name.

His development into a world-class player was also evident in the Fantasy Football player lists published in many national newspapers. He was the most expensive midfield player available and, perhaps a little unfairly, everyone anticipated that Cristiano would produce a repeat of his previous season's form. With his popularity vastly improved, he was high on every manager's shopping list. With free-kicks and penalties as obvious routes to goal, most expected Ronaldo to reach his 15-goal target again. United would need him to be at his best if they were to hold off their fellow title challengers, especially as their rivals had strengthened their squads over the summer.

For Cristiano, the summer of 2007 was the longest break he had enjoyed since arriving at United. While the absence of an international tournament had allowed him to give his body a proper rest and catch up with family, he had enjoyed touring the Far East and was impatient to get back into the groove of the new campaign. There was so much to look forward to in the 2007/08 campaign: defending the title; searching for Champions League glory; facing ex-team-mate Roy Keane's Sunderland team. There was sure to be no end of drama ahead. Neutrals were excited by the prospect of the most open title race in the history of the Premiership and the possibility of an English club winning the Champions League again. The other objective on the horizon for Ronaldo was qualification for Euro 2008. Portugal's early struggles meant that top spot in the group was far from confirmed and so Cristiano needed to be on his best form.

Ferguson spoke positively about Cristiano's character ahead of the 2007/08 season, praising his intelligence and the manner in which the winger was handling the intense media attention. He told the press, 'The problem comes when players get flattered by it and start enjoying it. But at the moment there's absolutely no sign that the boy will be wasted by it. He can cope. With Cristiano, a lot has happened to him in his time at Manchester United; but he has matured fantastically well.' Sir Alex famously fell out with David Beckham over his off-field distractions, but he seems to have more faith in Cristiano's decision-making.

When Mourinho publicly claimed that he had 'mellowed' and would be noticeably different during the upcoming season, most people were sceptical. Cristiano hoped that it would prevent the kind of verbal clashes with the Chelsea manager that had broken out towards the end of the previous campaign.

CONQUERING ALL
BEFORE HIM

NOW EVERYONE WAS asking: could Ronaldo repeat the heroics of the previous season and lead United to more glory? But his focus never wavered as he aimed to lift as much silverware as possible. He explained later in the season: 'To be the best in the world I have to win titles like the Champions League and the Premier League.'

But the campaign did not start as Ronaldo had hoped. A goalless draw on the opening day against Reading was frustrating. Cristiano went close to breaking the deadlock but the Royals held on. An injury to Rooney completed a miserable afternoon.

And it got worse. Ronaldo and his team-mates travelled to face Portsmouth in midweek and again collected just a point. With the score locked at 1-1, Pompey midfielder Sulley Muntari was sent off but as the Reds looked to capitalise, Ronaldo became involved in a fracas with Richard Hughes and was shown the red card. Ferguson looked on in dismay.

Already without Rooney, now he would lose Cristiano to a three-match suspension.

Ronaldo was equally unhappy. He hadn't got going yet and it was the worst time to be watching from the stands. To rub salt into the wounds, the Manchester derby was United's next fixture – a game he always relished.

Cristiano was sorely missed as the Reds stumbled to a 1-0 defeat. Suddenly, the media was questioning the team's title chances, just months after heaping praise on the players. One goal and two points from three games spoke for itself. Improvements were needed – and fast.

Gritty 1-0 home wins followed against Tottenham and Sunderland before Ronaldo was back in action away to Everton on 15 September. Again United struggled to find attacking fluency but took the points thanks to Vidic's late header.

On the positive side, it was the team's fourth clean sheet in six games and the Ferdinand-Vidic partnership was looking strong. Ronaldo knew that once the forward line started firing, there would be no stopping United.

This would happen soon but first the Reds grabbed three more spirited victories. The winger was in high spirits, despite the disappointment of two draws for Portugal in Euro 2008 qualifiers. He did, at least, add another goal to his qualifying tally.

United were drawn in Group F for the Champions League group stage, alongside Roma, Dynamo Kiev and Cristiano's former club Sporting Lisbon. Typically, Sporting would be the first fixture and, even more typically, Ronaldo stole the spotlight. He headed a 62nd minute winner to cap a successful return to the club that helped him progress to the highest level.

Back in domestic action, United faced their biggest test so far. On 20 September, Chelsea and Jose Mourinho had parted company after three action-packed seasons. The Portuguese would be missed. Avram Grant had taken over and his first game in charge was a trip to Old Trafford. The game turned on a controversial red card for John Obi Mikel for a challenge on Evra. Ronaldo was quiet but goals from Tevez and Saha clinched the victory, showing United would not surrender their title easily.

Cristiano finally opened his Premiership goal account for the season with a left-footed winner at Birmingham on 29 September. As he wheeled away in celebration, the worry for the rest of the league was that now Ronaldo was up and running, could anyone stop him?

Wigan certainly found it impossible when they visited Old Trafford. Cristiano, quiet in a midweek European win over Roma, scored twice against the Latics in a 4-0 win as he, Rooney and Tevez produced stylish link-up play, putting United top of the table.

After returning from two important qualifying victories for Portugal, Ronaldo began on the bench as United struck four again away to Aston Villa. He came on for the last 14 minutes but Rooney and Tevez stole the headlines. A 4-1 win at home to Middlesbrough made it 12 goals in three games.

It was the perfect preparation for a trip to face leaders Arsenal on 3 November. The result was a gripping contest. The visitors suppressed Arsenal's passing game in the first half, taking the lead through a deflected Rooney header before Fabregas equalised.

With eight minutes left, a draw seemed the likely outcome and Ronaldo had been quiet for long periods. But as is so typical of Cristiano, he popped up with a crucial contribution, by expertly converting Evra's cross. But United could not hold on. To Ronaldo's dismay, Gallas scored a last-gasp volley and the game ended 2-2. Nonetheless, Cristiano knew that United had shown they were more than a match for the Gunners.

A 4-0 home win over Dynamo Kiev in midweek clinched European qualification, with Ronaldo netting in the 88th minute. He had scored twice in a 4-2 win in Kiev and the Ukrainians were sick of the sight of him. Blackburn felt the same way at the weekend. The Portuguese struck twice in two minutes to clinch a 2-0 victory. Ferguson was impressed, claiming the current squad was his strongest ever.

'We've got young players led by Wayne Rooney and Cristiano Ronaldo and more in the likes of Carlos Tevez and Nani and Anderson,' he told the media. 'This team has to win something. They have a great chance of doing so.'

Ronaldo headed off for Portugal's last two Euro 2008 qualifiers safe in the knowledge that he was currently enjoying his best form of the season. The Portuguese ensured they reached the tournament, taking four points from the two games but allowing Poland to clinch top spot. Cristiano finished with a superb tally of eight goals in the qualifying group.

Back at United, Ronaldo's importance to the side was emphasised by a 1-0 defeat at Bolton while he was rested. Ferguson's decision not to even put him on the bench backfired as the Reds lacked creativity without their talisman. As if to prove this point, Ronaldo scored a sensational late free-kick in the midweek fixture against Sporting to snatch a 2-1 victory.

His goal-scoring run continued at home to Fulham on 3 December. A right-footed strike in the first half and a headed goal after the break kept the pressure on Arsenal at the top. A 4-1 demolition of hapless Derby surprised no one. The only shock was that it took Ronaldo until the last minute to get among the goals. He was rested in midweek as United drew 1-1 in Rome.

Next for Cristiano was a trip to Anfield for what Sky Sports dubbed Grand Slam Sunday – United clashed with the Merseysiders while Arsenal faced Chelsea. He had not enjoyed many productive afternoons against Liverpool and this match proved no different. Apart from a few flashes of brilliance, he was tightly marked. Tevez scored the winner as United escaped with a professional 1-0 victory.

Ronaldo fared better a week later with a double in a 2-1 victory over a stubborn Everton side. His first was a left-foot strike from outside the area, his second came late-on from the penalty spot. There was never any doubt about him holding his nerve from 12 yards.

The Christmas period often plays a pivotal role in the title race and United were determined to cash in. On Boxing Day, they beat Roy Keane's Sunderland 4-0. Ronaldo grabbed the third and was withdrawn before the hour mark. He watched contentedly as the team moved back to the Premiership summit.

Three days later, his header put the champions in front at Upton Park against West Ham. But, when presented with the chance to double the lead after 66 minutes, Ronaldo fired his penalty wide. Instead, West Ham rallied to stun United with two late goals.

Cristiano hung his head but Ferguson focused on poor

defending. He told the media: 'Scoring the penalty would have killed the game but if you lose goals to set-pieces you are not at your best.' Meanwhile, Arsenal won at Everton and went back to the top.

Ronaldo redeemed himself by setting up Tevez for the winner against Birmingham on New Year's Day and netted himself as the Reds left it late to beat Aston Villa 2-0 in the FA Cup Third Round.

Cristiano stole all the headlines a week later with his first hat-trick for the club as United battered Newcastle 6-0 at Old Trafford. The Reds scored all six goals in the second half and reclaimed top spot. After a slow start, these strikes were Cristiano's 14th, 15th and 16th league goals of the campaign.

His 17th came in United's next fixture at Reading and he netted two more in the FA Cup against Tottenham on 27 January, earning the Reds a place in the Fifth Round. Capitalising on Michael Dawson's red card, Ronaldo scored from the resulting penalty and was gifted a second when Tottenham keeper Radek Cerny allowed his shot to creep in. It was hardly the ideal way to reach 25 goals for the season in all competitions but Cristiano was not complaining.

January was also rumoured to be the month when Ronaldo began dating current girlfriend Spanish model Nereida Gallardo. Friends say the relationship is serious. She has already met the winger's family and has appeared in several photos with him.

There was no stopping Cristiano on current form and Portsmouth were the next to pay the price. Ronaldo scored twice in the first 15 minutes. The highlight of a dominant United display was Cristiano's second goal – a scorching 30-

yard free-kick that flew into the top corner.

Sir Alex was full of praise, claiming Ronaldo's strike rate from free-kicks was even better than David Beckham's or Eric Cantona's and that this effort was the best goal he had seen in Premiership history. He told the press: 'No keeper in the world would save that. The boy practises. It's a delight to see, terrific.'

`The team needed a late goal at Tottenham to salvage a point as Cristiano struggled to have his usual impact and United were below-par again at home to Manchester City in an emotional derby. To commemorate the 50 year anniversary of the Munich Air Disaster, Ronaldo and his team-mates donned replicas of the old kit. There were no names on the shirts so Cristiano ran out simply wearing the famous number 7.

Sir Bobby Charlton, one of the crash survivors, was involved in a moving pre-match dedication as United mourned the loss of so many talented footballers. But the occasion seemed to get to Ronaldo – and he was not alone.

City scored two first half goals and deserved the points. Ronaldo's pace had been an asset so often during the season but here he found Micah Richards in sublime form. The dressing-room was very quiet after the game.

The winger struggled to return to his best form in the Champions League Second Round. United were drawn against French champions Lyon and travelled to France for the first leg on 20 February. Ronaldo, rested while his team-mates destroyed Arsenal 4-0 in the FA Cup, was eager to be back in action.

The Reds collected a 1-1 draw but Cristiano again failed to hit his usual heights. The team played on the counter-attack but too often squandered possession. However, Ronaldo was certain that the Reds could win the second leg at Old Trafford.

Those worried about his dip in form were relieved to see Cristiano back to his irresistible best away to Newcastle. He set up Rooney's opener, then scored twice himself before Ferguson withdrew him with more than 20 minutes remaining as United completed a 5-1 demolition. Had he stayed on, a hat-trick seemed inevitable. Sir Alex continued to be cautious about Ronaldo's fitness, giving him just 20 minutes off the bench at Fulham. A 3-0 win kept the Reds on track for the title.

Ronaldo's winner against Lyon in midweek booked United's place in the Champions League quarter-finals. He reacted quickest to score the only goal of the game four minutes before half-time. The draw for the quarters paired the Reds with Roma – United's group stage opponents and the side on the end of the 7-1 demolition last season.

The team rolled into their FA Cup quarter-final against Portsmouth full of confidence – they had been phenomenal at Old Trafford all season. Ronaldo spent much of the game running at defenders but his frustration over physical challenges grew and grew. One particular challenge – by Sylvain Distin in the penalty area – saw Ferguson jumping up in anger. But the visitors clung on and struck a stunning late blow as Milan Baros was fouled by Tomasz Kuszczak, on for van der Sar. The penalty was awarded and the goalkeeper was dismissed. Ferdinand took over the gloves but could not stop Muntari's spot-kick. United were out and Ronaldo was at the centre of the post-match discussion as United fumed.

'The referee was unbelievable,' said the winger. 'Sometimes they just protect the defenders and I am thinking about having to change my game because it is difficult to play like that.'

The Portuguese's scoring touch was back at Derby on 15 March as he rescued his side from an embarrassing draw. With just 14 minutes to go, he finally broke the deadlock and his body language suggested he would carry United to the title if needs be. The previous season, Cristiano had saved some of his biggest contributions for late in the campaign and he was doing the same again. He scored both goals as United won 2-0 at home to Bolton, wrapping up the points inside 20 minutes. Arsenal and Chelsea, meanwhile, were struggling to keep up.

The second Grand Slam Sunday of the season again went United's way. Ronaldo was on target as Liverpool fell to a 3-0 defeat at Old Trafford. Chelsea then beat Arsenal 2-1 at Stamford Bridge to jump above the Gunners and cut United's lead to five points.

It was all going United's way but Cristiano refused to be complacent. He produced one of his best displays of the season as the Reds crushed Aston Villa 4-0 at Old Trafford on 29 March. He opened the scoring with a brilliant backheel and claimed the assists for the other three goals.

It was the ideal preparation for the trip to Rome in midweek. Cristiano knew that he needed to win European competitions if he wanted to be regarded as a truly great player – and he lived up to his billing as his pace and movement left Roma shell-shocked.

Sir Alex opted to play Ronaldo in a more advanced, central role to exploit the Italians on the counter attack. It worked perfectly. Cristiano opened the scoring after 39 minutes and was a menace all night, leading Scholes and Gary Neville to later call him the best player they have worked with.

Ferguson was thrilled, telling the press: 'Ronaldo's goal changed the game for us. It was a fantastic header. It was a centre-forward's header – it reminded me of myself.'

With six league games remaining, there was little margin for error for United. Their fate was in their own hands but there was still a trip to Stamford Bridge to come. Away to Middlesbrough on 6 April, Cristiano opened the scoring but two goals from Brazilian Afonso Alves put United in danger of defeat before Rooney snatched an equaliser. The chasers had been given encouragement.

More positive was a 1-0 win against Roma in midweek, sealing a comfortable 3-0 aggregate win. Ronaldo was named among the substitutes as an insurance policy but was not required. The game also saw Neville return from lengthy injury problems. He had not appeared for the first team since mid-March 2007.

United had known since the quarter-final draw that they would face either Barcelona or Schalke 04 in the Champions League semi-finals. It came as little surprise to Ronaldo and company when the Spaniards prevailed, setting up a mouth-watering clash.

Arsenal had looked likely to be involved all the way in the title race but a miserable March had left Wenger's side with only the slightest of chances. When they arrived at Old Trafford on 13 April, the Gunners knew that only a victory would be good enough. And they played like a team needing the three points, taking the lead shortly after the break. At that stage, it looked like an uphill battle for United. But a handball from Gallas presented Ronaldo with the chance to equalise from the penalty spot and he took it expertly. Hargreaves then won the game with a well-placed free-kick. Arsenal were out of the race and it was down to two.

But United could not shake off Chelsea. Ronaldo and company needed a late Tevez goal to earn a disappointing 1-1 draw away to Blackburn. This allowed the Blues to cut two more points off the Reds' lead as some questioned whether the champions had run out of steam. The lead was just three points with the clash at Stamford Bridge to come – but it was still in United's hands.

Cristiano tried to stay calm as the team entered the biggest week of their season. On 23 April, they travelled to Spain for their Champions League semi-final first leg with Barcelona. All the pre-match talk centred around the need for Ronaldo to play a starring role. Incredibly, he had a chance to shine within five minutes as United were awarded a penalty for handball. But to everyone's surprise, Cristiano fired his spot-kick wide. His reaction told the whole story – he was devastated.

It finished 0-0, meaning a victory at Old Trafford would take the Reds into the final. But all the talk post-match focused on Ronaldo's penalty miss. It was a crucial moment in a crucial match and for once the winger had fluffed his lines.

However, there was no time to dwell on it and Cristiano gave a positive response. He said: 'Today I didn't score – no problem. But now I will score in Manchester.'

At the weekend, United faced Chelsea in a massive title showdown. But, conscious of the return leg against Barcelona, Sir Alex left Ronaldo on the bench. With the score locked at 1-1, Cristiano was sent on for a 30-minute cameo. But Ballack's late penalty won the day, ensuring the title race went right to the wire. The two sides were level on points but United were ahead on goal difference – two wins from their final two games would be enough.

A raucous crowd welcomed United and Barcelona on to the pitch in midweek for the biggest European night at Old Trafford for years. With Rooney injured, even more was now expected of Ronaldo. However, it was Scholes, who had missed the 1999 final, who proved the match-winner, smashing an unstoppable strike into the top corner after 14 minutes.

Barcelona rallied through Lionel Messi but United held firm as Ronaldo and Tevez defended from the front. When the final whistle went, Old Trafford erupted. The next night, Chelsea overcame Liverpool in extra-time in the other semi-final. It would be the Reds against the Blues in the final in Moscow.

Back in Premiership action, Ronaldo ensured that there were no nervy moments at home to West Ham in United's last home game of the season. He was in sparkling form, scoring twice in the first 24 minutes to set up a 4-1 victory, and thoroughly enjoyed the lap of honour at the end. Chelsea won at Newcastle to send the title race to the final weekend.

There were two games to go – essentially two finals. Cristiano and his team-mates travelled to Wigan while Chelsea faced Bolton at Stamford Bridge. After a scrappy start, United took the lead after 33 minutes when Rooney was fouled in the area. Ronaldo, refusing to be haunted by his miss in Barcelona, took the responsibility and scored. He had been on target in eight of the team's final ten league matches. Giggs clinched the win and the title as he netted a second late-on.

The party began as the players celebrated with the

travelling fans and lifted the Premiership trophy. However, the feeling remained that the job was only half done. The season would still be disappointing if the Champions League trophy escaped their grasp.

With ten days off, Ronaldo and company got themselves into peak condition for the final and there was great excitement within the squad. While Giggs, Hargreaves, Evra and van der Sar had appeared in Champions League finals, this would be a new experience for many.

Moscow was rocking as the two teams lined up. Ferguson had waited nine painful years to return to the final and Ronaldo, who admitted doing the double was his dream, was determined not to let him down. Chelsea, though, were equally fired up.

The game began in typical cagey fashion but gradually opened up, allowing Cristiano to send a message to those who claimed he did not deliver in big games. A one-two between Brown and Scholes allowed the full-back to deliver a perfect cross and Ronaldo powered a header past Cech. After 26 minutes, United were ahead.

Ferguson's decision to play the Portuguese on the left wing proved shrewd. With Michael Essien playing out of position at right-back, Cristiano was able to exploit him with his pace and quick feet. But Chelsea struck, against the run of play, just before half-time. Essien's shot deflected to Lampard, who slotted home the equaliser. The midfielder had shown great courage to play in the semi-final after the death of his mother and had risen to the occasion yet again.

United spent the majority of the second half on the back foot as Chelsea dominated. But Ferdinand and Vidic were immense and Cristiano still looked the biggest danger on the counter attack. The game remained locked at 1-1 and even extra-time, which saw Drogba red-carded, could not separate the sides. The final would be settled on penalties.

It was decided that Ronaldo would take United's third kick and, with the score at 2-2, the winger stepped forward. His shootout record has always been excellent but he chose the worst moment to lose his nerve. Cech guessed correctly to make a vital save. A crestfallen Cristiano put his hands on his head. Had he blown it for the Reds?

After Nani netted United's fifth penalty, making it 4-4, Terry had the chance to win it for Chelsea. But the Blues skipper slipped as he struck his spot-kick and fired against the post. Ronaldo had been reprieved. The United fans jumped for joy. Anderson scored, Salomon Kalou scored. 5-5. Giggs, setting a new record of 759 appearances for the club, put United 6-5 up.

Anelka stepped forward for Chelsea's seventh kick. The Frenchman struck the ball to van der Sar's right but the Dutch keeper beat it out and United had done it. Ronaldo, who had feared his night would end with him sobbing in despair, instead cried tears of joy and relief while his team-mates mobbed van der Sar.

Ronaldo told the media: 'I thought we were going to lose. I had played well and scored but I had missed my penalty and it felt like the worst day of my life. Now it is the happiest day of my life.'

Ten days after the Premiership triumph, Cristiano lifted the Champions League trophy to cap off a tremendous season. He had made 48 appearances in all competitions, scoring an incredible 42 goals, and his phenomenal achievements were recognised when the end of season awards were handed out.

Speaking to the media after winning the PFA Player of the Year award, Ronaldo said: 'I feel very good but it is not just my award, my team-mates have helped me a lot. It is a great moment.'

However, his preparations for Euro 2008 were disrupted by speculation about his future. Long-term suitors Real Madrid continued to pursue Cristiano and United were left frustrated by his reluctance to give a definite answer about his plans. Clearly, the wide man was very tempted to swap the miserable English weather for sunnier climes.

Euro 2008 promises to be another showcase for Cristiano's remarkable talents as Portugal line up in Group A alongside co-hosts Switzerland, the Czech Republic and Turkey. Cristiano and company look favourites to top the group and the winger would love to add a third trophy to his double success at United. Considering that he has already surpassed the 50-cap mark for Portugal at just 23 years of age, there is no limit to how far Cristiano can progress. Certainly, 100 or even 150 caps is a target that is well within his reach, and by starting so young he has been given the chance to enjoy a long international career. Scolari and the Portuguese selectors have to take a lot of credit for spotting his potential so early and being prepared to throw him straight into the senior squad. The nation has earned a reputation for promoting good, young footballers and giving them the chance to prove themselves at international level. It is no coincidence that Ronaldo and so many others have been successful so early in their careers.

So long as he remains motivated and focused, he will surely go on to win many more trophies. He will be one of

Portugal's leaders going into Euro 2008 in Austria and Switzerland, and with the likes of Luis Figo now retired, the younger generation should get their chance to shine. Such has been the quality of his play, few would bet against him leading his national team to major tournament glory before he hangs up his boots.

He remains extremely proud of his roots and of being Portuguese. There is little chance of him following a growing trend of early international retirements. Team-mate Paul Scholes, Italian defender Alessandro Nesta and Czech midfielder Pavel Nedved, to name just three, have cut their international careers short in order to extend their club careers. But Ronaldo will surely not follow suit and may even have six major tournaments ahead of him – with the 2018 World Cup potentially being his international swansong. He has a very exciting future, which is a frightening prospect for defenders worldwide – they will be sick of the sight of him by the time he announces his retirement.

Similarly, Portugal and Madeira, in particular, continue to be very proud of Ronaldo, and he receives an incredible, frenzied welcome whenever he finds the time to return to the island. It is still home to him – despite spending so many years away on the Portuguese mainland and in England with United. He does not often get the opportunity to visit Funchal, but it will always have a special place in his heart. It is where his journey to the top started.

The remainder of Ronaldo's career is very hard to predict. His new contract at United binds him to the club in the short-term, but in the current climate it is impossible to be sure that he will see out his contract at Old Trafford. He has made no secret of his desire to play in Spain at some stage during his career. In the summer after the World Cup, during the contract negotiations, Real Madrid were linked with the winger and the interest has been even stronger since. The Spanish giants love to bring big stars to the club, especially attacking players. Growing up in Madeira, Ronaldo was very aware of Real Madrid's great history, both domestically and in European competitions. It is easy to understand the motivation behind a move to the Bernabeu. The same can be said for Barcelona's rich football history. If Ronaldo continues to play at the levels of the past two seasons, he will have his pick of all the clubs in Europe should he decide to leave Old Trafford at some point later in his career. An impressive Euro 2008 will add to the speculation. But he will be hard pressed to find a club that looks after its players better than United.

Ferguson will hope that Ronaldo soon settles down to a family life. It is well known that the United manager likes to see a player get married and adopt a quieter lifestyle, with fewer distractions. This, though, is not in the player's immediate plans though he is very happy with Nereida. Cristiano is already a well-balanced young man, and Sir Alex has been lucky that he has had no major problems with his winger's off-field actions – with the exception of the unfounded rape allegations. Strangely, Ronaldo has created more controversy for himself on the pitch than in his leisure time – the reverse of so many players in United's long history.

Eventually, Ronaldo will cast his mind to retirement and where that might take him. His family, still largely based in Madeira, seem likely to remain there, and perhaps one day

Ronaldo will return to live on the island. In fairness, he has not had much time to enjoy everything Madeira has to offer, having left for Lisbon aged just 12. He has become such a hero to the people there, who would be delighted to welcome him back to live in Funchal. Time will tell where Cristiano's future lies.

He will have plenty of off-field interests to keep him busy when he retires and has given himself all sorts of options. One suspects that Ronaldo will be much sought after, with television networks among those chasing his signature. He has a variety of tastes, and he will doubtless look to explore each and every one of them when he hangs up his boots in the distant future.

Back in Funchal, Madeira, Ronaldo has worked to set up a fashion store called CR7, which is managed by his sisters. A recent BBC documentary featured a picture of Cristiano's mother and sister standing outside the store. As one might expect, it is a stylish shop, advertised with a black sign with snazzy writing. Ronaldo also holds a fashion show in his hometown, which is attended by the mayor of Funchal. Wristbands are available with a printed message of 'There's only one Ronaldo', and increasingly he has become *the* Ronaldo, with his Brazilian namesake fading away in comparison. That, as much as anything, shows how far Cristiano has progressed over the past few seasons. It was a proud moment for him when he first heard the United fans chanting those very words in delight at one of his many special performances for the club.

Fashion is something that clearly interests Ronaldo, but he has suggested that he would be unwilling to throw himself into the world of fashion in the manner that David Beckham did. Referring to a Pepe Jeans campaign, in which he posed topless, he told *Four Four Two*, 'I like to do those things, and if it's done well and something I can identify with, it's liberating, but I'm no model.' Perhaps he will dedicate time to expanding his CR7 store into a chain outlet in the future when he hangs up his boots. Already Cristiano has been spotted sporting a number of designer bags, ranging from Gucci to Prada to Louis Vuitton. He poses for Pepe Jeans and his reputation in the industry is on the rise in Portugal. His interest in fashion appears genuine, and it may become his chief focus in years to come. Rio Ferdinand reveals in his autobiography that the United squad gave Ronaldo plenty of stick over the topless pictures. Ferdinand makes it clear that the winger is very well liked in the dressing-room and is always in the thick of the banter.

There is also a possibility that Cristiano will turn his hand to acting when his football career ends. Though his retirement is still a very long way off, he has admitted that he might enjoy the chance to follow in Eric Cantona's footsteps and pursue a career in Hollywood. With his profile sky-rocketing after leading United to the title, he may well get the chance. He certainly has the charisma to be a success as an actor, and he certainly relishes the opportunity to perform for an audience.

Further charity work is another area that Ronaldo might explore, as he takes great pride in using his own fortunate financial situation to help others in the world. He has taken a humanitarian trip to East Timor and is always eager to involve himself in good causes. He sees it as his way of giving something back to various communities. In his retirement, he may devote his free time towards more charitable organisations.

There is no sign of his fame disappearing any time soon. He continues to agree deals with a couple of eager sponsors. Firstly, he had the honour of inspiring 'Underworld Football', a game available on mobile phones. 'Underworld Football' is introduced with an image of Cristiano, and it offers the chance to save the game of football from extinction by using ball skills to wrong-foot monsters. It is easy to appreciate why this idea might have appealed to Ronaldo. Secondly, he has extended his contract with the Portugese bank Portugal Banco Espirito Santo (BES) until the end of the Euro 2008 tournament in Austria and Switzerland. The company uses his image for advertising, and Cristiano's face can be seen all over the country. He has also been used for campaigns promoting Portugal to tourists. So long as Ronaldo keeps winning trophies, his popularity will remain sky high. His management company is currently sifting through all the offers from companies fighting for an association with the man who is fast becoming the face of European football.

Whatever he does from this day onwards, and wherever he does it, one thing is for sure; he will seek to do the best that he can and to entertain as many people as possible along the way.